Homer's *Iliad* and *Odyssey*

HOMER'S

ILIAD

AND

ODYSSEY

A BIOGRAPHY

Revised and Expanded Edition

ALBERTO
MANGUEL

Yale

UNIVERSITY PRESS

NEW HAVEN & LONDON

Published with assistance from the foundation established in memory
of Calvin Chapin of the Class of 1788, Yale College.

2007 edition published by Grove Press.

First published in Great Britain in hardcover in 2007 by Atlantic
Books, an imprint of Grove Atlantic Ltd.

Yale University Press books may be purchased in quantity for educational,
business, or promotional use. For information, please e-mail sales.press@yale.edu
(U.S. office) or sales@yaleup.co.uk (U.K. office).

Set in Spectral and Shango types by IDS Infotech Ltd.
Printed in the United States of America.

Library of Congress Control Number: 2024932851
ISBN 978-0-300-27247-5 (paperback: alk. paper)

A catalogue record for this book is available from the British Library.

10 9 8 7 6 5 4 3 2 1

To Craig, in Ithaca

CONTENTS

Contents

A NOTE ON TRANSLATIONS AND EDITIONS

To simplify the reading, I've preferred to use common versions of the Homeric names. I use both "Odysseus" and "Ulysses" as appropriate but "Achilles" rather than "Akhilleus." As Samuel Butler noted in *The Authoress of the Odyssey*, "Neither do I think that Hekabe will supersede Hecuba, till 'What's Hecuba to him or he to Hecuba?' is out of date." (Though in our amnesic times, Butler may have to wait less time than he thought . . .)

I am aware that I use the term "Greek" incorrectly. The allied forces against Troy were composed of Achaeans, Danaans, and Argives, not of homogenous "Greeks," a name that was not invented until the expansion of the Roman Empire. However, in the context of this book, I use "Greek" as a kind of shorthand. Neither does the word "Hellenic" (which I have used once or twice) properly cover the historical and geographical ground of Homer's stories; it refers only to a limited territory in southern Thessaly. Regarding the use of the word "slave," I recognize that the preferred term in academia is "enslaved person" but I have chosen to retain "slave" to designate, for example, Achilles' Chryseis, for the sake of simplicity. In Homer's time there were a number of terms to distinguish various categories of slaves, from simple servant to war booty.

The scope of Homer's poems is limitless, that of this book is not. I have sought to follow Homer through many of the world's libraries but I have barely touched on his influence on the visual arts. I comment on some of the films that are based on Homeric themes, but there are many more that I do not mention. Since at least the seventeenth century, beginning with Claudio

Monteverdi's opera *Il ritorno d'Ulisse in Patria* (1639–40), composers have found fertile inspiration in the poems of Homer, especially the *Odyssey*, but I have decided not to venture into that field, which requires an ear more technically attuned than my own. Nor have I entered the worlds of video games and comics, rich realms in which Homer's influence can be commonly found.

The numbering of Homer's lines differs in the various translations. Throughout the book, I have used the versions of the *Iliad* and the *Odyssey* translated by Robert Fagles and published in 1990 and 1996, respectively, which to my taste are among the best and most graceful. Other translations of foreign works quoted, unless otherwise indicated, are my own.

Homer's *Iliad* and *Odyssey*

Introduction

Every great work of literature is either the *Iliad* or the *Odyssey*.
—Raymond Queneau, Preface to Flaubert's *Bouvard et Pécuchet,* 1947

It seems fitting that the two books which, probably more than any others, have fed the imagination of the Western world for over two and a half millennia should have no clear starting point and no identifiable creator. Homer begins long before Homer. In all probability, the *Iliad* and the *Odyssey* drifted into being gradually, indefinably, more like popular myths than formal literary productions, through the untraceable process of ancient ballads sifting and blending until acquiring a coherent narrative shape, ballads sung in tongues that were already archaic when the poet (or poets) whom tradition agreed to call Homer was at work in the eighth century BCE. The poems themselves, however, were most probably written down only toward the mid-sixth century BCE, probably in conjunction with performances at the Panathenaic festival in Athens.[1] The *Iliad* especially, but also the *Odyssey,* proved extremely popular: more than one thousand ancient manuscripts of Homer's work have survived. The earliest is a complete version of the *Odyssey* from the late tenth century BCE, though we have a Homeric papyrus with a few lines of the *Iliad* from the third century BCE.

For many centuries, the poor blind singer begging his way through ancient Greece was generally regarded as the author of the *Iliad* and the *Odyssey*; in time, he came to be replaced by a kind of inspired spirit, part fable and part allegory, the Ghost of Poetry Past. Nietzsche argued that "Homer as the composer of the *Iliad* and the *Odyssey* is not a historical tradition, but an *aesthetic judgment*."[2] Eventually, so widespread became the notion of an apocryphal Homer that in the 1850s Gustave Flaubert was able to mock it in his *Dictionary of Clichés*, a posthumously published handbook that purported to offer the bourgeoisie a correct social response for every utterance. "HOMER: Never existed."[3]

We don't know anything about Homer. It is otherwise with Homer's books. In a very real sense, the *Iliad* and the *Odyssey* are familiar to us before we open the first page. Even before we begin to follow the changing moods of Achilles or admire the wit and courage of Odysseus, we have learned to expect that somewhere in these stories of war in time and travel in space we will be told the experience of every human struggle and every human displacement. Two of our oldest metaphors tell us that all life is a battle and that all life is a journey; whether the *Iliad* and the *Odyssey* drew on this knowledge or whether this knowledge found its mirror in the *Iliad* and the *Odyssey* is, in the final count, unimportant, since a book and its readers are mirrors that reflect each other endlessly. Whatever their nebulous origins, most scholars now assume that the poems ascribed to Homer began as scattered compositions of various kinds that eventually coalesced and became perfectly interwoven to form the two lengthy stories we now know: one describing the tragedy of a single place, Troy, fought over by many men; the other telling the adventures of a single man, Odysseus, who makes his way back home through many dangerous places. For Homer's future readers, Troy came to stand for all cities and Odysseus for every man.

The biography of a book is not the biography of the man who wrote it. Yet in the case of Homer and his poems, one goes hand in hand with the other, since it is impossible to know which came first: the blind bard who sang of the destruction of the Trojan city and of the longing of a Greek king for his home, or the stories of the lure of war and the search for peace which required an author to justify their existence. Figures such as Homer that acquire the stature of legends are allowed to improve on their biography from generation to generation of readers; it can cause but mild surprise, for example, that in the early eighteenth century the learned philologist and Royal Professor of Greek antiquities at the University of Naples, Jacopo Martorelli, held Homer responsible for creating the first Chair of Greek Studies, which *Dottore* Martorelli had the honor of occupying centuries later.[4]

Writers and their work establish curious relationships in the eyes of their readers. There are books that through inspired wording conjure up a lifelike character who overshadows whoever the author may have been: Don Quixote and Cervantes, Hamlet and Shakespeare are cases in point. There are writers whose lives, as Oscar Wilde said of himself, are the recipients of their genius, and whose books are only the product of their talent.[5] Homer and his works belong to the former category, but there have been times in their long history when readers chose to consign them to the latter.

No one owns Homer, not even the best of his readers. Each of our readings is done through layers of previous ones that pile upon the page like seams in a rock until the original text (if there ever was so pure a thing) is hardly visible. So when we think, upon closing Homer, "Ah, now I've made the *Iliad* (or *Odyssey*) mine!" what we mean is that we have made ours a story that many others have long annotated, recast, interpreted, and adapted, and that, with their testimonies echoing more or less loudly in our ears, we have tried to impose our tastes and prejudices upon a cacophony of one-man bands, like Keats first looking into Chapman's Homer, or Elizabeth Barrett Browning proclaiming her childhood dream of being "the feminine of Homer," or Joyce hustling Ulysses through the crowded streets of Dublin.[6] In these attempts, strict adherence to official chronologies is not useful: readings influence one another back and forth across time, and we must not accuse Saint Augustine of anachronism for studying Homer under Goethe's guidance, or Pope for allowing himself to be prejudiced by the commentaries of George Steiner. All readers of the *Odyssey* and the *Iliad* bear Homer in mind, seek inspiration in his books, and build on his foundations. But, as the archaeologist Claude Sintes says, "Homer alone does not quote anyone else: he is the first."[7]

This palimpsest of readings does not alone hide from our eyes the original text (or what most scholars agree is the original text). It is said that an English divine, Richard Whately, waving the King James Bible at a meeting of his diocesan clergy, roared out, "This is not the Bible!" Then, after a long pause: "This, gentlemen, is only a *translation* of the Bible!"[8] Except for an increasingly small group of scholars upon whom has been bestowed the grace of knowing ancient Greek, the rest of us read not Homer but a translation of Homer. In this our fortunes vary: some may be lucky enough to fall upon the translations of Alexander Pope or Robert Fagles, or the luminous versions of Christopher Logue or Alice Oswald, Emily Wilson or Stephen Mitchell; others may be doomed to T. S. Brandreth's "literal" version of 1816 or to the pompous 1948 rendition by F. L. Lucas.

Translation is, in its nature, a questionable craft, and it is strange how, in certain cases, works such as the *Iliad* and the *Odyssey*, made out of words and therefore seemingly dependent for their success on how those precise words are used, can dispense with them and come across in languages that had not even been invented when the poems first came into being. *Mēnin aeide Thea Pēlēiadeō Akhilēos . . .* , "The wrath sing, Goddess, of Pelian

Achilles," is a more or less literal English version of the *Iliad*'s first line. But what did Homer mean by *aeide*, "sing"? What by *Thea*, "Goddess"? What by *mēnin*, "wrath"? Virginia Woolf noted that "it is vain and foolish to talk of knowing Greek, since in our ignorance we should be at the bottom of any class of schoolboys, since we do not know how the words sounded, or where precisely we ought to laugh, or how the actors acted, and between this foreign people and ourselves there is not only difference of race and tongue but a tremendous breach of tradition."[9]

Even among modern languages the "tremendous breach of tradition" persists. *Wrath* in English, with its old-fashioned ring that has echoes in Blake's tigers and Steinbeck's grapes, is different from the German *Zorn*, full of the military sound and fury evident in Emanuel Geibel's 1870 ballad about the "heil'gen Zorn ums Vaterland," "holy anger over the Fatherland"; or from the French *colère*, which, in existentialist Paris, Simone de Beauvoir defined as a passion "born from love to murder love."[10] Under such bewildering circumstances, what is a reader to do? Read, and bear the questions in mind. Translation may be an impossible task but its impossibility is countered by an infinite variety of possible interpretations. A reader can make bricks without straw; a translator cannot.

In spite of such uneasy conditions, a good book manages to survive, at times, the most unfaithful of translations. Even when we are reading "many soul-destroying things/In folded tablets" (as Brandreth self-accusingly has it), Achilles' anger or Odysseus's longing will somehow succeed in moving us, reminding us of our own passions and endeavors, touching something in us that is not just our own but mysteriously common to humankind.[11] In 1990, the Colombian Ministry of Culture set up a system of itinerant libraries to take books to the inhabitants of distant rural regions. For this purpose, carrier bookbags with capacious pockets were transported on donkeys' backs up into the jungle and the sierra. Here the books were left for several weeks in the hands of a teacher or village elder who became, de facto, the librarian in charge. Most of the books were technical works, agricultural handbooks, collections of sewing patterns, and the like, but a few literary works were also included. According to one librarian, the books were always safely accounted for. "I know of a single instance in which a book was not returned," she said. "We had taken, along with the usual practical titles, a Spanish translation of the *Iliad*. When the time came to exchange the book, the villagers refused to give it back. We decided to make them a gift of it, but asked them why they wished to keep that particular title. They explained that Homer's story reflected their own: it told of a war-torn country in which mad gods mingle with men and women who never know exactly what the fighting is about, or when they will be happy, or why they will be killed."[12]

"Myths," wrote Claude Lévi-Strauss, "operate in men's minds without their being aware of the fact."[13] In the final book of the *Iliad*, Achilles, who has murdered Hector, who in turn has murdered Patroclus, Achilles' beloved friend, agrees to receive Hector's father, King Priam, come to ransom his son's body. It is one of the most moving, most powerful scenes I know. Suddenly, there is no difference between victim and victor, old and young, father and son. Priam's words stir in Achilles "a deep desire/to grieve for his own father," and with great tenderness he moves away the hand that the old man has stretched out to grasp the hands of his son's murderer and put them to his lips.

> And overpowered by memory
> both men gave way to grief. Priam wept freely
> for man-killing Hector, throbbing, crouching
> before Achilles' feet as Achilles wept himself,
> now for his father, now for Patroclus once again,
> and their sobbing rose and fell throughout the house.

At length, Achilles tells Priam that they both must "put our griefs to rest in our own hearts."

> So the immortals spun our lives that we, we wretched men
> live on to bear such torments—the gods live free of sorrows.
> There are two great jars that stand on the floor of Zeus's halls
> and hold his gifts, our miseries one, the other blessings.
> When Zeus who loves the lightning mixes gifts for a man,
> now he meets with misfortune, now good times in turn.
> When Zeus dispenses gifts from the jar of sorrows only,
> he makes a man an outcast.[14]

To Achilles, and perhaps to Priam, and perhaps to their readers in the Colombian sierra, this is consolation.

Summaries of the Books

The *Iliad*

Before the beginning of the poem, Menelaus's wife, the beautiful Helen, has been kidnapped by Paris, son of the king of Troy, Priam, and of his wife, Hecuba. Among Paris's siblings are Hector, married to Andromache, and the visionary Cassandra. To rescue Helen, Menelaus's brother Agamemnon has laid siege to Troy, at the head of a coalition that includes, among many famous warriors, Ajax, Diomedes, Odysseus, old Nestor, and Patroclus and his friend, the greatest warrior of all, Achilles, son of the goddess Thetis. The siege has lasted ten long years with the gods continuously involved in the conflict. Their divine favors are divided: on the side of the Trojans are Aphrodite (whose son Aeneas is a Trojan), the sun god Apollo, and the war god Ares; on the side of the Greeks are Thetis, the goddess of wisdom Athena, the sea god Poseidon, and Zeus's wife, Hera.

Book 1
In the tenth year of the Trojan War, the Greek army, led by Agamemnon, is camped on the shore near the city. The priest of

Apollo, Chryses, has asked Agamemnon to allow him to ransom his daughter Chryseis, whom Agamemnon has claimed as his booty, and has been rudely rejected. Chryses prays to Apollo to help him, and the god sends a plague upon the Greeks. To pacify the god, it is decided at a general assembly that Agamemnon must return Chryseis. Agamemnon agrees but demands that he be given Achilles' concubine, Briseis, in exchange. Achilles feels dishonored and withdraws from the fighting, taking with him Patroclus and their soldiers. Achilles appeals to his mother for revenge, and the goddess Thetis convinces Zeus to side with the Trojans. Zeus and his wife, Hera, who supports the Greeks, have an argument, settled by Hera's son, the smithy god Hephaestus.

Book 2

Agamemnon has a dream in which he learns that he will take Troy. He tests the dream by suggesting to his army that they abandon the siege and return home. The plan backfires when the soldiers agree wholeheartedly. The commoner Thersites causes a disruption by rallying against the Greek leaders, but Odysseus restores order. The episode ends with a catalogue of the Greek and Trojan forces.

Book 3

The two armies meet on the plain outside Troy and settle on a truce, while Paris and Menelaus agree to fight in single combat for Helen. High on the ramparts of Troy, Helen points out the Greek warriors to Priam. Menelaus is close to killing Paris and ending the war, but Aphrodite saves him and transports him back into the city.

Book 4

The gods intervene again. Hera demands that the truce be broken. Athena persuades Pandarus, fighting on the Trojan side, to shoot at Menelaus, who is wounded.

Book 5

Helped by Athena, Diomedes attacks the Trojans. He even attacks Aphrodite, as she tries to help her son Aeneas, and the god of war Ares as he is rallying the Trojans.

Book 6

On the battlefield, Diomedes meets Glaucus, a Lycean fighting on the Trojan side, and they become friends and refuse to fight. Hector goes back to Troy to sacrifice to Athena. He speaks to Helen and to his wife, Andromache, and rebukes Paris for not being out on the field. Paris follows Hector's advice and joins the battle.

Book 7

Paris and Hector return to the fight. Hector challenges Ajax to a duel, but the outcome is unclear. The Trojans propose a truce so that both camps can bury their dead. In the meantime, following old Nestor's advice, the Greeks fortify the camp.

Book 8

Zeus encourages the Trojans, and also forbids the other gods to take part in the fighting. The Greeks withdraw to their camp and for the first time in the war the Trojans set themselves up outside their city walls.

Book 9

Worried about the advance of the Trojans, Nestor suggests that Agamemnon send Ajax, together with Phoenix (the old tutor of Odysseus and Achilles), to convince Achilles to join the troops again. In spite of being offered Briseis back, as well as the hand of Agamemnon's daughter in marriage, he refuses.

Book 10
Nestor now suggests that Diomedes and Odysseus go during the night to spy on the Trojans. They capture Dolon, an enemy scout, and based on his information succeed in killing several Trojans.

Book 11
Led by Hector, the Trojans succeed in pushing the Greeks back to their ships, wounding Agamemnon, Diomedes, and Odysseus. Achilles sends Patroclus to find out about one of the wounded whose body he sees being carried away. Nestor asks Patroclus to join the battle himself and to borrow Achilles' armor in order to frighten the enemy.

Book 12
Before Patroclus can return, Hector opens a breach in the wall of the Greek camp and passes through with his soldiers.

Book 13
The armies fight on the beach while the Trojans try to reach the Greek ships. Poseidon encourages the Greeks to fight back. Hector's advance is stopped by Ajax.

Book 14
Hera lulls Zeus to sleep so that Poseidon can continue to rouse the Greek army. Ajax gives Hector a stunning blow.

Book 15
Zeus awakes and speaks sternly to Hera, who then takes his message to the gods, ordering Poseidon to withdraw and Apollo to heal Hector. Once again, the Trojans drive the Greeks back to their ships.

Book 16

Patroclus returns to Achilles and borrows his friend's armor. In the meantime, Hector and the Trojans force Ajax and the Greeks back again and set fire to the first Greek ship. Dressed in Achilles' armor, Patroclus repulses the Trojans. Ignoring Achilles' warning not to drive them too far back, Patroclus reaches the walls of Troy and is stunned and disarmed by Apollo himself. The Trojan Euphorbus wounds him, and Hector kills him.

Book 17

Hector removes Patroclus's armor, but the Greeks manage to carry his body back to camp. The fighting continues, led by Menelaus and Ajax on the Greek side, Hector and Aeneas on that of the Trojans.

Book 18

Achilles hears that Patroclus has been killed. Full of rage and grief, he vows to avenge his friend in battle. Thetis promises him that Hephaestus will make him new armor but warns him that his own death must follow Hector's. Patroclus's body is brought into the Greek camp. Hephaestus makes Achilles new arms and a splendid new shield.

Book 19

Odysseus instigates a reconciliation between Agamemnon and Achilles. Achilles puts on his new armor. His faithful horse Xanthus foretells his death.

Book 20

Zeus reverses his decision, and allows the gods to intervene. Achilles begins a furious attack on the Trojans. Aeneas is rescued by Poseidon, Hector by Apollo. The Trojans retreat.

Book 21

The Trojan retreat is hampered by the river Scamander. As Achilles fills the river with corpses, it rises up angrily against him, but Hephaestus checks the swell with his fire.

The gods begin to fight among themselves: Athena wounds Ares and Aphrodite. The gods now retreat to Olympus, but Apollo distracts Achilles, allowing the Trojans to take refuge behind the walls of their city.

Book 22

Achilles finds Hector alone outside the walls, waiting for him. As Achilles approaches, Hector tries to run away. The gods intervene once more: after Zeus weighs Hector's life in the scales against Achilles' and Hector loses, Apollo withdraws his help, but Athena induces Hector to fight. Achilles kills him, then ties Hector's body to his chariot and drags it behind him around the walls of Troy and into the camp of the Greeks. Priam and his family watch in horror.

Book 23

During the night, Achilles is visited by the ghost of Patroclus, who demands a swift burial. The next day, Achilles gives his friend a magnificent funeral, followed by athletic games.

Book 24

For eleven days, Hector's body has lain unburied. Following advice from the gods, Priam visits the Greek camp and offers Achilles a ransom for his son's body. Achilles at length accepts, and after a shared meal Priam returns to Troy with Hector's remains. The poem ends with the funeral of Hector, while the Trojan women, led by Andromache, weep and lament their dead.

The *Odyssey*

The poem starts ten years after the fall of Troy. During the sack of the city, the disrespectful behavior of some of the Greeks annoyed the gods. Consequently, Odysseus has not been allowed to return to Ithaca where his faithful wife, Penelope, has been trying for seven years to ward off a crowd of suitors by delaying her answer until she has finished a tapestry depicting the shroud of Laertes, father of Odysseus, which she weaves during the day and then secretly unweaves at night. In particular, Poseidon and Apollo have sought to punish Odysseus, who during his travels has blinded Poseidon's son, the Cyclops Polyphemus, and whose companions have slaughtered the sun god's cattle for food. Odysseus is now stranded on a faraway island, the prisoner of the nymph Calypso, who has chosen him as her lover.

Book 1
At a gathering of the gods, Athena asks Zeus why he has forgotten Odysseus. Zeus answers that it is Poseidon's anger that has prevented Odysseus from returning to Ithaca, but that now, since Poseidon is away visiting the Ethiopians, Odysseus can begin the journey home. Athena disguises herself as Mentes, chief of the Taphians, and goes to see Odysseus's son Telemachus in Ithaca, telling him to take action against his mother's suitors. She instructs him to seek news of his father from King Nestor in Pylos and King Menelaus in Sparta.

Book 2
Telemachus calls an assembly to denounce the suitors. Speeches are made, but public opinion is not sufficiently roused against them. As a result, Telemachus leaves for Pylos in secret, accompanied by Athena, who disguises herself this time as Mentor, a friend of Odysseus.

Book 3
King Nestor tells Telemachus about the return of other Greek heroes who fought at Troy, among them Menelaus and Agamemnon, but can give him no news of Odysseus. He orders his son Pisistratus to accompany Telemachus to Sparta.

Book 4
At the court of Menelaus, Telemachus and his companions are entertained by the king and by his wife, Helen, now restored to her throne. Menelaus tells them that during his voyage back from Troy, the Old Man of the Sea informed him that Odysseus was being held captive by the nymph Calypso. Meanwhile, back in Ithaca, the suitors and Penelope learn of Telemachus's departure. The suitors plan to ambush him on his return and kill him.

Book 5
At a gathering of the gods, Hermes is sent to tell Calypso that she must release Odysseus. Calypso, sorrowful but obedient, provides him with wood to build a boat. Odysseus sails away but after only seventeen days, Poseidon discovers him and wrecks the boat in a storm. Naked and wounded, Odysseus manages to reach the land of the Phaeacians.

Book 6
Odysseus is discovered naked on the beach by Princess Nausicaa and her maids, who are washing clothes and playing ball. Odysseus begs her for hospitality; she gives him something to wear and tells him to go to her father's palace.

Book 7
Odysseus asks Nausicaa's parents, King Alcinous and Queen Arete, to help him. Without revealing his identity, he tells them only part of his story. The king suggests that he stay and marry Nausicaa.

Book 8

King Alcinous hosts a lavish party for his guest. The blind bard Demodocus sings about Odysseus and his quarrel with Achilles over whether craft or courage is the surest way of capturing Troy, and later about the ploy of the Wooden Horse. Odysseus weeps at the memory. During an athletics exhibition, he is taunted and forced to demonstrate his strength.

Book 9

At last, Odysseus reveals his name and tells his full story: how he and his companions left Troy on twelve ships, raided the Trojan allies in Thrace, reached the land of the Lotus Eaters, and finally landed on the island of the Cyclops, where they were captured by Polyphemus and kept in his cave to be eaten one by one. Odysseus explains how he succeeded in blinding Polyphemus, how he told his victim that his name was "Nobody," and how he escaped from the cave holding on to the belly of a ram. When, as he was sailing away, he revealed his real name, Polyphemus swore that he would ask his father, Poseidon, to avenge him.

Book 10

Odysseus continues his story: he and his companions reached the floating island of the god Aeolus, who gave them a bag containing all the winds except the west wind, to help them on their course. While Odysseus slept, his companions opened the bags and their ships were blown back to the god's island, but he refused to assist them again. They reached the land of the giant Laestrygonians, who destroyed eleven of their ships. On the surviving ship, Odysseus and his companions arrived at the island of the enchantress Circe, who turned some of the men into swine and took Odysseus as her lover. After a year on the island, Odysseus begged to be allowed to leave. Circe explained to him that he had first to travel to the Underworld and ask the ghost of the seer Tiresias for instructions.

Book 11
Odysseus tells of his visit to the Underworld: after he and his companions had conjured up the dead, the ghost of Tiresias told him that even after reaching Ithaca, he would continue to travel. Among the ghosts, Odysseus spoke to his dead mother, to King Agamemnon, to Achilles, and to Heracles.

Book 12
Odysseus concludes his story: after having lost some of his men to the monster Scylla, and after passing the whirlpool Charybdis and sailing past the luring Sirens, Odysseus and his companions reached the island where Apollo kept his cattle. Though they had been told not to touch the herd, hunger forced the men to kill and eat a few. The god complained to Zeus, who as a punishment destroyed their ships with a thunderbolt. Odysseus was the only one to survive. On a beam from his ship, he drifted for nine days until at last he reached Calypso's island. The rest of the story the king knows.

Book 13
King Alcinous sends Odysseus off laden with rich gifts. Odysseus falls asleep, and the Phaeacian sailors deposit him on the shore of Ithaca. Athena appears, disguised as a young man, and though he tries to hide his identity, she tells him that she knows who he is and that she will help him against the suitors. Athena dresses Odysseus as an old beggar.

Book 14
Odysseus in disguise is greeted by the swineherd Eumaeus, and makes up stories about himself to entertain his host.

Book 15
Telemachus leaves Menelaus and Helen, and sails for home, bringing with him the seer Theoclymenus. Back in Ithaca, Eumaeus

tells Odysseus the story of his life. Telemachus avoids falling into the hands of the suitors, who pursued him after he left Ithaca, and arrives on the island safely.

Book 16
Telemachus comes to the swineherd's hut, and Odysseus reveals himself to his son. He explains that they must be careful if they are to succeed against the suitors. The suitors sail back from their pursuit of Telemachus, and discuss what to do next.

Book 17
Telemachus returns to the palace and speaks with Penelope. In the meantime, the goatherd Melanthius, an ally of the suitors, seeing Odysseus with Eumaeus, insults the man he takes to be a beggar. As they approach the palace, Odysseus's dog Argos recognizes his master and dies of a broken heart. Odysseus begs the suitors for food; one of their leaders, Antinous, throws a stool at him instead.

Book 18
Irus, a professional beggar, taunts Odysseus, who knocks him out in a boxing match. Penelope appears and receives gifts from the suitors. One of the maids mocks Odysseus, who threatens to tell Telemachus of her behavior. Another of the leading suitors, Eurymachus, insults Odysseus. When Odysseus answers back, Eurymachus throws a stool at him but hits the wine steward instead.

Book 19
Led by Athena, Odysseus and Telemachus remove the weapons from the hall. The maid insults Odysseus again. Odysseus tells Penelope that he once entertained her husband and that the man is now not far away. The old nurse Eurycleia washes his feet and recognizes him because of a scar. Odysseus begs her not to reveal

his identity. Penelope explains that on the following night she will allow the suitors to try shooting an arrow through twelve ax handles with Odysseus's bow; the winner can claim her as his wife.

Book 20

Odysseus lies awake impatiently. The loyal cowherd Philoetius appears. Another of the suitors, Ctesippus, flings an ox foot at Odysseus to mock him. Seeing the suitors overcome by wild laughter, the seer Theoclymenus tells them they are all marked for death.

Book 21

Penelope brings out Odysseus's bow and announces the test: they are to bend the bow and shoot an arrow through the twelve ax handles. All the suitors try and fail, except Antinous, who postpones his turn. Odysseus reveals himself to Eumaeus and Philoetius. As Penelope leaves the hall, he grabs hold of the bow and shoots through the ax handles.

Book 22

Odysseus shoots Antinous and reveals his identity to the suitors. Helped by Telemachus, Eumaeus, and Philoetius, the slaughter of the suitors begins. The treacherous Melanthius brings several suits of armor for the suitors, but is caught. Odysseus runs out of arrows, puts on armor, and finishes off the suitors with spears. In a grisly ending, Melanthius is tortured to death and twelve of the maids are hanged.

Book 23

Penelope, told by Eurycleia of Odysseus's return, refuses to believe it. She tests him by telling Eurycleia to move their bed out of their room. Odysseus becomes angry, for he made the bed himself, and one of the posts is a living olive tree—unless someone has cut down the tree, the bed cannot be moved. At this last proof, Penelope recognizes her husband. The couple go to bed and tell each other their stories.

Book 24

Hermes leads the souls of the suitors into the Underworld, where they meet with the ghosts of Agamemnon, Ajax, Patroclus, and Achilles. In the meantime, Odysseus visits his father, Laertes, who has retired to a farm, and after some delay reveals himself to him. The relatives of the suitors plan revenge, but after lending Laertes the strength to kill one of them, Athena, still disguised as Mentor, imposes a lasting peace on Ithaca.

CHAPTER 1

A Life of Homer?

Homer, or another Greek of the same name . . .
—Oscar Wilde, *Oscariana*, 1910 (posthumous)

Homer, or the overwhelming presence we call "Homer," is a shadowy figure who his first biographers (or inventors) believed had been born at the end of the Bronze Age, not long after the sack of Troy, traditionally dated to 1184 BCE. Eratosthenes of Cyrene, librarian of Alexandria, who among other achievements accurately calculated the circumference of the earth, stated in his *Chronographiae* that Homer was a near contemporary of Hector and Achilles.[1] For the ancient Greeks, there was no question about the reality of Homer. He was simply the greatest of poets, a man of flesh and blood who in some remote age had composed the works on which all Greek culture was based, not only the *Iliad* and the *Odyssey* but also a number of hymns and other epics: a poem on Amphiaraus's expedition against Thebes, the so-called *Small Iliad,* the *Phoceis,* the *Cercopes,* and the *Battle of the Frogs and Mice,* most of which are now lost and many long discredited. In the fifth century BCE, the historian Herodotus doubted the attribution of some of these works to Homer but never the existence of the man himself. Thucydides, apparently quoting the funeral oration delivered by Pericles toward the end of the first year of the Peloponnesian War, wrote that "far from needing a Homer for our panegyrist, or other of his craft whose verses might charm for the moment only for the impression which they gave to melt at the touch of fact, we have forced every sea and land to be the highway of our daring, and everywhere, whether for evil or for good, have left imperishable monuments behind us." A few decades earlier, Aeschylus, none of whose plays is, as far as we know, based on either the *Iliad* or the *Odyssey*, stated that they were all "slices from Homer's big dinnerparty," thereby implying that there were other Homeric poems that had served him as inspiration; if so, they have not come down to us.[2]

His fame certainly has. An allegorical marble relief, carved by Archelaos of Priene in the late second century BCE, depicts Homer being crowned by Time (Chronos) and Space (Oikoumene, the "Inhabited World") and acclaimed by the Muses of History, Tragedy, Comedy, and Poetry, while his "children," the *Iliad* and the *Odyssey*, kneel by his side. Above the poet's apotheosis, in the upper section of the relief, Zeus appears in the pantheon, honored by the other gods. Zeus, Father of the Gods, is reflected by Homer, Father of Humankind.[3]

"Father of Humankind" implied the role of father of human history. Each of Homer's two great poems begins after a period of ten years: the *Iliad* a decade after the commencement of the siege of Troy, the *Odyssey* a decade after the city's fall. For the Greeks, these ten-year periods may have possessed a magical or legendary quality, marking the dividing line between the time of the gods and the time of humans; Greek history began, in their reckoning, the year of the destruction of Troy. Earlier dates were known and recorded (an inscribed slab known as the Parian Chronicle, now in the Ashmolean Museum in Oxford, notes what would be for us the year 1581 BCE as the first date in Greek history), but the fall of the fabled city was regarded as the conventional starting point of witnessed events.

Among the literary works of ancient Greece, the Homeric poems may have been the first to take advantage of the possibilities offered by written language: greater length, since the composition no longer needed to be short enough to be held in the poet's memory; greater consistency, both of plot and character, than that of oral poetry; greater continuity, because the written text permitted comparisons with earlier or later narrative passages; greater harmony, since the eye could assist the composing mind by enriching the purely aural rules of versification with those of the physical relationship between the written words. Above all, the poem set down in writing allowed the work a wider, more generous reach: the person who received the poem no longer needed to share the poet's time and space. And yet since an oral culture has no experience of a lengthy linear plot, "it hardly does justice to oral composition," wrote the linguist Walter J. Ong, "to describe it as varying from an organization it does not know, and cannot conceive of. The 'things' that the action is supposed to start in the middle of have never, except for brief passages, been ranged in a chronological order to establish a 'plot.'"[4]

An alphabetic writing system had reached Greece no earlier than the ninth or eighth century BCE; before that, there was a gap of two hundred to three hundred years following the collapse of Mycenaean culture and the disappearance of the writing system known as Linear B. The first examples of alphabetically written literary compositions are from the mid-eighth century: the "Phoenician letters" as Herodotus called them. In book 6 of the *Iliad,* Glaucus tells the story of how his grandfather was sent off with a message to the king of Lycia instructing him to kill the bearer (a device that Shakespeare would use in *Hamlet*): "[He] gave him tokens,/murderous signs, scratched in a folded tablet."[5] It is conceivable that the author of the *Iliad* had recourse to such signs and tablets, and that he composed some of his work in written form. Certain modern scholars suggest that it is possible that the original Ionian composer (or composers) of the *Iliad* and *Odyssey* wrote out the text of the poems not on tablets but on papyrus scrolls from Egypt. The Ionians of the seventh century BCE were enterprising merchants who set up shop as far as the western reaches of the Nile Delta and down to the Second Cataract; the names of the most adventurous ones appear engraved on the thigh of one of the colossal statues of Abu Simbel. From Egypt they brought home the wonderful invention of the papyrus scrolls, which, according to Herodotus, they continued to call *diphterai*, "skins," after their own books, which were made of vellum. If Homer did indeed write out his poems, then their length was in great measure determined by how much text one of these scrolls could contain: the division of the *Iliad* and the *Odyssey* into twenty-four books each is possibly the consequence of this physical limitation.[6]

Before deciding whether Homer composed orally or in writing, it was deemed useful to establish whether he existed in the first place and, if so, where he was born and how his life developed. The location of his birthplace became a much disputed question, and seven cities claimed to be the true one: Chios, Smyrna, Colophon, Salamis, Rhodes, Argos, and Athens. In time, the question suffered a variety of allegorical interpretations. In the seventeenth century, for instance, the English poet Thomas Heywood saw in the dispute over Homer's birthplace a parable of the poor artist who attains fame only after death:

> Seven cities warr'd for Homer, being dead,
> Who, living, had no roof to shroud his head.

Miguel de Cervantes recognized in the uncertainty of Homer's birthplace a sign of Fame's fair play, since it allowed more than one town to share in the poet's glory, as was the case with his Don Quixote "whose birthplace Cide Hamete was unwilling to state exactly, because he wished all villages and cities of La Mancha to contend among themselves to adopt him and claim him as theirs, as the seven Greek cities contended for Homer."[7]

One of the oldest traditions affirmed that Homer had come into the world on the island of Chios, and the late seventh-century BCE "Hymn to Delian Apollo" (attributed in antiquity to Homer) presented itself as the work of "the blind man who lives in rugged Chios."[8] Eventually, Chios asserted its preeminence, and visitors today are still shown the hollow in a rock about four miles from the island's main town where Homer and his descendants, known as the Homeridae, were supposed to have sat and sung poems to one another. Two further arguments sustain Chios's candidature. First the language of the poems is mainly Ionic, spoken by the early Greeks who settled on the west coast of Asia Minor and the adjacent islands, including Chios, although it may have been the conventional language of epic poetry, which Homer adopted for that very reason. Second, especially in the *Iliad*, there are references to the geography of this area, such as the mountain peaks of Samothrace seen from the plain of Troy, which could only be known to someone familiar with the landscape.

To compete with Chios, the island of Cos claimed to be Homer's burial place, a claim that Cyprus in turn contested. Cyprian tradition asserted that a native of Cyprus, a woman called Themisto, was Homer's mother and that Homer chose to die there, where her bones lay buried.[9]

During the fourth to the second century BCE, perhaps out of a need to lend further detail to Homer's evanescent character, several spurious biographies appeared, attributed, for the sake of verisimilitude, to well-known authors. The longest was thought to be the work of Herodotus (an attribution long proved false) and gave a list of Homer's many travels as well as a detailed genealogy:

a woman called Cretheis, not Themisto, is mentioned as Homer's mother.

The *Life of Homer* attributed to Herodotus was perhaps written by a native of Smyrna, since he gives Smyrna as Homer's birthplace in what is surely an attempt to glorify the city: "It may be seen from what I have said, that Homer was neither a Dorian nor of the island of Ios, but an Æolian," the author says, with admirable confidence.[10] Whatever the nationality of its author, the *Life of Homer,* like Homer's poems, was composed in Ionian Greek and shows a perfect familiarity with the dialect and customs of that area.

According to the story, Homer's grandparents died young and left their young daughter Cretheis in the care of their friend Cleanax. After a few years, Cretheis fell in love and became pregnant; for fear of scandal, Cleanax dispatched her to the newly built city of Smyrna. Homer's birth, the author explains, took place exactly 168 years after the sack of Troy, by the banks of the river Meles. Cretheis named the boy Melesigenes, after the river, as Milton reminds us: "Blind Melesigenes thence Homer call'd."[11] When the time came, Cretheis sent her son to school, where, because of his wonderful abilities, he was adopted by the teacher, who foretold a brilliant future for him and allowed him the run of the establishment. A visitor to Smyrna convinced Melesigenes to leave the city and take to the sea. From ship to ship, he crisscrossed Poseidon's realm and visited the places his Odysseus would stop at later, including, of course, Ithaca. On board, and for the first time, he began to compose poems to the great delight of his companions. From then on, the people he met became characters in the works that still lay in the future: the friendly Mentor from Ithaca; the bard Phemius; Mentes, lord of the Taphians; the leathersmith Tychios, who made the shield for Ajax. The lively author of the *Life of Homer* accuses others of making things up: for instance, he says that although the inhabitants of Ithaca claim that it was among them that the poet went blind, it happened, in fact, in Colophon—a point, he adds, on which all Colophonians agree. Apparently, the change of name from Melesigenes to Homer took place in Cimmeris, where the blind poet proposed to the local senate that in exchange for bed and board he would make the town famous with his songs. The senators (in the tradition of most government bodies up to our day) refused, arguing that if they set this dangerous precedent, Cimmeris would soon be overrun with blind beggars (*homers* in Cimmerian) seeking handouts. To shame them, the poet adopted the name Homer.

At the end of the first century CE, the philosopher known as Heraclitus the Grammarian or the Allegorist (to distinguish him from the pre-Socratic philosopher of the same name) accepted as a fact that Homer had died of humiliation on the island of Ios, after not being able to solve a children's riddle. One day, Homer heard a group of boys returning from fishing and asked them if they had caught anything. The boys answered, "Everything we caught we left behind and everything we failed to catch we bear away." In other words, they caught only lice: the few fish they caught they left behind when they were attacked by lice, but the lice they tried to pinch away were still on their bodies. According to Pausanias, Homer's inglorious death took place because he had failed to heed the oracle at Delphi. When Homer visited the oracle to ask about his origins, the answer he received was that his mother had been born on Ios and that this was where his bones would be buried, "unless he was careful of the conundrums of children." In the late eighteenth century, a picturesque figure, the Dutch count Pasch van Kreinen, after having read the story in Pausanias, organized an expedition to Ios, where he was told there was a site containing marble slabs with funeral inscriptions, one of them declaring, "Here under the earth lies the sacred head of heroic Homer." Because of certain grammatical mistakes in the epitaph, Count Pasch doubted its authenticity, and after having spent considerable time and money on Ios, moved on to pursue other not so ambitious archaeological endeavors.[12]

The author of the *Life of Homer* disputes the story that Homer died of chagrin and has him die instead of "a disease he had contracted on his arrival."[13] Throughout the *Life,* and with inspired hindsight, the author depicts scenes from the *Odyssey* in Homer's life, not only the ones already mentioned but others as well— Homer's mother cards wool and weaves like a faithful Penelope; the goatherd Glaucos receives Homer hospitably, just as Odysseus will be welcomed home by the faithful swineherd Eumaeus. The *Life of Homer* builds up the classical picture of Homer as the blind bard, traveling from place to place, singing his marvelous poems.

From early on, Homer was identified with one of his own characters, the blind bard Demodocus in the *Odyssey.* For his listeners and readers, Homer was, like Demodocus, a rhapsodist, a composer and performer of epic songs, who sometimes was called upon to compete with others, lending to his singing, as certain critics suggest, gestures to accompany the poetic events. Heraclitus the Grammarian thought that on one such occasion, Homer had competed with Hesiod in a recital contest. The description of Demodocus's performance appears in book 8 of the *Odyssey,* when, at the court of King Alcinous, the bard sings three stories to the sound of a kithara or lyre: first, a "song whose fame had reached the skies those days," The Strife Between Odysseus and Achilles; later, to please the crowds, The Love of Ares and Aphrodite; and finally, at Odysseus's leave-taking, the tale of the Wooden Horse and the sack of Troy. The first and last are wonderful moments of story within story, since Odysseus himself, unrecognized, is part of the audience and weeps at the memory of his retold past. (Another bard, the Ithacan Phemius, is described earlier on performing for Penelope's suitors at Odysseus's court.)[14]

Of the early bards or rhapsodists we know almost nothing, except that several of them were blind, traveled from town to town, and performed in public places and royal courts. However, there is a tradition reported by Pausanias that both Homer and Hesiod "failed to win the society of kings or else purposely despised it." Homer is said to have "deprecated the help afforded by despots in the acquisition of wealth in comparison with his reputation among ordinary men." And yet we know (Homer himself tells us) that they were meant "to sing the famous deeds of fighting heroes" (his word for poet is *aoidos,* "singer") and that they depended on the generosity of their listeners for bed and board. Reflecting on what he regarded as the exaggerated protraction of the final events in the *Odyssey,* his translator T. E. Lawrence (Lawrence of Arabia) observed, "Perhaps the tedious delay of the climax through ten books may be a poor bard's means of prolonging his host's hospitality."[15]

The traditional role of the poet-singer survived well into our time. In the 1930s, the American Milman Parry and his disciple Albert Lord discovered through their work on the bards of the former Yugoslavia a number of popular singers in the Muslim region of Serbia (*guzlars*) steeped in an ancient epic tradition very similar in form and style to that of Homer, whose poems show a high incidence of "formulaic" language. In broad terms, Parry and Lord challenged the traditional definition of a text and of how texts are shaped and acquire meaning over time. They suggested that the *Odyssey* and the *Iliad* might have been sung in a manner resembling that of these Balkan bards, whose songs were transmitted orally from generation to generation, and who, with the assistance of a string instrument, improvised on set texts and lent individual intonations and stresses to particular passages of a chosen poem.[16] That is to say, on the basis of established formulas, and using stories their audiences knew well, the bards sang poems that turned out to be newly perfected songs on each occasion.

Lord argued that the *Iliad* and the *Odyssey* did not mark a first stage in the sequence but the realization of a fully fledged performance in the hands of the gifted bard we call Homer. Lord further suggested that Homer, the putative author of one or both poems, could not write and that he dictated the verses to a scribe, giving birth to the text on which subsequent poets based theirs, a theory that Lord himself tempered late in life. Lord became interested not in discovering the "original" version of the *Iliad* and the *Odyssey* but in the many forms that the poems had acquired. "The word *multiform*," he wrote, "is more accurate than 'variant,' because it does not give preference or precedence to any one word or set of words to express an idea; instead it acknowledges that the idea may exist in several forms."[17]

Three centuries after Homer, by the fourth century BCE, the accoutrements of the bard had changed. Though he still remained "the interpreter of the poet's thought," he no longer used a lyre to accompany his words: now he dressed fashionably and carried an emblematic walking stick. "I am often envious of you rhapsodists in your profession," says Socrates, not without a certain irony. "Your art requires of you to go in fine array, and look as beautiful as you can, and meanwhile you must be conversant with many excellent poets, and especially with Homer, the best and most divine of all."[18]

How much of their poems the ancient Greek bards invented and how much they performed by rote, how strictly they were supposed to adhere to an original, and how the selection of their repertory was made are questions to which we have no clear answers. In 1997, Derek Walcott, the author of *Omeros*, a brilliant rendering of the Odyssean saga in a Caribbean setting, recognized his debt to Homer's poems but confessed that he hated the patronizing tone of academics digging for sources. "They are simultaneous concepts, not chronological concepts."[19]

Homer alone among the ancient bards emerged in the popular imagination as having perfected his art to such an extent that it became the measure of all excellence, never to be surpassed. An undated ordinance attributed to Solon, Pisistratus, or Hipparchus states that both the *Iliad* and the *Odyssey* should be recited in their entirety at the Panathenaia, a festival held in Athens in July in honor of the goddess Athena: Homer was the only poet thus honored.[20]

And yet the fact that Homer has a biography (or several) does not, of course, prove that he existed. "Some say," wrote Thomas De Quincey in 1841, "'there never was such a person as Homer.' 'No such person as Homer! On the contrary,' say others, 'there were scores.'" In 1904, Max Beerbohm drew a caricature of the many-personed Homer with "scores" of heads, strumming a lyre and carrying a label hung from his neck that reads "BLIND" in Greek.[21]

It may be that Homer was born not as a man but as a symbol, as the name that the ancient bards gave to their own art, turning a timeless activity into a legendary primordial person, into a celebrated common ancestor of all poets, the first and the best. When Milman Parry interviewed the Balkan guzlars and asked them for the names of the most admirable among them, several mentioned a master bard called Isak or Huso, a prodigy who lived longer than any normal man and whose birthplace was disputed. His repertory was immense, and it included all the best-known songs, but none of the witnesses had ever attended one of his recitals; they had only heard about him from other sources.[22] It is possible that Homer was born by much the same process.

The Albanian novelist Ismail Kadare met Albert Lord at a conference in Ankara, Turkey, in 1979; the meeting sparked Kadare's interest in Lord and Parry's theories and led to the writing of a novel, *The File on H*, published first in an Albanian magazine and later in a revised, shortened French translation in 1989. It tells the story of two Irish-American scholars who travel to Albania in the 1930s to record on mysterious machines called "tape-recorders" the performance of Albanian bards in order to discover how the

Homeric poems were composed. The Albanian authorities sus-
pect them of spying. Then one of the scholars begins to lose his
sight, which his colleague suspects is "Homer's revenge." The
mountain bards are told by the authorities to destroy the demonic
machines, and the two scholars leave for home. Miraculously,
the blind scholar is now capable of reciting the recovered poems
(which Kadare composed in the style of the traditional epics).[23]

Kadare had a short-lived political career in the 1970s as a
member of the Albanian Communist Parliament, a position that
enabled him to travel abroad and see his early books translated;
however, after he wrote a satirical poem about the dictator Enver
Hoxha, these privileges were withdrawn. Kadare continued to
write and occasionally publish, but in 1990 he fled to France,
where he claimed political asylum. Since his first novel, *The General of the Dead Army* (1963), Kadare has meticulously sought to
chronicle the story of his country, from the ancient days up to
the fall of communism, through the successive occupations by
the Romans, the Ottomans, the Italians, and the Nazis. Albania,
under Kadare's scrutiny, became a universal stage on which the
great tragedies of Europe's past were played out, in a vocabulary
with deep mythological roots. For Kadare, Homer offered the
archetype of all stories. Agamemnon, who is willing to sacrifice
his daughter Iphigenia for the sake of fair winds for his fleet, is
the model for every tyrant, Iphigenia the model for every victim.

Kadare found in Homer the language to speak of injustice in
our time. For Kadare's contemporary readers, as for Homer's first
audiences in the scattered Greek cities of his age, both the *Iliad*
and the *Odyssey* offered two unifying elements: common stories
and common gods. "Now in the contest between city and tribe,"
noted the historian Gilbert Murray, "the Olympian gods [Ho-
mer's pantheon] had one great negative advantage. They were
not tribal or local, and all other gods were. They were by this
time international, with no strong roots anywhere except where

one of them could be identified with some local god; they were full of fame and beauty and prestige. They were ready to be made 'Poliouchoi,' 'City-holders,' of any particular city, still more ready to be 'Hellânioi,' patrons of all Hellas."[24]

Homer's poems became the canonical texts that offered a cosmopolitan view of the gods and heroes; they were the reference against which documentary truths and metaphysical arguments could be tested. Two schools of thought reflected this dual reading. On one hand, historians argued that the legends were versions, more or less accurate, of actual facts. The historian Strabo, for example, argued that the *Odyssey* was written to teach geography: "Homer must be excused . . . if he mixed fantastic elements in his stories because they are meant to inform and instruct." On the other hand, the philosophers contended that the legends were allegories which concealed a sort of poetic proof. The Sophists in particular used Homer to illustrate and validate their discourse, while the Stoics were mostly inclined, not to read his work as if his poems were deliberate allegories, but to interpret certain passages and characters allegorically. Aristotle, however, refused to allegorize the mythical stories. His adamant position was mirrored centuries later by Bernard Le Bovier de Fontenelle, an inquisitive scholar whose life spanned one hundred years, during which he was celebrated for his writings, which made science accessible to the readers of the Enlightenment. In 1683, in his *Dialogues of the Dead*, the Sieur de Fontenelle imagined a conversation between Aesop and Homer in which the fabulist praises Homer for "his art of moral allegories." "Me?" says Homer in astonishment. "I never tried to do that." "What!" answers Aesop. "You haven't attempted to hide deep mysteries in your work?" "Not at all, I'm afraid," says Homer apologetically.[25]

"For the philosopher," concludes the historian Paul Veyne, "myth was an allegory of philosophical truths. For the historians, it was a minor deformation of historical truths."[26] For both,

Homer was the unavoidable reference. These two views of Homer echoed far into the future in the explorations and discoveries of the numerous schools of archaeologists who, following the early Greek historians, believed that the stories were true and that Homer described the events and their setting with illuminating accuracy, as well as in the countless new readings that surface in every age.

By the sixth century BCE, Homer had become not only the greatest of poets but the master whose view informed the entire Greek conception of the world, both of mortals and of gods, or of mortals who try to be heroes among gods who do not shine for their exemplary conduct. "Homer and Hesiod," wrote the philosopher Xenophanes, "have ascribed to the gods all things that are a shame and a disgrace among mortals, stealing and adultery and cheating on one another."[27] In this uncertain universe, as Homer made clear, human beings had to depend on their own resources and wit, not on the unreliable divine behavior. As a cautionary tale, few episodes are more atrocious than the gods' dealings with the Trojan Hector in the *Iliad*. At first, Hector is helped by Zeus and Apollo; then, at a certain arbitrary point, they abandon him to his fate. Worse still, the goddess Athena deceives him by passing herself off as one of Hector's own brothers and encourages him to fight Achilles, who, she knows, will certainly kill him. Homer's gods can be vicious con men.

And yet, in certain cases (though not by any means in all), the behavior of Homer's mortal heroes was something to which a just man might aspire. A professional ethos was developed among the Greek warrior class, recognizing that cool-headed tactics and loyal comradeship made better fighters, and so it became important to study in Homer the errors of Agamemnon, the devotion of Achilles to Patroclus, the resolution of Hector, the mulled-over experience of Nestor, the wily strategies of Odysseus. In this context, a formal education was deemed impossible without reference to Homer's work. The young Alcibiades, during a visit to a grammar school in around 430 BCE, asked the teacher for one of Homer's books, and being told that there was none, gave the poor man a blow with his fist.[28] A school without Homer was not a school; worse, it was a learning place without the means of learning excellence.

CHAPTER 2

Among the Philosophers

[Homer's work] forms a world in itself . . . which one can study to
the end of time and still feel that one is inside an epitome of the
entire literary cosmos.
—Northrop Frye, *The Secular Scripture and Other Writings,* 1975

From Homer's first interpreters in the sixth century BCE on, his
followers have seemed moved by a desire to tap into his prestige
rather than defend him against his detractors. Socrates (or rather
Plato, who made Socrates pronounce this encomium) tried to do
both. For Socrates, Homer might have been "the best and most
divine" but he also presented a philosophical dilemma. In the
Republic, Plato draws an analogy between human beings and the
societies they build. For Plato society can be seen as a reflection
of the human soul, divided into the governing, the military, and
the merchant classes, which loosely correspond to human intelligence, courage, and appetite (though this is a gross simplifica-
tion of Plato's complex and open view). From this ideal state, the
artisans of the false must be banned: that is to say, those who
make images of images have no place in a well-regulated world,
since they produce nothing that is true. An artist will, for example,
create a couch in a picture or in a poem, inspired by the couch a
cabinetmaker makes, in turn inspired by the archetypal idea of
a couch created by the godhead. Even Homer (and here begins

Plato's battle with the poet he most admires) cannot be allowed in the ideal republic because not only does he put forward images that are untrue, he presents men and women with whose faults we sympathize, and gods and goddesses whom we must judge as fallible. Literature, Plato says (and for Plato, Homer is the greatest literary craftsman), feeds that part in our soul that relishes "contemplating the woes of others," praising and pitying someone who, though "claiming to be a good man, abandons himself to excess in his grief." This is "the element in us that the poets satisfy and delight" and to avoid it, we should "disdain the poem altogether." Otherwise, "after feeding fat the emotion of pity there, it is not easy to restrain it in our own suffering." ("That's the price we have to pay for stability," says the Platonist Controller in Aldous Huxley's 1933 dystopia, *Brave New World*. "You've got to choose between happiness and what people used to call high art. We've sacrificed high art.") As Socrates tells his listeners, "high art" in particular corrupts us, whether we ourselves are good or bad, by pretending to offer spiritual enlightenment and a vicarious experience of the world, since in doing so it prevents us from seeking true self-knowledge and self-criticism. We think we know who we are by believing that we see our reflection in the characters of Achilles, Odysseus, Hecuba, Penelope. We stop defending Troy: we know that, whatever our struggles, the walls will crumble. We stop searching for Ithaca: we know that, whatever we do, we will reach home at last.[1]

Of course, as Plato knew, art and literature do not only offer us vicarious empathy and dangerous possibilities of inflated identities; they also carry the possibility of a vaster comprehension of the world. It is true that Mussolini found in the emblems of ancient Rome symbols to promote his fascist ideology and that in our time, during the assault on the American Capitol in Washington, on January 6, 2021, the mob carried flags embroidered with the phrase that the Spartan king Leonidas is said to have uttered when the Persian king ordered him to lay down his arms: *Molon labe,* classical Greek for "Come and take them," which has also become a slogan of American gun rights activists.[2] This is the noxious use of "the poets" that Socrates criticizes. But it is also true that art and literature (the "high art" of Huxley's Controller) are embedded in who we are, whether we participate actively or not in their enjoyment, simply as members of a literate society. Censorship of any kind can never suppress an idea entirely, but it can cause great damage by hiding from view the cultural evidence of a controversial subject, be it slavery, misogyny, or racism. The classics, Plato and Homer, imbue us with what the historian Mary Beard calls "a sense of wanting to rework the way we think about the past, by looking at slavery, debt, poverty, the fragility of democracy." She goes on: "History would be very dull if we weren't always trying to change how it was done. It's our conversation with the dead, and we practice a kind of ventriloquism in order to hear from the other side."[3]

According to Socrates, Homer was not an educator; he did not know how to make men better and he possessed no real knowledge, only the art of imitation, which is why he was neglected by his contemporaries. Had Homer and the other great poets been able to "help men achieve excellence," Socrates asks, would his fellow men "have suffered him and Hesiod to roam about rhapsodizing and would they not have clung to them far rather than to their gold, and constrained them to dwell with them in their homes, or failing to persuade them, would themselves have escorted them wheresoever they went until they should have sufficiently imbibed their culture?" Plato must have conceived these words with tongue firmly planted in his cheek, thinking of the fate of poor Socrates, the greatest educator of all, condemned to death by the society he strove to make better. Obviously Plato knew (all artists know) that society, whatever pittance it may accord an artist in grants, prizes, and memorials, always fails to honor and reward adequately those who, through craftsmanship and imagination, strive to make us better, and that its citizens, wherever and whenever, will always cling to their gold rather than to their goldsmith. As in all his dialogues, Plato presents Socrates as pursuing an argument to whatever corner it might lead, making no absolute claims and reaching no unimpeachable conclusions. "I cannot agree with you," says Hippias to Socrates in another of the dialogues. Socrates answers: "Nor can I agree with myself, Hippias, and yet that seems to be the conclusion which, as far as we can see at present, must follow from our argument." There speaks a man not afraid of allowing his thoughts absolute freedom to explore.[4]

Whether convincing or not, Plato's argument against Homer has haunted our societies since he first put it forward. It is the great paradox: we build societies in order to become happier and wiser; art, even the greatest art, grants us only the vicarious impression of both. Homer, who first and best created for us the spectacle of human shadows in constant battle, longing, suffering, and finally dying, is of all the most guilty, and must be held responsible for his progeny. When the Curate and the Barber decide to burn Don Quixote's library because, they believe, the books are responsible for the knight's madness, they come upon the *Amadís de Gaula,* the earliest of all novels of chivalry printed in Spain. "As the dogmatizer of such an evil sect," the Curate thunders, "we must, without any excuse, condemn it to the flames." But, counters the Barber, "it is also the best of all the books written in this genre and thus, as unique of its kind, it must be pardoned."[5]

The paradox is apparent in Plato: for all of art's supposedly noxious influence, Homer retains pride of place in Plato's library, surfacing at every occasion to illuminate a passage or provide a poignant reference: there are 331 references to Homer and his works in Plato's dialogues. "Do not you yourself feel [poetry's] magic and especially when Homer is her interpreter?" asks one of those who have listened to Socrates' arguments in the *Republic*. "Greatly," Socrates answers. And at the end of book 9, when one of the participants observes that such an ideal state as the Republic can be found in no place on earth, Plato lends Socrates an implicit reference to Homer that by its very use undermines the severity of the explicit ban. "It makes no difference whether it exists or ever will come into being," says Socrates. That is to say, it does not matter whether the Republic is built of stones and mortar or whether it remains an ideal, "a pattern of it laid up in heaven for him who wishes to contemplate it and so beholding to constitute himself its citizen."[6] What matters to Plato is the truth of the model, just as in the *Iliad*, for example, what matters is not the tragic outcome itself, but the "model" upon which the battle has been fought, as to us, its readers, the "models" of life set out in the two poems. These ideas, via Plato, will be the Homeric inheritance of the justice-seeking Don Quixote, of Dostoyevsky's idiot prince, even of Kafka's Josef K and of Melville's Ahab, each searching for the larger shape of his struggles and journeys within the little patch of universe he has been allotted. This then is Plato's (perhaps reluctant) reading of Homer: that our life must be lived to the best of our ethical abilities.

With Aristotle, the figure of the anecdotal man—the old blind wandering bard—faded into that of the literate, inspired poet. "Homer" came to mean his works, whether written by the poet himself or set down for posterity by others. For Aristotle too, Homer was the ultimate poetic reference, and not as an instance of a dangerous dream-life but as a craftsman's model, the example to be followed by those who aspired to high art, in tragedy as well as comedy. "As in the serious style, Homer is pre-eminent among poets, for he alone combined dramatic form with excellence of imitation, so he too laid down the main lines of comedy, by dramatizing the ludicrous instead of writing personal satire."[7] For Aristotle, Homer was not the ancient singer but the author of established texts, a master dramatist fully in control of his creation, and both the *Iliad* and the *Odyssey* (as well as a now lost mock-heroic poem called *Margites*) were exemplary solid works not subject to the fallible memory or the imperfect technique of the bards charged with performing them.

In the late nineteenth century, the German classicist Valentin Rose published a collection of fragments attributed to Aristotle that Rose judged spurious. The third edition, under the title *Aristotelis qui ferebantur librorum fragmenta* (Fragments of Books Attributed to Aristotle), included a number of questions supposedly posed by the Philosopher and answered by a mythical or literary interpretation: for instance, the seven flocks of fifty oxen slaughtered by Odysseus's men on the island of Helios (book 12 of the *Odyssey*) were a mythical representation of the solar days in a lunar year, and the head of Medusa on Athena's shield (book 5 of the *Iliad*) did not mean that the goddess displayed the actual head but that the shield had the same capacity to stun those who looked upon it.[8]

Though implicit references to Homer's books go back to the mid-seventh century BCE, in the works of poets such as Alcman of Sardis, Archilochus of Paros, and Tyrtaeus of Attica, the earliest acknowledged readings date from two centuries after his books were supposedly composed. According to Cicero, Homer's books were given their definitive written form in Athens under the tyrant Pisistratus, in the sixth century BCE.[9] The first known commentary on Homer (arguing that the Homeric books were allegorical, not historical accounts) is by Theagenes of Rhegium, a contemporary of Pisistratus, who produced an allegorical exegesis on the myths in Homer, substituting symbolic equivalents for the data of the story itself, and transposing them into the vocabulary of cosmology, physics, morality, and metaphysics. "Thus the myths are purified of the absurdities, implausibilities, or immoralities that scandalized the rational mind," wrote the historian

Jean-Pierre Vernant, "but at the price of renouncing what is essential in them, by refusing to take them literally and by making them say something other than what they simply intend to tell. This type of hermeneutic will find in Stoicism and Neoplatonism its most spectacular expression." In the fourth century BCE, the Attic orator Lycurgus, says Milton in the *Areopagitica*, "was so addicted to elegant learning as to have been the first that brought out of Ionia the scattered works of Homer," presumably edited for the common reader.[10] Four centuries later, commentaries on Homer were already so abundant and detailed that sixty-two lines from the *Iliad* (the famous Catalogue of Ships) provided a certain scholar, Demetrius of Scepsis, with material for thirty volumes, now lost.[11]

Not only scholars knew their Homer. Greek colonists exported his books to their many outposts. In Italy, about the time of the foundation of Rome in the eighth century BCE, the stories of Troy and Odysseus were deemed an essential part of a cultured person's world. The tomb originally thought to be that of a twelve-year-old boy from that time discovered in the Bay of Naples held, among various objects placed there to console the deceased in the afterlife, a cup inscribed with three lines of Greek. The first line is difficult to decipher, but the second and third read:

> I am Nestor's cup, good to drink from. Whoever drinks from
> this cup and drains it,
> Desire for lovely Aphrodite grabs him at once.[12]

The reference is to the *Iliad:* Achilles, seeing that the Trojans have pushed the Greek army back to their camp, sends his friend Patroclus to find out what is happening. Old King Nestor receives him in his tent, where drink and food have been set out, together with a notably splendid cup made of solid gold, studded with golden nails, fitted with handles, four all told, with two doves perched on each, heads bending to drink, and with twin supports running down to form the base.

> An average man would strain to lift it off the table when it was full,
> But Nestor, old as he was, could hoist it up with ease.[13]

The cup placed in the tomb might have served at drinking parties where participants would demonstrate their heroic strength by lifting it and perhaps quoting the appropriate Homeric lines. A moving comparison is implied between old Nestor, still able to lift the cup, and the boy who died too young, before being able to demonstrate his manly strength or enjoy the enticements of "lovely Aphrodite."

CHAPTER 3

Virgil

Virgil, it appears, was the first—in literature, at least—to apply
the linear principle: his hero never returns; he always departs. . . .
Had I been writing "The Divine Comedy," I would have placed
this Roman in Paradise: for outstanding services to the linear
principle, into its logical conclusion.
—Joseph Brodsky, "Flight from Byzantium," 1985

By the third and second centuries BCE, Homer's poems were
being studied at the Library of Alexandria by remarkable scholars
such as Zenodotus of Ephesus, Aristophanes of Byzantium, and,
perhaps the most erudite of all, the grammarian Aristarchus of
Samothrace. The editing method they followed, by and large,
was this: first, the authorship of a text was historically verified;
the text was then meticulously edited and divided into books or
chapters; finally, commentaries, exegeses, and scholia were gathered and annotated to facilitate its interpretation. Zenodotus
began work on Homer's poems by collating various copies of a
presumed lost original. He deleted obviously "foreign" elements,
marked questionable verses with a horizontal stroke to the left of
the particular line, and placed an asterisk next to passages about
which there might be some doubt but which, in his learned opinion, had indeed been composed by Homer.[1] Aristarchus revised
Zenodotus's work and added his own learned commentaries. For
philological reasons, Aristarchus suggested that certain sections
of the poems were later additions: among others, the story of the

nocturnal expedition during which the Trojan spy Dolon is captured in the *Iliad*, book 10, and the 120-odd verses at the end of book 23 of the *Odyssey*, in which Odysseus and Penelope, lying in bed, tell each other their adventures. Contemporary research has tended to agree with him.[2]

Aristarchus's painstaking erudition became legendary; in his wake, any exacting critic became known as an *aristarchus*. Thanks to the efforts of all these scholars, the texts of Homer's poems were largely stabilized; later work done in Byzantium during the early Middle Ages completed that of the Alexandrians. Available now in authoritative editions, Homer became the inspiration for the earliest Greek novelists, who from the first century BCE to the fifth century CE produced a series of popular love stories (*pathos erotikon*), for which they adopted not only Homer's subjects and themes but also his storytelling techniques and stylistic choices. Chariton, Xenophon, Longus (author of the famous pastoral *Daphnis and Chloë*), and Heliodorus made use of Homeric narrative devices such as the first-person account that Odysseus delivers at the Phaeacian court in books 9–12 of the *Odyssey*, the shifting points of view from the particular to the general and vice versa in the *Iliad*, and the beginning in medias res, in the middle of the story.[3] Thanks to them, these complex ways of creating character and plot, and of granting the reader emotion and conviction, became established as the primordial elements of fiction telling.

In the third century CE, the Neoplatonist philosopher Porphyry proposed to read Homer allegorically in order to find in the author of the *Odyssey* stories that would help him understand profound metaphysical questions. Porphyry had studied in Athens with the Greek rhetorician Cassius Longinus, who had suggested that the *Iliad* was composed in Homer's youth while the *Odyssey* was written in Homer's declining years, and then with the founder of Neoplatonism, Plotinus, in Rome. Porphyry wrote about everything, from astronomy to the nature of the soul, but

not much of his work has reached us. He applied Neoplatonism—
in very broad terms, the attempt to understand comprehensively
the universe and our place in it—to the tenets of pagan religion.
To achieve this lofty purpose, Porphyry sought to harmonize
the philosophies of Aristotle with those of Aristotle's teacher
Plato, and in doing so initiated a dialogue that extended over the
centuries. Reading in book 9 of the *Odyssey* an account of the
soul's travails, Porphyry interpreted the character of the Cyclops
as an incarnation of the bodily senses; when Odysseus tries
to kill the inhospitable monster, he is in effect trying to kill himself. That, according to Porphyry, is the act that Odysseus must
expiate.

> These gods must first be appeased by sacrifice and by the hard
> labor of the poor and by patience. . . . [Odysseus] will not be free
> of his labors until he has become completely free of the sea, and
> wiped out his very experience of the sea and of matter, so that
> he thinks an oar is a winnowing fan in utter ignorance of the
> business of seafaring.

The implication is that Odysseus has brought his misfortunes on
himself because he has forgotten his own nature and the universal
laws that guide us all. Later, in 523 CE, Boethius in his *Consolation
of Philosophy* has Philosophy herself explain to the author that the
state of exile is self-inflicted.

> You are overwhelmed by this forgetfulness of yourself: hence you
> have been thus sorrowing that you are exiled and robbed of all
> your possessions. You do not know the aim and end of all things;
> hence you think that if men are worthless and wicked, they are
> powerful and fortunate. You have forgotten by what methods the
> universe is guided; hence you think that the chances of good and
> bad fortune are tossed about with no ruling hand.[4]

In Rome, the *Iliad* and *Odyssey* were thought of as models to be copied or translated, to be then interpreted as allegories or taught as moral stories. What Homer said happened became both history and fiction, fact and symbol. In the third century BCE, Livius Andronicus, a Greek captive from Tarentum, produced a version of the *Odyssey* in Latin which Horace was to judge, 250 years later, as archaic, harsh, and vulgar. Nevertheless, the book became greatly successful and was used as a school text for the next three centuries. As if Greek history had been not only literally translated but spiritually transmigrated into the history of Rome, Roman children were introduced to Homer at the start of their schooling as a way to understand their own history. Commenting on the difficulty first-year law students experienced at the Roman court, Pliny the Younger wrote that "boys begin their career at the bar with Chancery cases just as they start with Homer in school: in both places they place the hardest first." Children were taught that Ulysses (the Roman Odysseus) ignored the Sirens in the same way the soul should ignore the temptation of the senses (the image was so popular that it appeared on tombstones), and that Achilles' anger showed how bad temper always turns against us. Horace, who learned Homer by heart at school under his teacher's cane, listed in one of his *Epistles* a number of these moral lessons and concluded, perhaps tongue-in-cheek, that through such stories "the Greeks must expiate their rulers' folly."[5]

Though Livius Andronicus had introduced Homer to the Latin reader, it was Virgil who made Homer a Latin author by adoption. Virgil's *Aeneid*, perhaps the greatest Roman literary achievement, is explicitly modeled on Homer's poems, and if Virgil owes an immense debt to Homer, the reverse is also true, because after Virgil, Homer acquired a new identity, that of Rome's earliest mythmaker. During the first Roman centuries, three legendary figures competed for the position of founder of the city: Romulus, who with his twin brother, Remus, was reported to have been suckled by a she wolf; Ulysses, the traveler; and Aeneas, the survivor of Troy. It was Marcus Terentius Varro, "the most learned of Romans" according to the rhetorician Quintilian, who in the first century BCE established Aeneas as the winner. Following the genealogy granted him by Homer ("Aeneas whom the radiant Aphrodite bore Anchises/down the folds of Ida, a goddess bedded with a man"), Varro established a detailed list of the ports of call on Aeneas's route from Troy (Ilion) to Italy and confirmed the claim of Julius Caesar that his family, the *gens Iulia,* was descended from the goddess of love via the Trojan refugee. But it was Virgil who transformed the legend into something resembling history, lending the defeated Trojans a posthumous victory over their enemy. Thanks to Virgil, the works of Homer, which had seemed until that point to be merely stories (albeit masterly) of battles and travel, were read as inspired premonitions of the world to come: first of Rome and its imperial power, and later of the advent of Christianity and beyond.[6]

The details of Virgil's life are thought to come mainly from a biography that has not reached us, written by a contemporary of Virgil's, the Roman poet Varius. Virgil (Publius Vergilius Maro) was born in the Etruscan town of Andes, near Mantua, on October 15, 70 BCE: his family name was probably Etruscan; his first name, a conventional Roman tag. Though his earliest biographies, written long after his death, made him out to be the son of a poor itinerant potter who married the daughter of one of his employers, Virgil was a Roman citizen by birth whose family held official posts of some importance in the Roman administration. Throughout his childhood and youth, of which we know very little, Italy was ravaged by civil war. Only in the year 31 BCE did the victory of Octavian (who was to become the emperor Augustus) at Actium put an end to the upheavals. Perhaps due to poor health, Virgil never held an administrative or military position, nor did he aspire to become a lawyer or a senator. He never married.

At the age of seventeen, Virgil left the countryside for Rome. An early short poem, in an anthology which may not be entirely by his hand, reveals Virgil's intention of abandoning youthful scribbles and dedicating himself to serious studies instead:

> Leave me Muses, you too, goodbye to you,
> Sweet Muses, because I will confess the truth,
> Sweet you have been, and yet you could sometimes
> Revisit my papers: decently: not often.[7]

In Rome, the young Octavian may have been Virgil's patron; in that case, it was probably for him that Virgil composed his *Eclogues* in the manner of the Greek poet Theocritus. The *Eclogues* made him famous. He was recognized and hailed in the streets, a painful experience for a shy man, who in such cases would seek refuge in the nearest house. Life in Rome became too exhausting, and Virgil retired to Naples, where he spent most of his remaining years. In 19 BCE, he set off with Augustus on a trip to Greece, but he became seriously ill and returned to die in Brindisium (present-day Brindisi).

Virgil wrote slowly: the *Eclogues* took him three or four years; the *Georgics*, dedicated to Augustus's chief minister, the rich Maecenas, seven or eight. We know that Virgil himself read the *Georgics* to Augustus in 31 BCE, and—whether through imperial encouragement or through a private sense of having acquired the necessary skills—the poet, now approaching forty, felt ready to undertake a more ambitious project. With renewed energy, at about this time Virgil started work on a new poem, which, like his two previous books, would carry a Greek name: the *Aeneid*.

At home, Virgil must have learned some Greek together with his Latin, since there were many Greek émigrés in Lombardy, but it was the poet Parthenius of Nicaea, author of a catalogue of erotic myths, who is said to have taught him in depth the language of Homer.[8] The Roman province of Greece, known as Achaea (a word that echoes Homer's designation), was for the Romans both a subservient colony and the ancient source of their own culture, with all the hierarchical implications of this dual identity. For the Romans of Virgil's time, Greece was attractive and exotic: the cultured Romans who traveled there visited the temples and palaces, studied the religious mysteries, brought back art objects to decorate their own households, and imitated the "Greek manner" by growing beards and taking boyfriends. In all this, however, they ostentatiously remained the masters. In the *Aeneid*, Aeneas's father warns his son never to forget that however magnificent the art and culture of other civilizations (meaning, namely, that of Greece), Romans are, and will remain, the rulers. Dante, in his political treatise *De Monarchia*, echoes this mandate and attributes it to Homer via Aristotle. "In the Philosopher's [Aristotle's] words, 'Every house must be ruled by the senior member.' And thus it behooves him, as Homer said, to bend the world to his rule and impose his laws on the rest." Many an imperialistic credo is built on a similar distinction and has for today's readers a familiar ring:

> Let others fashion from bronze more lifelike breathing images—
> For so they shall—and evoke living faces from marble;
> Others excel as orators, others track with their instruments
> The planets circling in heaven and predict when stars will appear.
> But, Romans, never forget that government is your medium!
> Be this your art:—to practice men in the habit of peace,
> Generosity to the conquered, and firmness against aggressors.[9]

Hearing that Virgil was hard at work, Augustus was eager to know exactly what the poem was about. He may have suggested to his favorite poet that an epic on the origins of Rome, glorifying of course his own rule, might be welcome. We know that Augustus wrote to Virgil from Spain, asking to see even a fragment. Virgil declined. Years later, Virgil agreed to read out loud to the emperor three books of the first half of the poem: the fall of Troy, the death of Dido, and Aeneas's visit to the Underworld. We know (because Virgil's secretary Eros tells us) that he wrote a page in the morning and then corrected it throughout the day until little was left of the original lines. He compared this method to a bear giving birth to her cubs and then licking them into shape. It is not obvious that Augustus understood him: "How could you ask that Caesar's pride admit the concept of metaphor, since Caesar never accepted the humility of perception?" asked Hermann Broch in his 1945 novel *The Death of Virgil.*[10]

Virgil was a keen, scholarly reader of Homer, not only of the poems but also of the ancient commentaries. Homer had told of the siege of Troy, distilling the agonies of a ten-year-long war into forty days of fighting; and later the return of one of the warriors, clever Odysseus/Ulysses, through a sea of troubles to his home in Ithaca. Virgil, accordingly, structured his poem in two parts, reversing Homer's order of events: the first (Aeneas's flight and travels) based on the *Odyssey;* the second (his battles leading up to the foundation of Rome) on the *Iliad.* Legend has it that before he died, Virgil asked his friends to burn the manuscript. Whether he was dissuaded or whether his friends chose to disobey, the book was soon afterward edited and widely distributed. Certain readers have felt that the second half of the *Aeneid* has something a little disappointing about it, less because Virgil did not have the time to polish it than, as the historian Peter Levi has perceptively pointed out, because Virgil "did not understand the fundamental principle in Homer's world, that poetry belongs to the defeated and the dead."[11] In Virgil's poem, Aeneas the hero was necessarily a victor, founder of the dynasty whose present inheritor was Augustus himself. There are no true victors in Homer.

For a number of reasons, Aeneas was the obvious Homeric hero to choose as the protagonist of a Roman epic, someone who intuits that, as Virgil has it, "An age shall come, as the years glide by,/When the children of Troy shall enslave the children of Agamemnon." Aeneas was the inheritor of the glory of Troy, a fate attributed to him implicitly in the *Iliad*, in which Achilles taunts "the great-hearted fighter" and asks him whether his courage will really allow him to challenge Achilles "in hopes of ruling your stallion-breaking friends/and filling Priam's throne." Aeneas became a famous hero: his escape from Troy, bearing his father, Anchises, on his back and leading away his infant son, was depicted on many frescoes, painted vases, and mosaics, and was therefore constantly present in the popular imagination. Early writers had continued his adventures all the way from Troy to the shores of Italy, and had suggested that he had conveniently settled in the neighborhood of what was to become Rome. Already in the third century BCE, the Latin poet Naevius had referred to Aeneas as "the father of the Roman people," and two centuries later, Lucretius began his lengthy poem *On the Nature of Things* by invoking the "Mother of the Aeneadae, darling of men and gods, increase-giving Venus."[12]

Homer's heroes have a rich complexity, a randomness of character that troubles the reader with endlessly nuanced interpretations. Outside allegorical readings, the psychology of Achilles, for instance, or of Odysseus is rewardingly bewildering. Achilles—sulking, egotistical, brave, faithful in his loves, lacking compassion toward his victims but capable of magnanimity, "a kill-ease" to use Lewis Carroll's pun—has a kaleidoscopic personality that never quite resolves itself, not even at the end of the book. The Australian writer David Malouf, in his novel *Ransom*, describes Achilles' complex character coming into being when the young adolescent first enters the world of warriors, slipping (Malouf says) "out of his hard boyish nature" to become "eel-like, fluid, weightless," as he discovers "a world of pain, loss, dependency, bursting violence and elation; of fatality and fatal contradiction."[13] Achilles' essential anger is multifaceted, impossible to define exactly. His anger at Agamemnon's military incompetence is not the same as his anger at Agamemnon's insulting treatment, which is again quite unlike his feelings after the death of Patroclus. "Wrath," "anger," even "mania" have been chosen to define the passion that triggers the narrative, each word qualified in turn to give it a particular tone.

Different translators have rendered the first line of the *Iliad* into English in a variety of ways. In 1616, George Chapman, whose translations so impressed John Keats, conceived it as: "Achilles' baneful wrath resound, O Goddess, that impos'd/Infinite sorrows on the Greeks." Thomas Tickell in 1715 suggested "Achilles' fatal Wrath, whence Discord rose/That brought the Sons of Greece unnumber'd Woes,/O Goddess sing." Alexander Pope published in 1715–20 a controversial *Iliad* that began like this: "Achilles' wrath, to Greece the direful spring/Of woes unnumber'd, heavenly goddess, sing!" In 1880, Henry Dunbar translated it as "The baneful wrath of Peleus' son, Achilles, goddess sing." Among the twentieth-century translations, A. T. Murray gave the line as "The wrath sing, goddess, of Peleus' son Achilles." W. H. D. Rouse summed it up as "An angry man—there is my story: the bitter rancour of Achilles, prince of the house of Peleus." H. D. F. Kitto's version was "Divine Muse, sing of the ruinous wrath of Achilles, Peleus' son." Richmond Lattimore's read, "Sing, goddess, the anger of Peleus' son Akhilleus/and its devastation." Robert Lowell came up with: "Sing for me, Muse, the mania of Achilles/that cast a thousand sorrows on the Greeks." Robert Fagles, whose translations are used in this book, rendered it simply as "Rage—Goddess, sing the rage of Peleus' son Achilles."[14]

A similar sampling of tempers (and equal problems of range) arise in every language into which Homer has been translated.

Juan de Mena, in 1519, translating from a Latin version, was plod-
dingly explicit: "Divinal musa, canta conmigo, Omero, la ira del
sobervio hijo de Peleo—es dezir Achilles" (Divine muse, sing with
me, Homer, the ire of the haughty son of Peleus, that is to say,
Achilles). In 1793, the German Johann Heinrich Voss began his
Ilias with the simplest rendition: "Singe den Zorn, o Göttin, des
Peleiaden Achilleus" (Sing the wrath, O Goddess, of the Pelian
Achilles). Almost a hundred years later, Charles-Marie Leconte de
Lisle attempted le mot juste: "Chante, Déesse, du Pèléide Akhil-
leus la colère désastreuse" (Sing, Goddess, of the Pelian Achil-
les the disastrous wrath). The twentieth-century Brazilian poet
Haroldo do Campos was concise: "A ira, Deusa, celebra do Peleio
Aquiles" (The anger, Goddess, celebrate, of Pelian Achilles).[15]
"To call Achilles' anger 'terrible,'" wrote the nineteenth-century
scholar Juan Valera, commenting on a later Spanish version that
spoke of *terrible cólera,*

> is to translate badly. [The word Homer uses] comes from the
> Greek verb "to lose, to destroy" and means "fatal, pernicious,
> unfortunate, harmful," all of which are not terrible but something
> more than terrible. There are terrible things in the world that lead
> to no harm whatsoever, but Achilles' anger was not one of them.
> . . . The sound Apollo's arrow makes when shot is terrible, the eyes
> of Minerva shine in a terrible manner, a terrible fire burns over
> the head of magnanimous Achilles. Finally Priam, when Helen
> comes to see him, seems in her eyes venerable and terrible, and
> yet Priam intends no harm to Helen, nor does he hurt her in any
> way; rather he treats her with fatherly kindness, even though he
> fills her with terror and shame. Who has been harmful is Helen,
> harmful to Priam, without for that reason having been terrible.[16]

Why is anger, Achilles' anger, the subject of the *Iliad*? Because,
in Homer's telling, it is the driving force of the war, without which

there would be no story. "Anger" (*amertume*, "bitterness"), says the French historian Frédéric Gros in *Why War?*, "is a formidable destructive force ... and we are obliged to recognize that many wars are not fought *in aid of* history but *against* it."[17] And yet, Achilles' anger is neither constant nor clear. It covers a vast range of angers, and Homer carefully describes the circumstances under which they arise—fury at Agamemnon's insult, pique at the suggestion of giving up Briseis, spite when begged to join his comrades, sullenness when Patroclus asks to borrow his armor, frenzy at Patroclus's killing, murderous rage against Hector. Even when dead, Achilles is not rid of his anger. In the Underworld, when Odysseus visits him, he bridles at the suggestion that death might be a good thing.[18] The historian Nancy Sherman, discussing the makeup of the military mind, argues that though anger is as much a part of war as weapons and armor, it is of military value only when held in control. The Stoics believed that anger, like all emotions, was a voluntary state, but they denied that it was an acceptable warrior-like quality, since it distorts our view of the world. Sherman notes that to temper the feeling of anger, the Stoics proposed an *apatheia*, "a freedom from passions in which there is no frenzy or rage, no annoyance or bitterness, no moral outrage." In the nineteenth century, Stendhal associated this steadfast state with the heroes of Greece and Rome. "I forgot to be angry!" says Fabrice in *The Charterhouse of Parma*. "Am I perhaps one of those great courageous beings of which antiquity has given the world a few examples? Am I a hero without knowing it?" If Fabrice is an ancient hero, he is certainly not a Homeric one. There is no apatheia among Homer's heroic characters.[19]

In Virgil, this variety of emotional traits is much simplified. The psychology of the characters is not less believable; it is less ambiguous, with the exception perhaps of Queen Dido, who casts her abused, mournful shadow well into our time. Aeneas, however, has appeared to some readers as too single-minded, too word perfect. "We will always admire more the Achilles described by Homer, with all his defects, than the perfect hero incarnated by the Aeneas of Virgil, because of the illusion and persuasion that render the former more believable," observed the nineteenth-century poet Giacomo Leopardi, careful reader of both.[20]

In the *Iliad* and the *Odyssey*, the heroes are in the hands of gods who, if not mad, at least behave in an erratic manner. In the *Aeneid*, because their designs, however whimsical, have already been laid out by Homer, the gods seem to have a clearer purpose, so the misfortunes that befall Aeneas or the difficult decisions he must make (to leave Dido, for example) acquire a specific meaning in the fateful story: the show must go on. In Homer, the funeral of Hector and the arrival in Ithaca are powerful moments in the dramas, and the last ones, but they are not conclusions. The implicitly announced foundation of Rome is not only the conclusion of the *Aeneid*; it is its raison d'être. "How shall it end now?" asks Jupiter to Juno in the final lines. And then, following Juno's answer, the god commands:

All will be Latins, speaking
One tongue. From this blend of Italian and Trojan blood shall arise
A people surpassing all men, nay even the gods, in godliness.[21]

Augustus could not have wished for a better ending.

CHAPTER 4

Christian Homer

When he [the seventeenth-century French rhetorician Claude Belurgey] was asked what his religion was, he answered that it was that of the great men of Antiquity, Homer, Aristotle, Cicero, Pliny, Seneca.

—Gui Patin, letter of 1662

After Virgil, from the first centuries of the Christian era on, the church fathers attempted not so much to reconcile Homer with the godliness of the authority of the *vera religio* but to find in the tenets of that religion gaps into which Homer might fit. God had created the book of the world in which we are all written, and his son had corrected in his blood our errors; now the new stories were forced to share the shelf on which the first place had been allotted until that point to Homer.

For the great thinkers of the early church, the apparent conflict between the old pagan literature and the dogma of the new faith presented a difficult intellectual problem. One of the most learned of these Christian scholars, Saint Jerome, attempted throughout his long life to reconcile the two. Jerome realized that he could never honestly disclaim Homer as his own intellectual beginning, nor could he ignore the aesthetic pleasure Homer's books had given him. Instead, he could create a hierarchy, a *gradus ad Parnassum* of which Homer and the ancients were the necessary grounding and the Bible the highest peak.

Jerome was born in Dalmatia around 342. Though his parents were Christian, he was not baptized until his eighteenth birthday. He studied Latin in Rome under the guidance of the celebrated scholar Aelius Donatus, author of the most popular medieval grammar book, the *Ars grammatica.* Thanks to Donatus, Jerome became thoroughly familiar with the great names of antiquity, names which he later quoted copiously in his writings. In his thirties, he traveled to Syria, where he learned Hebrew from a distinguished rabbi and lived among the hermits in the deserts near Antioch. He was ordained a priest but did not exercise his office; instead he became secretary to Pope Damasus I, who ordered him to revise the Latin translation of the New Testament from the Hebrew and Greek.[1] Jerome did more than revise it: he rewrote most of it, as well as translating afresh a large part of the Old Testament. The colossal achievement, the Latin Bible known as the Vulgate, ensured his intellectual fame and became the standard version of Scripture for Catholics for the next fifteen centuries. The long hours he toiled on this commission, urged on by his impatient patron, the meticulous research he undertook to overcome the obstacles presented by the original, and the pittance he received in payment for all his work inspired the Catholic Church to name him the patron saint of translators.

In an autobiographical letter to a friend, Jerome recounts a dream which soon became famous. To follow his religious vocation and in compliance with the precepts of the church, Jerome had cut himself off from his family and renounced the luxuries (especially "dainty food") to which he was accustomed. What he could not bring himself to do was abandon the library that "with great care and toil" he had put together in Rome; racked by guilt, he would mortify himself and fast but "only that I might afterwards read Cicero." A short time later, Jerome fell deathly ill. Fever caused him to dream, and he dreamt that his soul was suddenly caught and hauled before God's judgment seat. A voice asked him who he was, and he replied: "I am a Christian." "Thou liest," said the voice, "thou art a follower of Cicero, not of Christ. 'For where your treasure is, there will your heart be also.'" Overcome with dread, Jerome promised God that "if ever again I possess worldly books, or if ever again I read such, I have denied thee." But the great oath was too onerous and seemed impossible to keep: every reader's memory furnishes him with remembered books, whether he desires it or not, and even if Jerome had firmly resolved never to read worldly books again, the ones read in his youth would open their pages to him, calling up line after line in front of his mind's eye, and he would have broken his oath through powers beyond him. Jerome then changed his promise to one that seemed more reasonable: "to read the books of God with a zeal greater than I had previously given to the books of men." Jerome promised God to make use of the ancient authors in order to better read his word.[2]

In his childhood, Jerome had befriended a boy called Rufinus, who in later years became his strongest intellectual opponent. Rufinus, intent on persecuting his one-time friend, prompted a Roman orator called Magnus to raise once more the question of pagan versus Christian culture, and ask Jerome why he so often made use of the writings of the ancients in his ecclesiastical work, "contaminating the sacred with the profane." Jerome answered with an impassioned defense of the classics, giving arguments that were used for centuries afterward. He suggested that every reader, by culling and interpreting, transforms an old text into a new one, one capable of shedding light upon problems ignored by the original author. "My efforts," wrote Jerome of his readings, "promote the advantage of Christ's family, my so-called defilement with an alien increases the number of my fellow servants." Above all, were not the words of Christ to be treated with the uttermost respect, and therefore translated into the best and purest words available? And was not the best and purest tongue that of the old masters, whose devices and styles needed therefore to be studied? Erasmus, who in the early sixteenth century annotated Jerome's letters, pointedly asked, "Is the profession of Christ at odds with eloquence? If Cicero speaks eloquently about his gods, what prevents a Christian from also speaking eloquently about holiness and true religion?"[3]

A contemporary of Saint Jerome's, Saint Augustine, was also, in his youth, a great reader of the classics, but when the problem of conflicting cultures presented itself to him, his answer was not that of Jerome. Augustine was born in Thagaste, in what is now Algeria, in 354. His mother was a Christian, and though she tried to teach her son the faith of her church, he was clearly more drawn to the old stories of Greece and Rome—more of Rome than Greece since, as he tells us, Greek held little charm for him as a child, and even as an adult he was not able to understand the language fully. Perhaps because he could not read it properly, he disliked Greek literature. "Homer," he wrote, "as well as Virgil, was a skilful spinner of yarns and he is most delightfully imaginative. Nevertheless, as a boy, I found him little to my taste. I suppose," he added apologetically, "that Greek boys think the same about Virgil when they are forced to study him as I was forced to study Homer."[4]

In Carthage, where he was sent to complete his education, Augustine set up house with a young woman with whom he had a son; following his parents' orders, he left her to marry another woman whom his mother had picked for him, but the marriage did not take place. Augustine became a teacher, working in Rome and then in Milan, where he was instructed by the aged Ambrose, an old friend of his mother's. In his youth, Augustine had been seduced by the Manichaeans, whose doctrine proclaimed that the universe was the fruit of two independent principles, Good and Evil, permanently in conflict. Now, under the influence of Ambrose and of the writings of Plotinus and the Neoplatonists, he abjured the Manichaeans (he was to become one of their fiercest enemies), accepted the religion of his mother, and decided to devote his life to God. He returned to Africa, where he founded a religious community. In 396 he was made bishop of Hippo. The Vandals invaded North Africa in 428, and two years later besieged Augustine's city. Augustine was then seventy-six years old. He died in the fourth month of the siege, on August 28, 430.[5]

All his adult life, Augustine was conscious of the haunting shadow cast by the books he had read in his past; he knew that his old love for Virgil colored all his reading and writing, and the alluring influence of the pagan classics troubled him deeply. Horace (whom Augustine had also read in his youth and much admired) had written an epistle to a young student of rhetoric, Lollius Maximus, telling him that he was rereading Homer and that, in his opinion, Homer, better than any rhetorician, could show us "what is fair, what is foul, what is helpful, what not": "Now, while still a boy," Horace urged, "drink in my words with clean heart, now trust yourself to your betters. The jar will long keep the fragrance of what it was once steeped in when new."[6]

Augustine turned Horace's words around and used them as a warning against allowing young children to read Virgil: "They take great draughts of his poetry into their unformed minds," he wrote, "so that they may not easily forget him." Horace, Augustine agreed, was right: the books we loved best in our youth keep haunting us throughout our life. Therefore, since he could not uproot them from his soul, he needed to find a method to convert these ancient stories into cautionary tales in spite of themselves, thereby satisfying both Augustine's taste for good literature and his demand for higher morals—in effect, having his classical cake and eating it too. "Can any schoolmaster in his gown," Augustine asked, "listen unperturbed to a man who challenges him on his own ground and says 'Homer invented these stories and attributed human sins to the gods. He would have done better to provide men with examples of divine goodness'? It would be nearer the truth to say that Homer certainly invented the tales but peopled them with wicked human characters in the guise of gods. In this way their wickedness would not be reckoned a crime, and all who did as they did could be shown to follow the example of the heavenly gods, not that of sinful mortals."[7]

Augustine put his own advice into practice. His *City of God*, for example, begins with a long analysis of the various ways in which the ancient authors described and commented on the fall of Troy—authors other than Homer, since the *Iliad* ends before the destruction of the city. This classic example allowed Augustine better to praise the building of a heavenly city, and to cite the heroes of Greece and Rome in order to enhance the greater example of the Christian martyrs. The arguments are mostly convincing because Augustine is an extraordinary rhetorician, well versed in the methods of Cicero, and yet at the same time, the reader feels that the scent of the early wine has not vanished entirely, and that the boy who wept for Dido and "was sad not to be able to read the very things that made me sad" is still there, lusting for his beloved books.[8] In his attempt to reconcile past and present cultures, it is not clear whether Augustine eventually came to understand that he did not have to forgo either. For Christianity, the reading of the ancient authors lent the new faith a prehistory and a universality. For the ancient world, it meant continuity and transmission of intellectual experience.

Fifteen hundred years after Augustine, one of his distant readers, the German poet Heinrich Heine, gave the division between pagans and Christians yet another twist, forcing a choice between that which Homer and the Greeks represented—an archetypal conception of Beauty—and that which the Judeo-Christian world sought to impose: a dogmatic and divinely revealed Truth. In the last poem he wrote, a fortnight before his death in Paris in 1856, dedicated to his beloved and barely literate French mistress

Mouche, Heine described a disturbing dream. He sees a dead man (Heine himself is that man) lying in an open sarcophagus, surrounded by bits of broken sculpture. The sarcophagus is decorated with scenes taken from both classical mythology and the Old Testament. Suddenly, quarreling voices break into the quiet of the place.

> Oh, the argument will never end.
> Always will Truth quarrel with Beauty.
> The human army will always split
>
> Into the Greeks and the Barbarians.[9]

CHAPTER 5

Other Homers

Achilles only exists because of Homer.

—François-René de Chateaubriand, Preface to *Les Natchez*, 1826

Almost a century and a half after Augustine's death, a quaestor of the Ostrogoth king Theodoric and minister to three of his successors, Flavius Magnus Aurelius Cassiodorus Senator, wrote a treatise on religious and civil education called *Institutiones divinarum et saecularium litterarum* in which, for the first time, instructions were given on how to study the liberal arts in the context of Christian doctrine. Time abbreviated both the author's name and that of his book, which became known as Cassiodorus's *Institutiones* and was considered an essential learning tool well into the Renaissance. The *Institutiones* is divided into two parts. The first is a guide to scriptural study and the art of collecting and copying manuscripts; the second is an encyclopedic treatment of the seven liberal arts. According to Cassiodorus, all the arts, ancient and modern, are to be found "in essence" in the Holy Scriptures: all wisdom and all art comes from them, and even the pagan writers (such as Homer) received their illumination from the eternal word of God, not yet revealed but ever-present. One of Cassiodorus's early works is the *Expositio Psalmorum*, a detailed and methodical examination of Psalms. Here Cassiodorus analyzed the text that would sustain the argument of the *Institutiones*. Did not Psalm 19 clearly say that "the heavens declare the glory of God" everywhere and in all time? Did it not declare that "there is no speech nor language, where their voice is not heard"? For Cassiodorus, anyone in any age was therefore capable of learning from that all-embracing voice. But which was the best language in which to learn this heavenly wisdom?[1]

In 324, shortly before the birth of Augustine, the Roman emperor Constantine transferred the seat of government to Byzantium and gave it his own name. As Constantinople, the city was to become the center of all important political and cultural activities of the empire. By the eighth century, even though the laws of old Byzantium, in order to satisfy both the western and the eastern regions of the vast empire, were being translated into Latin and Greek, only Greek was held to be the natural language of literature and philosophy, and therefore the business of monasteries and colleges. Children from the age of eight on were taught elements of Greek grammar not only through pious works but also by means of anthologies of the classics that included selections of Homer. After learning the rules of the language by heart, the students composed poems and speeches imitating the ancient models. These formal tasks reached their absurd peak with a teaching exercise called the schedograph. This consisted of the dictation of a text with as many homonyms and rare words as possible, so that the student would have to learn the spelling of the first by context and of the second by memorizing an abstruse vocabulary. Memory played an important part in Byzantine education: after several years of schooling, students were expected to know the *Iliad* by heart.

Principal among the schools of higher learning was the Royal College of Constantinople, whose president was pompously called the Sun of Science, while his twelve assistants, the twelve professors of the various faculties, were known as the Twelve Signs of the Zodiac. The college possessed a library of between forty thousand and seventy thousand volumes, including a majority of Greek works, among them a manuscript of Homer written on a roll of parchment 120 feet long, said to be made from the intestines of a fabulous serpent.[2]

In the seventh century, Egypt had ceased to be part of the empire, and parchment began to replace the Egyptian papyrus, just as papyrus had, in the seventh century BCE, replaced parchment among the Greeks. The invention of lower-case cursive allowed scribes to produce more copies at a lower cost, since fewer pages were needed to hold a given text. More readers were therefore able to become familiar with the whole of an original work, rather than with a selection that had been compiled into an anthology in order to transcribe or annotate it. For the Byzantines, the craft of literature was above all copy and gloss, and originality was deemed a worthless endeavor, except when displaying one's knowledge of arcane words and phrases. A deliberate preciousness clung to the Byzantine appreciation of the classics, and the Greek writers of Constantinople imitated the ancient models without aspiring to either their charm or their power. "Their prose," wrote the historian Edward Gibbon, "is soaring to the vicious affectation of poetry: their poetry is sinking below the flatness and insipidity of prose. The tragic, epic, and lyric muses, were silent and inglorious: the bards of Constantinople seldom rose above a riddle or epigram, a panegyric or tale; they forgot even the rules of prosody; and with the melody of Homer yet sounding in their ears, they confound all measure of feet and syllables in the impotent strains which had received the name of *political* or city verses."[3]

Gibbon's judgment is perhaps too harsh. If the wordsmiths of Constantinople were not as admirable as their ancestors, they nevertheless produced some remarkable work, especially in the realms of history and biography, in which Homer's influence was heard as a distant beat. For any educated person at the court, familiarity with some of Homer's work was a mark of distinction. An anecdote recorded in the eleventh-century *Chronographia* of Michael Psellus illustrates the point. During a court procession, an onlooker, seeing the beautiful imperial consort Sclerena go by, softly quoted the first part of a line from the *Iliad,* in which the Trojans, speaking of the beautiful Helen, say: "It were no shame [that Trojans and well-greaved Achaeans should suffer pain long time for a woman such as she]" but did not complete it. At the time, Sclerena "gave no sign of having heard these words, but when the ceremony was over, she sought out the man who had uttered them and asked him what they meant. She repeated his quotation without a single mistake, pronouncing the words exactly as he had whispered them. As soon as he told her the story in detail, and the crowd showed its approval of his interpretation of the anecdote, as well as of the Homeric reference, she was filled with pride and her flatterer was rewarded for his compliment." Sclerena had not read the *Iliad,* and yet in her eyes, apposite knowledge of Homer granted the courtier a certain prestige.[4]

By the end of the fourth century, the division between the Greek East and the Latin West in the Roman Empire became more evident. In the East, church and state lent citizens the sense of living in a divinely appointed Christian realm, while in the West, service to the emperor and service to the Christian authorities were seen as two separate duties. Intellectually, the East held as essential the traditional study of the classics, both Greek and Latin; in the West classical scholarship was judged to be part and parcel of pagan beliefs. Therefore, while Homer continued to be edited, studied, and read in Constantinople, in Rome he all but faded from the memory of readers. Many Roman Christians now believed that their intellectual duty was exclusively to the revealed Gospels and felt no deep attachment to the old written culture;

consequently, they may have experienced no compunction in throwing away the old papyrus scrolls in which the classical texts were preserved. Whereas in the East, Bishop Athanasius told holy virgins to "have books in their hands at dawn," in the West, Christians quoted Augustine, who had written approvingly of holy men who lived through "faith, hope and charity—without books."[5]

The dispute that had preoccupied Jerome and Augustine between Roman Christianity and ancient Rome was largely to blame for the neglect of classical culture. In 382, the statue of the goddess Victory, symbol of Rome's glory since the time of Augustus, was removed from the altar of the Senate House by imperial orders to placate the Christians among the senators. The spokesman for the pagan majority was Quintus Aurelius Symmachus, father-in-law of Boethius (both of whom, years later, under Ostrogothic rule, would be accused of treasonable dealings with Constantinople and tortured to death). Symmachus argued eloquently not for the suppression of Christianity but for Christian tolerance "for the age-old cult of his class," noting that surely the emperor had nothing to gain by outlawing the rites of his own ancestors. "Was not Roman religion (and here is the heart of the matter) inextricably tied to Roman law? If one part of the heritage went, must not the others follow?" Symmachus's quiet argument was answered by the bishop of Milan, Augustine's instructor Saint Ambrose. He accepted the points made by his opponent, and yet the question, he said, was not an intellectual but a political one. If the emperor agreed with the pagans, the bishops would withdraw their support of the government. The Christians' threat won the battle.[6]

When the Gothic king Alaric, who had invaded the Italian peninsula in 401, besieged and entered Rome nine years later, the fall of the city was perceived as a punishment willed by the ancient gods on the followers of the new one. The Goths too were Christians: they had been converted in the mid-fourth century by a Greek preacher called Ulfilas, who, being a follower of the Arian heresy, taught that while God the father was divine, Jesus his son was not. For the Roman Christians, the fact that the invaders were heretics compounded Rome's humiliation. It no longer seemed important to attempt reconciliation with the pagan past. For a time the ancient texts were still preserved and studied in monasteries and abbeys, and copied in both secular and religious workshops. But with the fall of the Gothic kingdom, after the sack of Rome by the Vandals in 455 and the beginning of the long wars that devastated the Italian peninsula, the culture of books, in which libraries were the traditional vessels for preserving the memory of a society, all but disappeared from everyday life.[7] For a people who had undergone two sieges in the space of four decades, books became objects and relics rather than vessels for stories, and even the archetypal tale of the siege of Troy vanished into the obscure past. Homer became a monument, known by hearsay to have existed somewhere and dutifully respected from afar.

In the East, however, Homer continued to be read and was recognized as part of the social imagination. Though only certain sections of the poems were quoted or glossed, and knowledge of his work was, by and large, reduced to a few set pieces, Homer's presence was felt across the entire cultural landscape. Perhaps a sense of this ghostly influence can be perceived if we consider the many attempts to contradict, undermine, and even deny his stories. Though Homer's poems were, for the Byzantine scholars, exalted literature worthy of imitation, several other texts competed with them for preeminence, and these in turn gave rise to a vast secondary literature. According to a certain Proclus probably writing in the second century CE (not the fifth-century CE Neoplatonist of the same name), there existed a group of epic poems known as the "Epic Cycle," composed in Homer's time or earlier, from which Homer himself might have drawn his material. Of the six epics dealing with the Trojan War only a few quotations survive, but their titles and contents were preserved in a manuscript of the *Iliad* now in Venice. The longest extant text is the *Cypria*, a sort of prequel to the *Iliad*, which begins with the Judgment of Paris, when Aphrodite promises the Trojan prince the love of Helen as a reward for declaring her the most beautiful of the goddesses. The *Aithiopis* follows on from the funeral of Hector at the end of the *Iliad* up to the death of Achilles and the dispute between Ajax and Odysseus over his armor. The *Little Iliad* (once attributed to Homer himself) continues the story from the awarding of the armor to Odysseus to the entry of the Wooden Horse into Troy. The narrative is then picked up by the *Iliou Persis* (The Sack of Ilion), of which only ten original verses survive. It chronicles the fall of the city and ends with two sacrifices and a departure: Polyxena slaughtered at the tomb of Achilles and Hector's son killed by Odysseus, while the Greeks sail home threatened by an angry Athena, whose altar has been violated by Ajax. Finally, the five books of the *Nostoi* (The Returns) follow the fate of the victors: Menelaus's voyage to Egypt and his successful homecoming, Agamemnon warned by the ghost of Achilles that he will be murdered by his wife, Clytemnestra, the shipwreck and death of Ajax, and the long journey home of Achilles' son Neoptolemos. Odysseus's further adventures are told in the *Telegony*, a sequel to the *Odyssey*: after Penelope's suitors are buried, Odysseus sails off to Thesprotia (a last adventure forecast by Tiresias), where he marries the queen, fights a war, returns to Ithaca, and is killed there by his son Telegonos, born from Odysseus's union with the enchantress Circe. Upon discovering his mistake, Telegonos, accompanied by Penelope and Telemachus, takes the body back to his mother, who makes them all immortal.[8]

The Epic Cycle was at the origin of what has been called "the Trojan genre," and it served as source material for innumerable writers. Notable among these was Quintus of Smyrna, an educated Greek living in Asia Minor in the third century, who wrote a "complete" (and grisly) history of the Trojan War known as the *Posthomerica*, in a style imitating Homer's. But the most famous of all the Trojan stories were two firsthand accounts purportedly written by a couple of soldiers who had taken part in the war, Dictys of Crete and Dares the Phrygian, that were thought to antedate Homer's poems by several centuries. A number of Byzantine writers based their stories on Dictys's account, *A Journal of the Trojan War*, fewer on that of Dares, *The History of the Fall of Troy*, perhaps because Dictys offered the Greek version of the facts, while Dares told that of the Trojans. Furthermore, Dictys's narrative went on to tell the story of how the Greek victors returned to their homelands, thereby providing a useful bridge from the *Iliad* to the *Odyssey*. Far from being authentic records of the events, both accounts were probably composed in Greek in the first century CE. These original versions have not survived, with the exception of a small fragment of Dictys's text, discovered in 1899 on the back of an income tax return for the year 206.[9]

Both stories were translated into Latin, and in this new version, Dares' account, since it narrated the events from the point of view of Aeneas's people, became more popular than his Greek colleague's among the inheritors of the Roman Empire. Dares' text was quoted as the primary source by all those who retold the history of Troy, overtaking the popularity of the *Iliad*. As mentioned, Homer had been criticized for depicting the gods as prone to all the human foibles and interfering with the affairs of mortals. Dares, and also Dictys, referred to the gods only as figures of reverence and placed the responsibility for the fighting on the shoulders of human beings alone. For many centuries, the chronicles of Dictys and Dares were considered to be authentic documents, written, as it were, one against the other. Not until the beginning of the eighteenth century did confidence in their veracity diminish, when the scholar Jacob Perizonius proved beyond doubt that both authors (whoever they might have been in real life) were consummate forgers.[10]

Around 1165, a clerk from Normandy, Benoît de Sainte-Maure, serving in the entourage of the British king Henry II, based his account of the Trojan War, *Le Roman de Troie*, on the chronicle of Dares. One day, says Sainte-Maure, in Athens, a scholar named Cornelius "was searching all over in a library for learned books, when he came across the history that Dares had composed in the Greek tongue." Cornelius translated it into Latin, and it was this translation that Sainte-Maure claims he followed "word by word" in his own book. Though Sainte-Maure acknowledged Homer as "a clerk of extraordinary talent and full of wisdom," Dares' chronicle was, in his opinion, even better, since the Trojan soldier had taken part in the events he described, whereas Homer had obtained his facts by hearsay. Sainte-Maure acknowledges that he has not read Homer himself, but asserts that he obtained his information on the poet "from the source" (i.e., Dares). Sainte-Maure presents himself simply as a translator for the benefit of those who cannot read Latin script (the *illiterati*), explaining that he intends "to translate it into Romance from the Latin in which I found it, if I have the intelligence and the skill, so that those who do not understand [Latin] letters can nevertheless delight in the story."[11]

Sainte-Maure, the apocryphal translator, was himself subjected to many so-called translations. One of the most curious ones was conceived in Italy in the early fourteenth century by a cleric, Binduccio dello Scelto, of whom we know almost nothing except that he was from Siena. In 1322, his *Storia di Troia* (History of Troy) in the Tuscan tongue was copied out by order of the aristocratic Andrea degli Ugurgieri, keen reader of the literature of chivalry.[12] The original manuscript of Binduccio was lost, but Ugurgieri's copy was lovingly preserved. Binduccio's version follows the text of Sainte-Maure but with the addition of innumerable colorful details and lively episodes: the wrath of Achilles is interwoven with that of the witch Medea, wife of Theseus, and life in Priam's court sounds like scenes of courtly life in Tuscany. Aeneas's escape from Troy is told in tandem with the parting of the Trojan prince Troilus from his beloved, Cressida (named Briseida in Sainte-Maure's *Roman de Troie*), an episode that caught the imagination of the many who "delighted in the story." Briseida is forced to leave the city when her father, Calchas, defects to the Greek side. The Greek warrior Diomedes sees her and falls in love with her, and, after some hesitation, Briseida accepts Diomedes' proposal. She gives him, as a token of her love, the right sleeve of her dress, and the forlorn Troilus is killed in battle by Achilles. For later generations of readers, Cressida and her Troilus will acquire a life of their own.

Two centuries later, around 1300, an Irish version of Ulysses' travels after the fall of Troy was composed by an anonymous bard under the title *Merugud Uilix maic Leirtis* (The Wanderings of Ulysses Son of Laertes) that lent the troubled hero two homecoming surprises: Ulysses discovers Penelope in bed with a young man who turns out to be Telemachus, innocently lying by his mother's side; the faithful dog Argos is not a feeble hound dying heartbroken at his master's feet but a rainbow-colored mastiff full of life.[13]

A contemporary of the imaginative Irish bard, the Sicilian writer Guido delle Colonne, wrote (without acknowledging the source) a Latin prose version of Sainte-Maure's *Roman de Troie* which was later translated into English by John Lydgate, but it was Geoffrey Chaucer who first rendered Sainte-Maure's chronicle into English. In his version of his *Troilus and Criseyde*, Calchas, a Trojan priest who is able to foretell the future, becomes aware that Troy will fall and decides to leave the city with his daughter, the beautiful Criseyde. Troilus, a Trojan warrior, has the audacity to mock Eros, the god of love, and is punished by falling helplessly in love with Calchas's daughter. Assisted by Pandarus, Criseyde's uncle, Troilus and Criseyde exchange letters and eventually spend an amorous night together. In the meantime, Calchas persuades the Greeks to exchange a prisoner of war, Antenor, for his daughter. Troilus asks Criseyde to elope with him, an offer she refuses, but she promises to return to him in ten days. Once in the Greek camp, Criseyde decides that her promise cannot be kept and allows herself to be seduced by the great warrior Diomedes. Realizing that his beloved Criseyde will not return, Troilus curses Fortune, and goes into battle, where he eventually gets himself killed. Throughout the poem, Chaucer emphasizes the responsibility of the Trojans in their own destruction, their faults mirroring the ones Chaucer found in the turbulent England of his time, after the death of King Edward III in 1377. The summation of Troilus's story, "fro wo to wele, and after out of joie" (from woe to riches, then back into misery), is also that of Troy and, by extension, of Chaucer's own society. While Troilus is the poem's explicit protagonist, a victim of Eros, it is Criseyde who acquires, in Chaucer's hands, a memorable complexity. Idealized by Troilus according to the rules of courtly love as a flawless work of art, Chaucer's Criseyde is revealed as a much richer, much more troubled character. Although, following the moral code of his time, Chaucer cannot excuse her unfaithfulness, he succeeds in portraying Criseyde as a vulnerable, suffering, hesitant woman who is forced to change her allegiances in order to survive. "She is as the world is," noted the American critic Charles Muscatine, "and goes as the world goes."[14]

Whereas Chaucer's direct source was the story of Saint-Maure (and, according to Chaucer himself, the chronicle of Dares), it was contemporary Italian writers such as Boccaccio who led Chaucer to develop his original English decasyllabic line for the poem. "Seeing the kind of things that the Italian poets were doing inspired a kind of experimental frenzy in Chaucer and liberated him to indulge in his fascination for 'newfangelnesse,'" noted the Chaucer scholar Marion Turner.[15] Chaucer's newfangelnesse was to inspire his followers, such as the Scottish poet Robert Henryson, who produced a sequel, *The Testament of Cresseid*, which was far less forgiving toward the Trojan heroine. In Henryson's poem, the unfaithful young woman is punished by the gods with leprosy and dies after receiving alms from Troilus, who fails to recognize her in her pitiful state. In 1474, William Caxton included the story (by then extremely popular) in his *Recuyell of the Historyes of Troye*.[16]

William Shakespeare, who according to Ben Jonson had "small Latin, and less Greek" and therefore almost certainly had not read Homer in the original, made use of these various English versions as sources for his *Troilus and Cressida* (1609). Throughout the centuries, critics have found the play intensely problematic. In the seventeenth century, John Dryden rudely branded it a "heap of rubbish," and proceeded to write a "corrected" version (*Troilus and Cressida; or, Truth Found Too Late*) in which Cressida, following the conventions of Dryden's day, turns out to have remained faithful to her Troilus, eventually killing herself as proof of her innocence, and Troilus kills Diomedes but then himself falls in battle.[17]

Critics have been puzzled by the fact that in Shakespeare's version of the story, Homer's heroes are stripped of their mythical stature and are shown as petty, ambitious, conniving men and women. The War of Troy is depicted not so much as a confrontation between two civilizations, the Trojan and the Greek, but as a vast and petty family quarrel in which the men seek to assert their power and the women employ their wiles to back the male of their choice. Ulysses, for example, is portrayed as an artful politician, uncannily recognizable among the political villains of our day, a man seemingly defending the authority of Agamemnon as the supreme Greek commander and yet at the same time not relinquishing his own ambitious grip on the political reins. Shakespeare's Cressida, like Chaucer's, escapes the narrow definition of the unfaithful mistress. Even in the eyes of the love-torn Troilus, shattered by the realization that Cressida has become Diomedes' mistress, she remains a complex, undefinable creature alive with unsolved contradictions:

> This she? No, this is Diomed's Cressida.
> If beauty have a soul, this is not she;
> If souls guide vows, if vows be sanctimonies,
> If sanctimony be the gods' delight,
> If there be rule in unity itself,
> This was not she. O madness of discourse,
> That cause sets up with and against itself;
> Bifold authority, where reason can revolt
> Without perdition, and loss assume all reason
> Without revolt. This is and is not Cressid.[18]

Whereas Troilus is only briefly mentioned in the *Iliad* by King Priam, who in book 24 lists him among the sons he has lost, Cressida, under the name Chryseis, is an important secondary character. She makes her appearance in the poem as Agamemnon's war booty, with no connection with Troilus, Diomedes, or Calchas. With none of the psychological complexity of either Chaucer or Shakespeare's heroine, Homer's Cressida is nonetheless a powerful figure of revenge who succeeds in having the god Apollo send the plague that sweeps through the Greek army at the start of the poem, forcing Agamemnon to return her and claim Achilles' concubine Briseis for himself, an act that triggers Achilles' anger and sets the poem in motion.

CHAPTER 6

Homer in Islam

There is not only Arab poetry: foreign nations also have their own.
There have been Persian poets and Greek poets. For instance,
Aristotle, in his *Logic,* praises the poet Umatîrash (Homer).

—Ibn Khaldun, *Al-Muqaddima,* 1377

Whereas in Byzantium the study of Greek was, by and large, the
study of antique models, in the centers of Arab culture (first Baghdad, and later Cairo, Damascus, Córdoba, and Toledo) the study of
Greek literature was perceived as a conversation among contemporaries. Aristotle and Plato were not figures from a misty past:
they were active voices in constant dialogue with their readers,
readers who were also their promulgators and conveyors through
translation and commentary. In the ninth century, the great Abū
'Uthman 'Amr ibn Baḥr al-Kinānī al-Baṣrī, known simply as al-
Jahiz, accused scholars of preferring Aristotle to the Qur'an, without acknowledging that he himself had followed the philosopher
in several of his books.[1]

Although translation of foreign literature into Arabic can be
said to have begun in the mid-eighth century during the rule of
the celebrated Abassid caliph al-Mansur with the Indian story
collection *Kalila and Dimna,* Ptolemy's *Almagest,* and Euclid's
Geometry, among others, the great tradition of translation
from the ancient Greek was firmly established a century later.

It all started with a dream. One night in Baghdad, the Caliph al-Ma'mun, known as "Lover of Knowledge" and son of the famous Harun al-Rashid (who, as a character in the *Arabian Nights* would delight the European imagination in later centuries), saw a pale, blue-eyed man with a broad forehead and frowning eyebrows. With the assurance of dreamers, the caliph understood that the stranger was Aristotle. Al-Ma'mun and Aristotle talked all night. In the morning, as a result of the encounter, the caliph ordered that a library should be founded in Baghdad that would house a translation center devoted mainly to the works of the philosopher. The center was placed under the direction of the scholar Hunayan ibn Ishaq al-'Ibadi, who, assisted by a school of disciples, translated into Syriac and Arabic almost the entire corpus of Greek and Hellenistic philosophy and science known at the time.[2]

Hunayan often made use of his knowledge of Homer (Ùmìrùs or Umatîrash) to help clarify certain obscure images, unidentified names, and difficult analogies in the classical Greek texts. Because Hunayan knew his Homer, or however much of Homer he was able to gather, he was able to explain to his readers that, for example, the monster mentioned in a certain book was "a giant whose name was Cyclops," and that when the monster Scylla received the epithet "Hound of the Sea," it was because Homer had compared her cries to the yelping of a pup.[3] According to a contemporary, the scholar Yusuf ibn Ibrahim, Hunayan had begun his scholarly career as a brilliant though over-inquisitive student in Baghdad. He had shown such a passionate curiosity in class that his teacher, exasperated by the constant flow of questions, had ordered him out of the lecture hall, and the young man, taking the dismissal to heart, had left Baghdad without letting anyone know where he was going. Two years later, Ibrahim found himself called to the bed of a patient of Greek ancestry, whose Greek aunt had been a slave of Harun al-Rashid. There he noticed a strange man, his hair falling over his face in the fashion of Byzantium, who was reciting Homer in the original to his ailing host. The stranger was Hunayan, returned to Baghdad with a word-perfect knowledge of Homeric Greek.[4]

Beyond the fame acquired for the excellency of its translations, the center's prosperity was largely due to monetary incentive: sponsors paid generously for translated works that lent them intellectual and social prestige among the Baghdad aristocracy. Translators were highly specialized; they had no overall knowledge of Greek but acknowledged being familiar with the style and vocabulary of certain authors. For instance, translating a medical text by Galen, Hunayan comes upon a quotation from a play by Aristophanes and confesses to the reader: "But I am not familiar with the language of Aristophanes, nor am I accustomed to it. Hence, it was not easy for me to understand the quotation, and I have therefore omitted it."[5] (Hunayan was aware that Aristophanes did not write the same Greek Homer did.) Not all translators displayed (or display today) such disarming honesty.

Although poetry was not part of the center's mission, a few fragments of Homer were translated as well, as attested in several collections of philosophical sayings, some reliable and some apocryphal, and in Arab versions of Greek authors who had quoted Homer, such as Aristotle himself. Avicenna, the tenth-century Persian polymath, for example, in his commentary on Aristotle's *Poetics,* repeats the Philosopher's praise of Homer and says that he is the model of the "laudatory poet."[6] So great was the thirst for these ancient texts that to the recognized works of acclaimed writers were added pure inventions, as for instance the *Kitab al-Tuffaha* (Book of the Apple), a gloss of Plato's *Phaedrus* accompanied by a series of meditations supposedly jotted down by Aristotle on his deathbed. Biographies of Homer, "the wandering poet" as he was known, were included in dictionaries and encyclopedias.[7]

Just as the pagan authors had served in Christian Europe as a source of analogies to prove the superiority of the religion of Christ, so the Islamic writers made use of the Greek corpus (and to a lesser extent, the Latin one) to prove the truth of the Qur'an. Examples drawn from the Greek authors served to illustrate the laws that rule the soul according to the words of the Prophet. The tenth-century scholar al-Farabi, the foremost logician of his time, was one of the most influential of these commentators. After studying in Baghdad with the disciples of Christian scholars from Alexandria, al-Farabi settled in Damascus, where, in relative seclusion, he wrote the critical treatises on Aristotle, Plato, and Galen that earned him his fame. In these, al-Farabi set out his belief that philosophy, like religion, can help us attain the truth, following a different path and beckoning to all kinds of travelers. Each of these paths, both the religious and the philosophical, offered two levels of pursuit. The highest, that of metaphysical inquiry, was meant for the few whose intelligence or gifted spirit allowed them to comprehend complex abstract formulations; the other, available to the common majority, was followed through stories, myths, riddles, and parables. In an ideal society, the two paths, and both levels in each path, coexisted with more or less ease, though there were scholars who thought that the exponents of the lower level (poets and mythographers such as Homer, and "everyday prophets," as the philosopher al-Saraksi called ambulant preachers) were charlatans. Plato had put it more sternly when he called them "falsifiers of the truth" and banned them from his Republic. Al-Farabi was less severe. Muhammad had declared that the ideal community of the faithful constituted an *umma*, a perfect city-state; for al-Farabi, Plato's ideal republic and Muhammad's umma were two incarnations of the same idea, and though one disallowed poets and the other did not, both spoke of the same holy place. In this context, Homer's poems, though not as exalted as the works of Aristotle and Plato, deserved to be read because, despite their watered-down, vulgar idiom, they too held inklings of the truth.[8]

As far as we know, no version of Homer's work was produced during the golden period of Arabic translation. A few Abassid scholars were aware of the contents of the two major poems, and fragments of the *Iliad* and the *Odyssey* appeared in popular narratives: for instance, several of Odysseus's adventures surface in the stories of Sindbad the Sailor. A late thirteenth- or early fourteenth-century anthology of military exploits, the *Raqa'iq al-hilal fi Daqaiq al-hiyal* (Cloaks of Fine Fabric in Subtle Ruses), includes a potted version of Achilles' wrath and the killing of Hector. The source, of course, may not be Homer but one of the many other retellings of the story of Troy.

> We are told how the King of the Greeks of Byzantium used cunning when he invaded Ifriqiya [Phrygia] and the population learned of this well enough in advance for them to organize resistance and entrench themselves in a city [Troy] that he besieged for a long time to no avail. The city gate withstood all his attacks. Among the citizens there was a man called Aqtar [Hector] who was very daring and courageous. Anyone who fought him was invariably killed. The King of the Greeks [Agamemnon] was told of this.
>
> He had a commander named Arsilaous [Achilles], unsurpassed for his bravery throughout the world. Following an outburst of anger from the King, he had refused to take any part in the war. The King had asked him to, but he did not obey. The King then said: "Spread the rumour that our enemy Aqtar has captured the brother of Arsilaous."
>
> The latter was distressed when he heard the news. He looked everywhere for his brother, but could not find him. Then he asked for his weapons and went out against Aqtar. He fought against him and took him prisoner, and led him before the King of the

Greeks. The latter put Aqtar to death. The people of Ifriqiya and all their supporters were terrorstricken when they found out that their hero was gone. The King of the Greeks, with Arsilaous, attacked the city, inflicting heavy losses on the enemy and conquering the region.[9]

Two important changes are introduced in this version of Homer's story. Hector has not captured Achilles' "brother"—it is only a rumor spread by Agamemnon. And Achilles does not kill Hector; he only captures him, and it is Agamemnon who orders the execution. In the Arabic telling, Agamemnon is the secret protagonist of the story.

The great Arabic translation schools began to decline toward the end of the tenth century, but the impulse to bring into one's own language the wisdom expressed in another continued long afterward. The Arab scholars who had rendered the Greek works into their tongue and enlivened them with their own comments had done so less out of a will to preserve the Greek culture (the Persian heritage was for them as important as the Greek) than for the sake of what has been called "appropriation and naturalization," absorbing another culture into their own.[10] Now, from the eleventh to the thirteenth centuries, many of these Arab versions of the Greek classics were in turn translated into other languages, particularly Latin and Hebrew. In Sicily and, especially, in Spain (al-Andalus), the works of Aristotle annotated by al-Farabi, Avicenna, and Averroës acquired a new life through fresh glosses and interpretations. Some fiction and poetry, too, entered Europe in Arabic versions and was then rendered into local tongues, so that the handful of Homeric episodes that had metamorphosed into an Arabic setting underwent a further transformation and became Spanish *romances*, Provençal *canzones*, French *fabliaux*, and German *Märchen*.

Centuries later, in 1857, Wilhelm Grimm, one of the brothers of fairy-tale fame, suggested that Homer's stories, which in the original were told as legends with a historical basis that happened in a specific time and place, had been carried throughout the world and had changed over the centuries in the telling. They became folktales set in the indefinite past ("Once upon a time") and featured generic heroes with names such as Hans, Elsie, or Jack. How far Homer's poems traveled is a matter of conjecture, but, for instance, scholars have recognized in an Icelandic saga composed about 1300, *The Story of Egill One-hand and Asmundr the Berserks' Killer,* the influence of the *Odyssey,* in particular the encounter between Odysseus and the Cyclops which later, in English folklore, became the tale of Jack and the Beanstalk.[11]

The twentieth-century English translator and collector of folktales Andrew Lang asked a number of questions regarding the ancient origins of the character of Odysseus, which he saw as a puzzle. "How did a petty chief, in the remotest part of Greece, manage to inherit ... the fame of adventures which are widely rumoured not only through Europe," Lang wondered, but throughout the world? "Why did he whose native realm was distant and obscure, come to be more gloriously renowned than Agamemnon, Menelaus, and all the great heads of the royal houses in Achaia, in Thessaly, in Bœotia, in Crete?"[12]

It must be said that Arab translators were not solely responsible for the renewed European awareness of its Greek heritage.[13] Most of the great poetry and theater arrived much later and through different byways. And yet, either as translated text or read in the original Greek, through commentaries and glosses or as literary hearsay, broken up into stories and specific characters or retold in their entirety, whether as historical facts or as allegories and symbols, the poems of Homer gradually filtered back into the imagination of medieval Europe. Writing in the early sixteenth century, Juan de Mena, in the preface to his *Iliad,* attempted to explain the mechanics of this late transmission to King Juan II. Authors such as Avicenna, he said, were like silkworms who wove their books out of their own entrails, while he worked like the bees "who steal the substance from mellifluous blossoms in other men's orchards." "A great gift I bear," Mena assured his king, "if my thieving and looting do not corrupt it, nor my bold and fearless daring, and that is to translate and interpret such a seraphic work as Homer's *Iliad*, from Greek carried into Latin and from Latin into vulgar Castilian, our mother tongue."[14]

A book's influence is never straightforward. Common readers, unrestricted by the rigors of academe, allow their books to converse with one another, to exchange meanings and metaphors, to enrich and annotate each other. In the reader's mind, books become entwined and intermingled, and every library is delightfully chaotic, so that we no longer know whether a certain adventure belongs to Arsilaous or to Aquiles, or where Odysseus's adventures end and where Sindbad takes them up again.

CHAPTER 7

Dante

Dante—known to that gentleman as an eccentric man in the nature of an Old File, who used to put leaves round his head, and sit upon a stool for some unaccountable purpose, outside the cathedral at Florence.

—Charles Dickens, *Little Dorrit*, 1855–57

Toward the end of the Middle Ages, scholars and poets returned once again to the questions that had preoccupied Jerome and Augustine regarding the relationship between Homer's stories and the stories of the Bible. Allegorical interpretations continued, but these were accompanied by a search for literal correspondences between what the ancients had told and what the church had revealed, establishing a sequence of parallel readings that honored one without dishonoring the other. In both art and literature a tradition of typological commentaries on the Old and New Testaments was already common, setting side by side episodes of the former with those of the latter: for instance, the tree from which Adam ate the forbidden fruit was depicted next to the wooden cross on which Christ died for our salvation. Accordingly, a similar typology was established between Homer and the Bible: between, for example, Achilles in the *Iliad* and David in the Old Testament, or between the stages of Odysseus's return and the troubled exodus of the Hebrews from Egypt. In the early fourteenth century, Albertino Mussato, the most celebrated of the members of the *cenacolo padovano*, the Paduan Circle of Latin poets, argued that the pagan writers had expressed the same ideas as those found in Scripture but in the form of enigmas or riddles in which they had secretly announced the coming of the true Messiah. Their poetry, Mussato boldly declared, was "a second theology," a notion that Petrarch was later to invert as "theology is poetry that comes from God."[1] Scholars in the twenty-first century have resumed Mussato's reading and further explored the relationship between the ancient poets and the Bible from a mythographical point of view, finding parallels between the stories in the *Odyssey*, for example, and several in the Old Testament, especially the book of Genesis, as well as in the Gospels, canonical and apocryphal.[2]

When Mussato spoke of pagan poetry, he meant, first and foremost, Homer. Even though the Latin classics had pride of place in the libraries of the Renaissance, Homer was considered the fountainhead, the primordial spring without whom there would have been no culture. For that reason, when Dante meets the great writers of antiquity in the first circle of his Hell, he has Homer, brandishing a sword to indicate the supremacy of epic poetry, appear at the head of the delegation of writers. Homer and his colleagues come forward to greet Virgil—"Honour the highest of poets, his shadow, which had left, returns"—and then, to Virgil's amusement, they welcome Dante; that is to say, first the master poet who sang of the triumph of Rome, and second (but this is in the future) the master poet who sang of the triumph of Christianity.[3]

Homer exercised on Dante and his contemporaries an influence in some ways similar to that which the gods of Olympus effected on the ancients. As depicted in the *Iliad* and the *Odyssey*, Zeus and his fellow divinities walked among the mortals, inspiring them, haunting them, seeking their glory or their death, or just being a nuisance (as when, in the *Iliad*, Athena pulls Achilles' hair).[4] They were phantom presences in heaven and material representations in marble and bronze in the temples, but they were also alive in bedrooms and markets and battlefields, sitting by mortals in their studies or accompanying them on their voyages. After Plato's death, his disciples defended Homer's notion of the gods as "spies in disguise," which Plato himself had ridiculed; in his gossipy books, Plutarch spoke again and again of the appearance of the gods among men; and the emperor Marcus Aurelius meditated on the divine beings "visible as the stars in the sky but also present as friends and instructors in dreams."[5] For Augustine, however, only one God filled the world with his presence. Seneca, writing in the first century CE, offered a middle way. For him, not the gods but the great writers and thinkers of antiquity lived among us. "Only men who make Zeno and Pythagoras and Democritus and the other high priests of liberal studies their daily familiars, who cultivate Aristotle and Theophrastus, can properly be said to be engaged in the duties of life," he wrote. "It is a common saying that a man's parents are not of his own choosing but allotted to him by chance. But we can choose our own genealogy." Pointing at his library, Seneca argued that these great men could share with us their experience.

> Here are families with noble endowments: choose whichever you wish to belong to. Your adoption will give you not only the name but actually the property, and this you need not guard in a mean or niggardly spirit: the more people you share it with, the greater will it become. These will open the path to eternity for you and will raise you to a height from which none can be cast down. This is the sole means of prolonging your mortality, or rather, of transforming it into immortality.[6]

For Mussato, Dante, and their contemporaries, Seneca's argument was commonplace. To the company of the poets of Greece and Rome were assimilated the fathers of the Catholic Church, so that in the same way that Mussato could address Livy as his master in his *Historia Augusta*, Petrarch could later engage in a dream dialogue, the *Secretum meum*, with Saint Augustine.[7] These relationships were devotional, similar to those that readers have with their favorite books.

Only Dante's case is different. Dante was the first nonclassical writer to be treated by his contemporaries as equal to the great Greek and Latin authors, a position that he himself did not find surprising:

> The sea I travel is no longer traveled.
> Minerva fills my sails, Apollo leads me,
> And the Nine Muses point me toward the Pole Star.[8]

Even then, Dante knew that he could not tell his story all by himself; he required divine guidance. Homer had started the tradition by which the poet establishes his authority not as the inventor but as the performer of tales that a divine voice has dictated. Both the *Iliad* and the *Odyssey* begin by asking the Muse to sing the chosen subjects: the rage of one man, the cunning of another. There is, however, a difference between the two beginnings. In the *Iliad*, Homer humbly leaves the stage to the Muse alone: "Goddess, sing the rage . . ." But in the *Odyssey*, the poet allows himself to appear as the receiver of the song that he will transmit to his audience if he so chooses: "Sing to me of the man, Muse . . ." Virgil and Dante profit from the daring intrusion of that "to me." Virgil, in the *Aeneid*, asks the Muse to recall for him the cause of the war that set Aeneas on his journeys. Dante too, in his *Commedia*, invokes the Muses for help, but so that his memory, capable of "setting down" what he saw on his marvelous journey, might now reveal to him in his role of scribe, as he later calls it, its excellence in the telling.[9]

G. K. Chesterton remarked that we do not have to read the classics in order to accept the fact that they are classics; in other words, we can take it as read that Cervantes, Shakespeare, and Dostoyevsky are "important" writers, in the sense that they have carried import for successive generations of readers.[10] When we finally come to them (if we finally come to them) singly and on our own terms, we rescue from the blanketing notion of classic a primary judgment and a personal meaning: "I like—or I don't like—Homer's books, and this is what they say to me." Dante's own knowledge of the classics was limited to what was available in the Latin originals, especially Horace, Seneca, and, of course, Virgil. Of the great Greek tragic poets that Statius mentions to Dante and Virgil in Purgatory, suffering their cleansing in order to ascend to Paradise—Euripides, Antiphon, Simonides, Agathon, "and several other Greeks with laurel wreaths"—Dante had no knowledge except by hearsay; neither Sophocles nor Aeschylus is mentioned because in the fourteenth century their names had fallen into oblivion, and Dante had never heard of them. Even Euripides was known only by name since none of his works was available.[11]

Dante and his contemporaries accepted the time-honored glorification of Homer as an undisputed fact, and read him, if at all, in Latin translations such as the popular anonymous paraphrase of the *Iliad* known as the *Ilias latina*, probably written in the first century CE. Petrarch kept, with devotional care, a Greek manuscript of Homer which he did not know how to read. To the friend who sent it to him from Constantinople, he wrote, "Your Homer lies mute by my side, while I am deaf by his, and often I have kissed him saying: 'Great man, how I wish I could hear your words!'" At Petrarch's suggestion, and with the help of Boccaccio, their friend Leonzio Pilato, a Calabrian monk of Greek origin, translated the *Odyssey* and the *Iliad* into Latin, both badly.[12]

Dante acquired his Homer through Virgil. "If indeed he knew nothing of the Greek original," George Steiner remarked, "Dante's clairvoyant genius intuited, discerned the Homeric presence in the *Aeneid.*"[13] In this sense, Virgil was not only Dante's guide through Hell and up Mount Purgatory, he was also his source and inspiration, and through him Dante was able to enjoy the experience of Homer's work. Virgil was for Dante, among other things, a poet who had clearly identified the Roman Empire as a unified cultural world, a world that in Dante's time aspired to that same unification: spiritual, under the scepter of a God-chosen pope, and material, under that of a God-chosen emperor. Those who obeyed the laws of God as dictated by his two servants were rewarded; those who broke them had either to undergo a redemptive purge or, if the fault were too serious, to suffer a dreadful and eternal punishment. Dante's *Commedia,* the account of his cautionary excursion to the Kingdom of the Dead, is therefore divided into three parts. The first, Hell, is the dwelling place of those condemned absolutely, a funnel-shaped pit that runs from the Northern Hemisphere to the center of the earth; the second is Purgatory, where souls are redeemed after death, a high mountain that rises on an island in the Southern Hemisphere atop which sits the Garden of Eden; the third and last is Paradise, a place beneath the nine heavens of medieval astronomy which form all together one single heaven where God's bliss is equally enjoyed.

The model for Dante's *Commedia* is perhaps a composite of many sources, from Homer (via Virgil) to Arabic accounts of Muhammad's journey to the other world, the Mi'raj. One version of the latter was translated into Castilian by order of Alfonso X, and then into Latin, French, and Italian, the last of which Dante might have read.[14] Even though the complex architecture of the afterlife realm is, to a large degree, Dante's own, the foundation stone is Homer's.

CHAPTER 8

Homer in Hell

"The noise, my dear! And the people!"
—Unknown, often attributed to Ernest Thesiger on being
asked about serving in the First World War

Homer's Hell has no remarkable physical features. According to the *Odyssey*, it is a simple, schematic dwelling place for the souls of the dead, ruled unobtrusively by the god Hades. There, according to the witch Circe, Odysseus must travel in search of instructions for his voyage home when, after keeping him for a year as her lover, Circe at last consents to let him go. But first she tells him that he must "travel down/to the House of Death and the awesome one, Persephone,/there to consult the ghost of Tiresias, seer of Thebes." Odysseus is terrified. "Circe, Circe," he cries, "who can pilot us on that journey? Who has ever/reached the House of Death in a black ship?"[1]

Circe gives Odysseus precise instructions. Driven by the North Wind, his ship will cut across the River Ocean and reach the dark, desolate coast of Persephone's Grove. From there he must descend to the Kingdom of Hades and the waters of the Acheron, into which flow two smaller rivers, that of Fire and that of Tears (the latter a branch of the Styx, or Stream of Hate). Here Odysseus must make offerings to the dead and wait for them to appear, and eventually the ghost of Tiresias will tell him by what means he may return to Ithaca. Odysseus follows Circe's instructions to the letter. (Later, in book 24, there will be a second excursion to the Underworld, when Hermes leads the ghosts of the slaughtered suitors "past the White Rock and the Sun's Western Gates and past/the Land of Dreams" into the "fields of asphodel." No doubt there are several routes to Hell.)²

Homer had described a place without graded categories, an Underworld in which souls wander about, incorporeal and listless, like the inmates of a retirement home, some still suffering from regret for what they have done or left undone on earth, others undergoing hideous tortures decreed for them by the gods: Tityus devoured by vultures, Tantalus condemned to eternal hunger and thirst, Sisyphus ineffectually rolling his boulder up the hill. Though Pindar, in the sixth century BCE, located specific areas in the Underworld for the "happy shades," Homer's dead are never pleased to be where they are. "No winning words about death to *me*, shining Odysseus!" says the ghost of Achilles when he sees him. "By god, I'd rather slave on earth for another man . . . than rule down here over all the breathless dead" (a sentiment echoed in Ecclesiastes 9:4, where it is written that "a living dog is better than a dead lion").³

Homer's account proved not vivid enough for Virgil. In the *Odyssey*, since Circe has described in detail the route to the realm of Hades, there is little for Odysseus to do in the next episode but follow her instructions. Twelve lines suffice to chronicle his journey, a further sixteen to narrate the sacrificial offerings to the dead. Then, as Circe had predicted, the ghosts arrive in awful droves:

> Brides and unwed youths and old men who had suffered much
> and girls with their tender hearts freshly scarred by sorrow
> and great armies of battle dead, stabbed by bronze spears,
> men of war still wrapped in bloody armor—thousands

swarming around the trench from every side—
unearthly cries—blanching terror gripped me![4]

The arrival of the dead is horrible; compared to the overwhelming menace of the moaning crowd, the individual spirits
who thereafter speak with Odysseus are tame in their demeanor.
It is the swarm of souls that haunts the reader, as Homer knew it
would, since he repeats it at the end of the section, with almost
identical words:

> the dead came surging round me,
> hordes of them, thousands raising unearthly cries,
> and blanching terror gripped me.[5]

Homer's ghastly picture of the dead as a confused mingling
of sexes and ages, occupations and social classes, extends across
many hundreds of future years and will eventually take on its most
recognizable shape toward the middle of the fourteenth century
in the danse macabre, a human chain in which Death leads by the
hand all men and women on earth, from pope to humble peasant.
The earliest depictions of the danse macabre appeared in Europe
in the early fifteenth century: on the walls of the Cimetière des
Innocents in Paris, in the cloister of old Saint Paul's in London, in
the Marienkirche of Lübeck.[6] A century later, Hans Holbein the
Younger produced a series of woodcuts illustrating the Dance of
Death that became the subject's standard iconography, translated
in the twentieth century as the Triumph of Death in Ingmar Berg-
man's 1957 film *The Seventh Seal* and later as its mirror image,
the Triumph of Life, at the end of Federico Fellini's 1963 film *8½*.

The sight that confronts Odysseus is one of wretched things
rising in the air, a storm of howling ghosts conjured up by the
sacrificial offerings, all generations mingled. But not only death
as the end of adult life is common to us all: in order to round the

circle of human life, Homer broadens the image to include the newly born. In book 6 of the *Iliad,* on the bloodied battlefield, the Lycian Glaucus, fighting on the side of the Trojans, is taunted by the Greek Diomedes, who will reveal himself to be Glaucus's friend. Glaucus says:

> Like the generations of leaves, the lives of mortal men.
> Now the wind scatters the old leaves across the earth,
> now the living timber bursts with the new buds
> and spring comes round again. And so with men:
> as one generation comes to life, another dies away.[7]

The souls that meet Odysseus are like an autumn whirlwind. Glaucus describes the dead as "old leaves" but recalls their counterpart, left unmentioned in the *Odyssey:* the promised new budding in the spring. In the twentieth century, Philip Larkin blended both notions in one image. His poem "The Trees" begins with "The trees are coming into leaf/Like something almost being said," and ends with hope: "Last year is dead, they seem to say/Begin afresh, afresh, afresh." And Alice Oswald, in her retelling of the *Iliad,* brings back the image to the common course of human time: "Like leaves who could write a history of leaves/The wind blows their ghosts to the ground/And the spring breathes new leaf into the woods."[8]

A similar throng of leafy souls confronts Virgil's Aeneas in the Underworld. In Homer, the ghosts descend upon Odysseus; in Virgil, the ghosts crowd the shore in front of Aeneas, forced to wait one hundred years before they are allowed to cross over (like a throng of refugees, the twenty-first-century reader will say). The frightening description ends with one of Virgil's most famous, most beautiful lines: *tendebantque manus ripae ulterioris amore.* (Elizabeth Cook, in her novel *Achilles,* describes the scene as "layer upon layer of longing.")[9]

Virgil, remembering his Homer, uses in the *Aeneid* the leaf metaphor of the *Iliad* to illustrate the phantom hordes in the *Odyssey*, and with that overlapping of images the dead become innumerable, including all generations of men and women, falling to the ground autumn after autumn. Suddenly the reader realizes: I too shall be one of them.

> Matrons and men were there, and there were great-hearted heroes
> Finished with earthly life, boys and unmarried maidens,
> Young men laid on the pyre before their parents' eyes;
> Multitudinous as the leaves that fall in a forest
> At the first frost of autumn. . . .
> . . . .
> So they stood, each begging to be ferried across first,
> *Their hands stretched out in longing for the shore beyond the river.*[10]

Dante has this Virgilian reading firmly in mind when he describes the corresponding scene in his *Commedia*. Led by Virgil, Dante has crossed the Gate of Hell and reached, like Odysseus and Aeneas before him, the shores of Acheron and the legions of dead.

> As in Autumn the leaves detach and fly
> One after the other, until the branch
> Sees on the ground all its mortal coils.[11]

In Homer, the dead surge up in crowds, and men come and go like leaves: the accent is on the cyclical nature of succeeding generations. In Virgil, the dead are as many as the leaves that must fall when autumn comes: the accent is on the number. And now, to the notions of perpetual movement and infinite quantity, Dante adds that of individual fate, of each leaf coming to its own singular end, "one after the other." André Malraux, describing the death of his protagonist in the 1930 novel *La voie royale*, has him say this: "There is no . . . death . . . There's only . . . me . . . me . . . who's dying . . ."[12] Where Virgil has used *cadunt* (they fall) to describe the action of the leaves, Dante uses *si levan* (they fly off; they detach themselves), granting each leaf and, by implication, each soul a voluntary individual movement. Death is our allotted end, Dante seems to say, but it is also an act for whose quality we ourselves are responsible. That each of us dies is decreed; the act of dying is ours, individually. (In the Second Circle of Dante's Hell, the souls of the lustful are tossed about like leaves in a howling wind, but each separate soul has its own story.) Dante insists that the verb "to die" must always be conjugated in the first person singular.

Dante's inheritors took advantage of his reading of Homer through Virgil. Milton, in *Paradise Lost*, placed the composite image in a Virgilian landscape to describe Satan's legions at the edge of the Sea of Fire.

> Thick as autumnal leaves that strow the brooks
> In Vallombrosa, where th'Etrurian shades
> High over-arch'd embow'r.

Two centuries after *Paradise Lost* was published, Paul Verlaine, with Dante in mind, reverted to Glaucus's image as depicting not the numerous dead but the poet himself.

> And I depart
> On an evil wind
> That carries me off
> This way and that
> Exactly like
> A leaf that's dead.[13]

Verlaine employed the plural image in the singular; Gerard Manley Hopkins, contemporary of Verlaine, held it up as a mirror to a child, addressing her in the second person:

Margaret, are you grieving
Over Goldengrove unleaving?
Leaves like the things of man, you
With your fresh thoughts care for, can you?
....
It is the blight man was born for,
It is Margaret you mourn for.[14]

In a famous letter to the imperial vicar Can'grande della Scala, Dante explained that every image in the vast pageant of the *Commedia* is to be read in four senses: literal, allegorical, anagogical (spiritual), and analogical (by analogy). That is to say: one, the dead are as "thick as autumnal leaves"; two, all men will suffer "the blight man was born for"; three, we must accept death as the "evil wind" God has willed for us, but we must attempt to depart gracefully, carried "this way and that"; four, as we are told in Ecclesiastes 1:4, "One generation passeth away, and another generation cometh: but the earth abideth forever."[15]

Percy Bysshe Shelley, describing the ruins of Pompeii in the autumn of 1820, gave the image a further twist. He inverted the sense of the comparison and lent the falling leaves the quality of wandering ghosts.

I stood within the City disinterred;
And heard the autumnal leaves like light footfalls
Of spirits passing through the streets.[16]

Like several of Dante's images, the autumnal dead illustrate the Thomist tenet in which Dante believed: that humans can attain perfection only in the afterlife by reaching their end in the correct manner—though the poet may have been unable to make explicit the exact meaning of "correct." At the same time, by association with terrestrial things (trees, wind, earth) Dante's images ground in our everyday experience the higher metaphysical realities.[17] This latter point is important: what happens on the Otherworld journey attracts Dante's attention only if it relates to the spiritual outcome of the subject; in the case of the ghostly crowd, numerous as leaves, what matters to him is the fact that the dead risen in the *Odyssey* were once the seasonal flesh and blood described in the *Iliad*. Homer made the observation, Virgil saw the association, Dante drew the conclusion.

CHAPTER 9

Greek Versus Latin

When a Prince lacks a Homer, it means that he is not worthy of having one.

—Fénelon, *Dialogues des morts*, 1692–96

Given Homer's role as founding father of these narratives, why does Dante place Homer in Hell? For Dante the pilgrim, Hell is not absolute, as it is for the souls condemned to abide there: it is a cautionary place that he by divine grace is allowed to see while he still has the opportunity to repent of his sins. In this vision of the afterlife offered to him, Dante lodges Homer, together with the other pagan poets, in a sort of suburb of that Hell, its First Circle, as a charitable alternative that is Dante's own invention.

In Dante's Hell, souls descend as a result of the life they have led to endure the punishment their own sins have constructed for them; the greater the error of a soul's conduct on earth, the deeper its place in Hell. The divisions are strict and many. First comes the vestibule of intellectual cowards, where are sent the souls of those who remained undecided in their choice between good and evil: Hell does not want them and Heaven rejects them. Next, on the edge of the pit of Hell, begins the First Circle, or Limbo. Here dwell the souls of infants who have died unbaptized and of those who, having practiced a moral life, chose not to enter the Christian fold, such as Avicenna and Averroës. This is also the home of the virtuous pagans such as Homer, whose "honored names echo in your life and won them grace in heaven," but who, having lived before the coming of Christ, "were not able to adore God properly." Movingly, Virgil adds, "Of that lot am I."[1] To Homer and his friends, Dante grants a moated castle surrounded by seven walls and a green meadow. Allegorically, the moat represents earthly possessions or the art of rhetoric; the walls, the seven liberal arts or the intellectual and moral virtues. Even in Hell, Homer remains exalted.

The artists of the Renaissance adopted the notion of Homer as first among these ancient virtuous pagans. In about 1470, in his Palace of Urbino, the duke Federico da Montefeltro, said to be the most learned man of his learned court, placed in his study twenty-eight portraits of celebrated historical figures: Ptolemy next to King Solomon, Virgil next to Saint Ambrose, Seneca next to Thomas Aquinas, and, of course, Homer leading the lot. Though Federico preferred the philosophers to the poets, Homer could not be absent in a cultured man's workshop.[2]

When, three decades later, in 1508, Raphael was asked by Pope Julius II to decorate the papal chambers in the Vatican, the twenty-three-year-old painter chose for the room overlooking the Belvedere Gardens the theme of Mount Parnassus, home of the pagan gods, and gave Homer pride of place. In the days of ancient Rome, the Vatican Hill had been consecrated to Apollo, and it was Apollo that Raphael decided to depict, playing, instead of the classical lyre, the Italian *lira da braccio,* a sort of lute of nine strings popular in the Renaissance, to symbolize the contemporary presence of the god. Around Apollo are grouped eighteen poets, ancient and modern, with blind Homer presiding, stage right, over a sort of secular Trinity, Dante on his right and Virgil on his left. The grand mural was completed in 1511.[3]

Greek scholarship flourished some time after Boccaccio and Petrarch's incipient efforts, thanks largely to the Greek exiles fleeing the Turkish invasions. After the conquest of Constantinople by Mehemet II, on May 29, 1453, a number of accomplished Hellenists migrated to Florence, Rome, Padua, and Venice, setting up schools of Greek and working on editions of Greek manuscripts. In Venice, thanks to their erudition, the printer Aldus Manutius was able to produce some of the most exquisite versions of the classics, notably, around 1504, several editions of the *Iliad* and the *Odyssey*.[4] Familiarity with the classics became essential for a person of social standing. The sophisticated scholar Tommaso Parentucelli, who in 1447 was elected pope under the name of Nicholas V, was said to be "as fond of books as the Borgias were of women" and to have paid ten thousand gold pieces for a translation of Homer.[5]

The educational treatises of the time underline the importance of teaching Homer and Virgil to young children, because "this is a knowledge which all great men have possessed."[6] "Homer, the prince of poets," wrote the philosopher Battista Guarino, "is not difficult to learn, as he seems to have been a source for all our [Latin] writers. Their minds will delight in Virgil's imitation of him, for the *Aeneid* is like a mirror of Homer's works, and there is almost nothing in Virgil that does not have an analogue in Homer." Aeneas Silvius Piccolomini, who became Pope Pius II, found an exquisite reason for studying the ancient authors: "The commerce of language," he wrote, "is the intermediary of love." The French poet Jean Daurat, member of the prestigious sixteenth-century literary group known as La Pléiade, lectured on the *Odyssey* at the Collège Royal in Paris and defended Homer as a source of encyclopedic knowledge culled during a kind of Pilgrim's Progress toward virtue. His student Joseph Scaliger thought all this was too much. "The man," Scaliger said of his former teacher, "has begun to debase himself and amuse himself by finding the whole Bible in Homer."[7]

Like Piccolomini, Popes Paul II and Paul III had a good knowledge of Greek, but they did not share his firm belief in the importance of the survival of the ancient cultures. Paul II, an eclectic collector, a lover of sports and lavish parties, and the founder of Rome's first printing press, issued a ban forbidding schools to teach the pagan poets to children. Paul III, a patron of artists such as Titian and Michelangelo, established in 1542 the Congregation of the Roman Inquisition, or Holy Office, whose mission, among many others, was the banning of heretical and pagan works.[8] Between 1468, when Paul II ordered the suppression of the prestigious Roman Academy, which he suspected of performing pagan rituals under cover of studying the classics, and Paul III's death in 1549, interest in Greek studies on the Italian peninsula began an irreversible decline.[9] There were, however, a few enlightened interludes. Shortly after his election to the Holy See in 1513, Leon X, second son of Lorenzo the Magnificent, ordered that the Roman Academy be reopened and that a college for young Greek students be founded under the direction of the eminent scholar Giovanni Lascaris. The Quirinal College was active for approximately seven years, during which it educated a select number of young boys of Greek ancestry in Greek language, literature, and thought. A letter has been preserved from a Greek notary established in Venice which gives a detailed account of the ceremony during which the children welcomed the pope with elaborate salutations in ancient Greek, using terms borrowed from the classical authors, notably Homer.[10]

Greek scholars started to immigrate to the northern countries, and humanists such as Erasmus, Thomas More, and Guillaume Budé, benefiting from their knowledge, carried on the work of commentary and editing. "In letters, we are nothing without the Greeks," Erasmus wrote to his English colleague John Colet. Peter Schade (Petrus Mosellanus), a twenty-four-year-old friend of Erasmus and professor of Greek at Leipzig University, published in 1518 a book titled *Discourse on the Need to Learn Different Lan-*

guages in which he ardently defended a multilingual culture. To the opposition's argument that God had punished humankind with the plurality of tongues after Babel (according to Genesis 11:1–9), Schade answered with the notion that God is a polyglot ("God understands the tongues of all people") and that angels and saints, being our intercessors, are also polyglots by necessity. "Indeed, if they did not understand prayers conceived in any language, it would be useless for a German or a Frenchman to murmur a prayer in their mother tongue addressed to saints of other nationalities. Certainly, they would be thus no less ridiculous than if they attempted to speak to the dead."[11]

The dead might speak to God in their myriad tongues, but to us mortals they often speak in translation. While in the West, as we have seen, Homer was translated early on into Latin and later into several of the endemic tongues of Europe, in the East, in China, Japan, and Korea, Homer proved less popular. In China the earliest translations of sections of Homeric epics date from the late Ming Dynasty in the seventeenth century, but Chinese readers had to wait for more than three hundred years to see the first complete version of the two poems.[12] In Japan, Tatsusaburo Uchimura attempted a verse translation of the *Iliad* for the first time in 1904 and published books 1 to 4 under the title *Toroi no Uta* (The Song of Troy). Nonohito Saito was the first to translate the *Odyssey* into Japanese, but his death from tuberculosis prevented him from finishing it: the first sections were printed posthumously in 1913. The first complete *Iliad* in Japanese was published in 1940 and a complete *Odyssey* in 1943.[13] In Korea, the poet Yoo Yeong, who translated Milton into Korean, published in 1959 his versions of both the *Iliad* and the *Odyssey*.[14]

In Ottoman Turkey, no translation of Homer existed before 1885, when Na'im Fraseri translated the first book of the *Iliad*, noting in his preface that "until now, no other poet in the world has reached the level of Homer." The Turks, however, knew about

Homer long before the nineteenth century. *The Book of Dede Korkut,* the classic saga of the Oghuz Turks that originated as an oral epic sometime in the early eleventh century and was first recorded five centuries later, has numerous similarities with Homer's poems. Among its many episodes, it tells of various sporting competitions of the warriors such as those described in the *Odyssey,* and of the adventures of the hero Basat, who ends up killing the frightful Cyclops Tepegöz. By the end of the nineteenth century, the Homeric sagas were clearly part of the Turkish imagination. Exploring the differences between Homer's stories and those of the Ottoman Muslims, the great twentieth-century novelist Ahmed Tanpinar remarked, "In the *Iliad,* the whole Greek world, including the cosmos, the gods, the lives, the works and the arts of the Greeks and Greek civilization are gathered in the narrative of one event. The story of the *Iliad* is an entity; details are disregarded or ingeniously integrated in the whole. The *Book of Kings* [the epic poem by the eleventh-century Persian poet Ferdowsi], on the other hand, is a rectilinear narrative that treats every detail with the same precision."[15]

In most of Europe, as we have seen, Homer enters the libraries much earlier. And yet in the Catholic countries, after the Reformation, the number of translations of Homer came to a virtual halt for several decades. Latin was confirmed as the accepted language of the Catholic Church and Greek that of Protestant culture (not counting, of course, the endemic languages into which the Protestant Bible was translated). The Council of Trent (1545 to 1563) forbade Catholics the reading of the Greek and Hebrew Bibles except in the case of appointed scholars, and in the eyes of the Church of Rome, students of Greek became synonymous with heretics. As a consequence, several Greek scholars were burnt at the stake in 1546 as offenders of the faith by the Catholic king of France, François I, in spite of the royal devotion to the arts and letters. In the Protestant countries, the study of Greek was assiduously encouraged, and even in the Protestant colonies Greek became part of the standard school curriculum. In 1788, for instance, in the Danish Virgin Islands, the Rector Hans West opened in Christiansted a school to teach the children of planters the works of Homer and other classical poets.[16] Not knowing Greek became, in Protestant countries, a mark of ignorance. In Oliver Goldsmith's 1766 novel *The Vicar of Wakefield*, the foolish principal of the University of Louvain in Belgium makes this boast: "You see me, young man, I never learned Greek, and I don't find that I have ever missed it. I have had a doctor's cap and gown without Greek; I have ten thousand florins a year without Greek; I eat heartily without Greek; and, in short, ... as I don't know Greek, I do not believe there is any good in it."[17]

This division, while not absolute, had far-reaching consequences: from the seventeenth century on, Homer was being rigorously studied in English, German, and Scandinavian universities, while in Spain, France, Portugal, and Italy he was being neglected for the sake of Virgil and Dante. The first Spanish translation of the *Odyssey* made directly from the Greek, by Gonzalo Pérez, was published in Amberes in 1556 and hardly distributed; the *Iliad*, in a version by García Malo, also from the Greek, had to wait until 1788 and met with as little success. For centuries, Spanish-language readers learned their Homer through quotations in classical texts or through a handful of Latin translations. This remained the norm long into the nineteenth century. When Miguel de Unamuno was given the chair of Greek at the University of Salamanca in 1891, it was pointed out that the celebrated intellectual had no Greek. Juan Valera, chairman of the committee that had selected him, explained, "None of the other candidates knows Greek, so we selected the one most likely to learn it."[18] (Unamuno's students later recalled his fluency in ancient Greek.) The first encyclopedia written in Spanish, the *Silva de varia lección* by Pedro Mexía, was published to great acclaim in 1540 in

Seville. Though it purports to be a compendium of "books of great authority," its references to Homer, since the author knew no Greek, are few and most likely taken either from a Latin translation of the *Iliad* that appeared in Basel in 1531 or from quotations of Homer by other authors. When Mexía does mention Homer's works, he chooses only the best-known episodes, such as Hector addressing his horses in book 8 of the *Iliad* or Aeolus giving the number of winds in book 10 of the *Odyssey*.[19]

Only a handful of Spanish writers defended Homer against his disparagers. The poet Francisco de Quevedo, for instance, mocked the ignorance of those who invented "shameless lies against Homer and false testimonies in order to raise altars to Virgil" and, in somewhat convoluted prose, accused these pseudo-scholars of perjury: "In all ages there have been infamous men who have preferred to lend infamy to those who are famous rather than become famous themselves, being as they are, infamous."[20]

The learned Mexican poet Sor Juana Inés de la Cruz published in 1689 a curious imitation of Luis de Góngora under the title "The Dream" in which she mentioned Homer as the "sweetest of poets" who wrote of "Achillean feats and Ulysses' martial subtleties." Though she had only read Homer quoted in the works of other contemporary writers, such as the German scholar Athanasius Kircher, this did not prevent her from exalting his perfection: "It would be easier," she said, "to remove from the fearful Thunderer his lightning ... than half a line of verse dictated to [Homer] by propitious Apollo."[21]

For Francis Bacon, instead, writing in 1609, Homer was a familiar instrument of poetical instruction, to be consulted carefully and constantly. To dismiss the poets of old because of their "casual licentiousness" (as the Council of Trent had decreed) "would be rash, and almost profane; for, since religion delights in such shadows and disguises, to abolish them were, in a manner, to prohibit all intercourse betwixt things divine and human."[22]

For Sor Juana, Homer was an uncontested, unread reference; for Bacon, he was a sourcebook to be studied and analyzed. This divided inheritance was passed on in the nineteenth century to the Americas and was reflected in lifestyles and libraries. In the United States, the elite chose to model its architecture after the tenets of the Greek Revival, while in Latin America the bourgeoisie chose to fashion its houses after the French and Italian baroque. "He who first reads Homer in America," wrote Ralph Waldo Emerson in his journal, comparing that wise future reader to the founder of Thebes and to the second king of Rome, "is its Cadmus & Numa, and a subtle but unlimited benefactor."[23] In the north, Emerson, Whitman, and Thoreau read Homer; south of the Rio Grande, José Martí, Rubén Darío, and Machado de Assis read Virgil.

CHAPTER 10

Ancients Versus Moderns

"How unlike the home life of our own dear Queen!"
—A Victorian lady upon seeing Shakespeare's *Antony and Cleopatra*
starring Sarah Bernhardt in 1899

Michel de Montaigne, writing in the last decades of the sixteenth
century, chose Homer as one of the three "most excellent of men"
of all time. (The other two were soldiers, Alexander the Great
and the Theban commander Epaminondas.) Confessing that his
Greek was not up to truly appreciating Homer, whom he knew
mainly through Virgil, Montaigne granted the blind bard primacy
because of the far-reaching power of his invention. "Nothing
lives on the lips of men," wrote Montaigne, "like his name and
his work: nothing is as known or accepted as Troy, Helen, and
his wars—which may never have taken place on real ground. Our
children are still given names which he forged over three hundred
years ago. Who does not know of Hector and Achilles? Not only
individual lineages but most nations seek their origins in Homer's
inventions. Mehemet II, Emperor of the Turks, wrote thus to our
Pope Pius II: 'I am amazed that the Italians should band against
me, since we both have a common Trojan origin and, like the
Italians, I have an interest in avenging the blood of Hector on
the Greeks whom they, however, favor against me.' Isn't all this

a noble farce in which Kings, Republics, and Emperors all play their parts over many centuries, and for which this vast universe serves as a stage?"[1]

To his cast of farce players, Montaigne could have added writers and scholars. From the mid-seventeenth to the mid-eighteenth century, the study of Homer in France became embroiled in what came to be called "the Battle of the Ancients and Moderns," a hundred-year-long quarrel in which both sides held confused and contradictory opinions. In 1781, the classical scholar Jean-Baptiste-Gaspard d'Ansse de Villoison discovered a tenth-century manuscript of the *Iliad* in Venice of which he published an extremely learned edition eight years later.[2] Villoison's Homer served as the basis for most subsequent French editions: the fact that the French scholar was challenged by other European scholars did not perturb the Gallic self-confidence of Villoison's fellow countrymen, both the *anciens* and the *modernes.*

According to the anciens, the classics were the admired model to be imitated and continued; according to the modernes, traditional literature was a creative millstone and writers and artists ought to be able to invent something distinctively new. The modernes defended Christianity over paganism; the anciens, the official power of the king at Versailles against the mundane intellectuals of the Paris salons. The debate covered many subjects: the use of Olympic gods or of angels and demons in epic poetry; the language, Latin or French, in which public inscriptions should be written; the inclusion of colloquialisms and vulgar actions in literary compositions. With aristocratic haughtiness, modernes such as Charles Perrault, author of the famous fairy tales, admitted Homer's importance but scoffed at him for being vulgar: for comparing the retreating Ajax to a stubborn ass beaten by children, or for presenting a princess who declares that she must go down to the river to do her brothers' laundry.[3] Perrault's attitude toward Homer, wishing that he were purged of vulgarity, was compared by the critic Charles-Augustin Sainte-Beuve to that of the child who wants his mother to read him a story, saying, "I know it isn't true, but tell me the story anyway."[4] The anciens said that they admired Homer in spite of his occasional coarseness and incivility. For most of the anciens, as well as for the modernes, Homer remained a phantom, "visible but absent."[5] When Pierre de Ronsard, a precursor of the modernes, declared, "I want to read in three days Homer's *Iliad*" undisturbed, he was probably in earnest in his desire to conjure up Homer's ghost, though he added that if someone came with a message from Cassandra, the messenger should be let in at once.[6]

There were of course exceptions. Jean Boivin, who would become in 1692 head of the Royal Library of France, was taught Greek by his older brother Louis after they lost their parents and Louis became Jean's tutor. Louis's pedagogical methods were strict but effective. He locked the ten-year-old Jean in the attic with a volume of Homer in Greek, a dictionary, and a grammar, and did not release him until the boy was able to explain in Latin and French a number of Homer's verses. Jean acquitted himself so well that decades later, at the age of forty-three, he was appointed professor of ancient Greek at the Royal College of France.[7]

One of the anciens, the twenty-three-year-old Jean Racine, whose mastery of Greek, even at that age, was remarkable, responded to the modernes by praising Homer's sense of "what is true." Racine had little patience with what he considered pretentious niceties. "Those husbandry terms," he wrote, "are not as shocking in Greek as they are in our tongue, which has little tolerance for anything, and which will not approve of composing eclogues about farmers, as Theocritus did, or that one speak of Ulysses' swineherd in heroic terms. Such delicate sentiments are nothing but weakness of character."[8]

Racine had the knowledge, memory, and literary acumen to back his opinions. Born in 1639 and orphaned at a very young age,

Racine was educated at the Cistercian School of Port-Royal. He completed his education in Paris and after considering and rejecting an ecclesiastical career settled there in 1663 to become a writer. When he was still an adolescent at Port-Royal, he discovered the novel by Heliodorus, *Aethiopica; or, The Loves of Theogonis and Charicles*, a *pathos erotikon* (romance) written in the late second century CE and inspired by the stories of Homer. The *Aethiopica* was an example of the kind of literature frowned upon by the Cistercian monks. Therefore, the sexton, finding the boy reading it in the abbey forest, pulled it out of his hands and threw it into a bonfire. Racine managed to secure a second copy, which was also discovered and condemned to the flames. He then bought a third copy and learned the text by heart. Then he handed it over to the sexton, saying, "Now you can burn this one too."[9] (Readers today will recall that this strategy to circumvent censorship was employed by Ray Bradbury's rebels in *Fahrenheit 451*.) Racine also memorized much of the *Iliad* and the *Odyssey*.

At Port-Royal, the adolescent Racine became familiar not only with the classics of Greek literature but also with the strict tenets of Jansenism. The doctrine of Jansenism took its name from the theologian Jansenius, who in the early seventeenth century, under the influence of Augustinian theology, taught the doctrine of predestination, according to which it is not good deeds that can save humankind from the eternal fire but what Saint Thomas Aquinas called "the gratuitous gift of God's grace alone."[10] Augustine had suggested a similar argument against the Pelagian heretics (who believed that good actions on earth led to salvation in heaven) but had defended the notion of man's free will in his debate against the Manichaeans. For twenty-two years, Jansenius worked on his thesis, which he ambitiously called *The Augustine of Cornelius Jansen, Bishop; or, On the Doctrines of Saint Augustine Concerning Human Nature, Health, Grief, and Cure Against the Pelagians*, but he died of the plague in 1638 before he was able to deliver it for publication. Two years later, his friends had it published under the abridged title of *Augustinus*. Outraged by its self-confidence, Pope Urban VIII declared several of its propositions heretical, and the book was condemned by the Inquisition in 1641. Blaise Pascal, defending Jansen's argument, wrote in his *Pensées*, "We understand nothing of the works of God, if we do not start from the principle that he blinds some and enlightens others."[11]

At least two of these heretical propositions run through most of Racine's work. First, because of the lack of powers granted to us, some of us are unable to obey God's commands; second, since we are all victims of Adam's sin, in order to merit or deserve punishment we need not be free of interior necessity but only of exterior constraint. According to Racine, both these notions are evident in Homer's depiction of the relationship between mortals and gods; for this reason, Homer (together with Pindar, Euripides, and Plutarch) is Racine's essential inspiration for some of his later great plays, notably *Andromaque* and *Iphigénie*. Inspiration in the sense of source: Homer's conclusions are Racine's starting points.

In the *Iliad*, Homer had shown the desperate Andromache clutching her son and bidding her husband, Hector, not to leave her to go fight the Greeks. "Andromache," he says to her,

> Dear one, why so desperate? Why so much grief for me?
> No man will hurl me down to Death, against my fate.
> And fate? No man alive has ever escaped it,
> neither brave man nor coward, I tell you—
> It's born with us the day that we are born.[12]

This is a Jansenist argument if there ever was one, and Racine explores it in great depth in *Andromaque*. The play follows the story of Hector's widow, allotted among the spoils of war to Achilles' son Neoptolemus (also known as Pyrrhus). Fate has wrought a chain of unrequited loves: that of the Greek envoy Orestes for the

Greek princess Hermione, of Hermione for Pyrrhus, of Pyrrhus for Andromache, and of Andromache for her dead husband, Hector. Orestes declares his position clearly: "I give myself blindly to the fate [*destin*] that drags me along." But Racine realized that this statement was too simple: something more than the power of fate is at play. The first edition of *Andromaque* was published in 1667. A year later, Racine revised the line for the 1668 edition. In the new version, Orestes says, "I give myself blindly to the rapture [*transport*] that drags me along." Fate, yes, but in the form of rapture, an obsessive fate that grants each man and each woman a peculiar emotional strength, an impulse greater than our realization that it will lead us to misfortune or catastrophe.[13]

This "emotional strength" is not to be confused with human instinct. An example of the dichotomy is made clear in the episode of Odysseus and the Cyclops in book 9 of the *Odyssey*. While the Cyclops is driven by cannibal appetite, which he satisfies through brute force, Odysseus survives through his *mētis*, a Greek word that means "clear thinking," "clever reasoning," "cunning." In the first case, the action and the person who performs it are one; in the second, the actor is master of his acts.[14] Not that a hero must always override his instincts—on the contrary, they are proof of his humanity—but he must be conscious of them. After Odysseus is forced to watch in horror his companions being devoured by the monster Scylla, "screaming out, flinging their arms toward me," he and the survivors go ashore for the night and "adeptly" prepare their supper of roasted mutton. They eat and drink, and only then do they recall their "dear companions" and weep, and "a welcome sleep came on them in their tears."[15] Aldous Huxley, commenting on this passage, remarks that Homer's description of the men eating and drinking after seeing the slaughter of their friends rings astonishingly true. "Every good book," says Huxley, "gives us bits of the truth, would not be a good book if it did not. But the whole truth, no. Of the great writers of the past, incredibly few have given us that. Homer—the Homer of the *Odyssey*—is one of those few."[16]

It is this individual God-granted emotional strength, managed through mētis, that allows human fate to be fulfilled in a myriad of ways. According to Racine, Andromache is forced to marry the victorious Pyrrhus, but she succeeds in following her apparent fate (to incarnate Troy's victimhood after Hector's death) and also in overturning Troy's defeat in the same action (since Pyrrhus effectively abdicates in her favor and that of Hector's son, by saying, "I give you … my crown and my faith:/Andromache, reign over Epirus and me").[17] Giving herself to Pyrrhus, she will become his queen, while her son, a Trojan, will inherit the Greek throne. It is not love that prompts Andromache (who will pay for this mētis with her life) but something else, which she can neither identify nor ignore. To go back to Pascal's phrase, God has both blinded and enlightened her, forced her to obey her fate and at the same time to assume consciously her rapture as well.

Racine's annotations, scribbled on the margins of his copies of the *Odyssey* and the *Iliad,* give us a fair idea of his reading of Homer. Racine was especially interested in the methods by which Homer achieved verisimilitude. He notes, for instance, that Telemachus's kind reception of Athena in a stranger's guise (in book 1 of the *Odyssey*) might have been inspired by a similar welcome granted to the wandering Homer on his own travels; he points out that the *Iliad*'s story takes forty-seven precisely timed days: five of fighting, nine of plague, eleven for Poseidon's sojourn in Ethiopia, eleven for Patroclus's funeral, and eleven for that of Hector. Racine's notes cover the subjects of food, dress, geographical descriptions, appropriate metaphors, the efficacy of certain gestures, the pleasure derived from weeping. In book 5 of the *Odyssey,* Odysseus has jumped overboard to escape the wave Poseidon has sent to destroy him. He has spent two days adrift at sea, the *pontos atrygetos* or "unharvestable sea," and on the third day he sees land with "the joy that children feel/when they see their father's life dawn again, /one who's lain on a sickbed racked with torment." But just as he is about to reach the rocky shore, Poseidon sends another battering wave, which would have flayed him alive against the stones had Athena not intervened. Grasping the rocks, the skin of his hands ripped off in strips, striking the reef "like pebbles stuck in the suckers of some octopus/dragged from its lair," Odysseus prays to the River God whose mouth he has reached:

> Hear me, lord, whoever you are,
> I've come to you, the answer to all my prayers—
> rescue me from the sea, the Sea-lord's curse!
> Even immortal gods will show a man respect,
> whatever wanderer seeks their help—like me—
> I throw myself on your mercy, on your current now—
> I have suffered greatly. Pity me, lord,
> your suppliant cries for help![18]

In our own anxious times, the forced migrations, the stubbornly hopeful refugees, the shipwrecked asylum seekers washed up on the European coast all have their reflection in the character of Odysseus striving to find his island. In a 1992 study by a researcher at the University of Guadalajara, Mexico, one of the migrant workers described his experience of trying to reach the United States: "The north is like the sea," he said. "When you travel as an illegal, you are dragged like an animal's tail, like rubbish. I imagined the way the sea washes the rubbish ashore, and I thought: maybe it's just like being in the ocean, tossed and tossed again."[19] The experience, the emotional strength, the image are the same.

Racine also remarks that Seneca, during his painful forced exile in Corsica, summed up this passage in four words: *Res est sacra miser* (Wretchedness is a sacred thing). And Racine adds, "This sentiment is made even more beautiful by the fact that it is engraved in the heart by Nature herself."[20] It is also the sentiment at the heart of the poems of Homer.

Not all the combatants in the century-long *querelle* between the anciens and the modernes were driven by literary, philosophical, or aesthetic motives. Some motives were political. Anne Dacier, daughter of a noted humanist and one of the best-known Greek scholars of her time—her work on the *Iliad* was to influence Pope's translation a few years later—sided with the anciens and published in 1714 an ancien handbook, *On the Causes of the Corruption of Taste.*[21] Together with scholars such as Pierre-Daniel Huet and Jacques-Bénigne Bossuet, she oversaw a series of Greek and Latin texts trimmed and purged for the use of the dauphin, the eldest son of the king of France, and *ad usum Delphini* became an expression to denote an expurgated book. Although Dacier's editions of Homer were famous, the Homer ad usum Delphini timorously excised not only certain scenes that might have been considered ribald (such as Odysseus naked in front of Nausicaa in book 6 of the *Odyssey*) but several disrespectful references to kings as well (e.g., Achilles' insulting speech to Agamemnon in book 1 of the *Iliad*). The ancienne Dacier thought that the dauphin might be affected by a different kind of vulgarity from the one that offended the moderne Perrault. Much the same impulse drives editors and school boards in the twenty-first century to suppress African American history books and to publish classic children's writers such as Roald Dahl and Dr. Seuss in "corrected" versions stripped of "offensive" passages, ad usum English-speaking Delphinorum.[22]

For Madame Dacier's fellow anciens, some of the motives to trim Homer were religious. For instance, François de Salignac de la Mothe-Fénelon argued that Homer might indeed serve as a source of inspiration to the young but only if his stories were told in the appropriate pedagogical tone and with a devout Christian purpose. Gifted with a brilliant mind and an easy style of story-telling, Fénelon seemed to be destined for an exalted career as the tutor of the dauphin. He was elected to the French Academy, appointed archbishop of Cambrai in 1693, and enjoyed fame as the author of several literary books of instruction. But in 1696 he fell out of favor with Madame de Maintenon, King Louis XIV's second wife, for having befriended Madame de Guyon, a devout promoter of Quietism among the young. Quietism, a Christian doctrine linked to certain trends of Spanish mysticism, encouraged abandonment to the will of God and favored silence over prayer. Madame de Maintenon and Fénelon's own teacher Bossuet feared that such passive habits would lead to moral indifference. To justify his position, Fénelon published in 1697 *Explanation of the Maxims of the Saints,* in which he attempted to defend, point by point, the disputed doctrine, but his arguments did nothing to convince his opponents. Less than two years later, Bossuet managed to have the book condemned both by the pope and by the king. To add to the dishonor, at about the same time, Fénelon was discharged from his duties as royal tutor.[23]

Before his fall from grace, Fénelon, in order to provide his royal pupil with a manual of mythology and civic morals, devised in 1699 a pedagogical fable in which he continued the story of Telemachus, interrupted in book 4 of the *Odyssey.* In Homer's poem, Telemachus and Nestor's son Pisistratus arrive at the palace of Menelaus and Helen, where they hear the story which the Old Man of the Sea had told the king, that Odysseus has been imprisoned by Calypso on a faraway island. In the *Odyssey,* Telemachus does not appear again until book 15; Fénelon decided to recount the missing adventures of Ulysses' (as Fénelon calls him) son. Accompanied by Athena disguised as the faithful Mentor, Telemachus is shipwrecked on Calypso's island, falls in love with a nymph, is rescued from the attachment by Mentor, and finally reaches the port of Salente. Here Mentor establishes an ideal city-state, in which the good of the people and the independence of the church take precedence over the pleasures and powers of the king. In the meantime, Telemachus is sent off on various missions (including a descent into the Kingdom of Hades) until at last they both sail back to Ithaca, where Telemachus and Ulysses are reunited. In the climate of suspicion and fear of Versailles, the anonymously published *Adventures of Telemachus* was seen less as a pastiche of Homer than as a treasonable criticism of Louis XIV's regime. From his own cathedral pulpit, Fénelon was forced to read out the pope's ordinance against his *Explanation* and lived the rest of his life exiled from the court. Fénelon died in 1715, only eight months before his fractious king.[24]

Eventually the dispute between these various readings of Homer acquired a reputation for absurdity. In 1721, Charles-Louis de Secondat, baron de Montesquieu, author of the influential *De l'esprit des lois* (On the Spirit of the Law), made fun of the French society of his time in an anonymously published epistolary novel that purported to be the gossipy correspondence between Usbek, a Persian traveler, and his friends back home, on subjects that ranged from the traditional and oppressive oriental order to the silly laissez-faire of France. Remarking that he is shocked by how Parisians waste their talent on puerile things, Usbek gives his friend Rhédi (who is in Venice) a telling example. "When I arrived in Paris, I found them becoming heated in a quarrel about the flimsiest matter imaginable: the reputation of an ancient Greek poet, whose homeland for the past two thousand years remains unknown, as well as the time of his death. Both parties admit that he was an excellent poet; the only question was how much or how little merit was to be attributed to him. Each one wished to contribute something of his own; but among these distributors of reputation, some carried more weight than others. That's what the quarrel was about!"[25]

In the end, the *querelle* was left appropriately unresolved. In 1757, the scholarly baron Frédéric-Melchior Grimm reached this conclusion: "We can truthfully say, without wishing to depress the *modernes*, that nothing has made the sublime singer [Homer] so admirable as the work of his successors, from Virgil to Monsieur de Voltaire."[26]

CHAPTER 11

Homer as Poetry

Have I not made blind Homer sing to me?
—Christopher Marlowe, *Doctor Faustus*, 1604

A century earlier, at about the same time that the querelle between the anciens and modernes began, Rembrandt van Rijn painted a portrait of a bearded man in a large-brimmed hat, rich sleeves, and a gold chain, his right hand on the skull of an ancient bust. Though Rembrandt himself did not give the painting a title, it came to be known as *Aristotle Contemplating the Bust of Homer* (now called *Aristotle with a Bust of Homer*). Around 1632, Rembrandt had moved from Leyden, his hometown, to Amsterdam, where he had set himself up as a portrait painter. His reputation grew and with it his fortune, increased by his marriage to the well-to-do Saskia van Uylenborch, who became the model for many of his paintings. But after 1642 his business declined, and when, ten years later, the commission for the portrait came, he was only four years away from declaring bankruptcy. Rembrandt accepted with alacrity.

The work had been commissioned by a rich Sicilian merchant, Antonio Ruffo, who, when he received it, imagined from the pile of books in the background that the subject was an intellectual character of some sort, and entered the painting in his inventory as "a half-length of a philosopher made in Amsterdam by the painter Rembrandt (it appears to be Aristotle or [the doctor of the church] Albertus Magnus)."[1] A third character appears in the composition: a helmeted head on a medallion hanging from a gold chain and recently identified as that of Alexander the Great, Aristotle's most famous pupil. Alexander is the link between the philosopher and the poet: it was Aristotle who, according to Plutarch, prepared the edition of the *Iliad* that Alexander kept "with his dagger under his pillow, declaring that he esteemed it a perfect portable treasure of all military virtue and knowledge."[2] The art historian Simon Schama makes a good case for the bearded man being the Greek painter Apelles rather than Aristotle, but what matters is that the contemplated bust is indeed Homer. Rembrandt portrayed Homer on other occasions: in a drawing that shows him reciting his poems and in a preparatory sketch for a canvas (poorly preserved) that shows the bard with his hands on his cane and his eyes in shadow. These portraits, albeit imaginary, depict a flesh-and-blood person, made vividly present in the act of speaking or composing, his eyes convincingly blind while "above them," writes Schama, "within the shining skull of the poet, visions are nonetheless forming."[3]

The bust, however, is a convention, not Rembrandt's conception of a poet, or even of the poet Homer, but the reproduction of a popular icon, a mass-produced trinket, equivalent to a Lourdes crucifix, "a portrait-type," notes Schama, "commonly, but entirely speculatively, identified as the bard."[4] An inventory of Rembrandt's possessions lists precisely such a bust. And yet, because it is not a particular interpretation of Homer, the bust serves in the painting as the allegorical image for an all-embracing idea of poetry, perhaps of all the literary arts. Aristotle or Apelles, or whoever the bearded man might be (and he is very much a particular man), is contemplating in Homer's bust an immemorial flow of emotions and thoughts, born out of the heartening belief that the experience of the world can be distilled and preserved in words and images that will reflect that experience in the eyes of a reader. The man in Rembrandt's portrait is contemplating not a bust of Homer but the creative act itself. In the same way that the art of poetry might have been, for the early bards, symbolically incarnated in a mythical being called Homer, now, more than two thousand years later, the icon of Homer has been turned upon itself and come to mean the art of poetry.

"There is something unprecedented (and unrepeated) about the way the poetry of the *Iliad* and the *Odyssey* affects reader and audience," wrote the poet and critic Michael Schmidt in his book on the early Greek poets, "something which even a decent translation communicates to the attentive ear. This 'something' has to do with how the language relates to the things it names, how the words relate to the world they portray. It is more than a matter of using verbs, active verbs, much more frequently than most Greek poets do, in some passages more frequently than nouns; it is more than how he enacts thought, embeds it in the action through the use of such verbs, *embodies* it. . . . It starts in the unique nature of the language that is deployed."[5]

But what was the "unique nature" of Homer's poetic language? For Sir Philip Sidney in the late sixteenth century, "the art of poetry" was the art of imitation, "a speaking picture, with this end: to teach and delight." For Francis Bacon, a quarter-century later, it was the art of sublimation. "Poesy," he wrote, "was ever thought to have some participation of divineness, because it doth raise and erect the mind, by submitting the shows of things to the desires of the mind; whereas reason doth buckle and bow the mind unto the nature of things." For the eighteenth century it came to mean the art of inventiveness or invention, "to be original with the minimum of alteration," as T. S. Eliot put it, though he also warned, "It is dangerous to generalize about the poetry of the eighteenth century as about that of any other age; for it was, like any other age, an age of transition." And it is perhaps in translation that transition is best expressed and most clearly seen, since in a newly translated text, whatever is meant by "originality" can be shown by comparison to previous efforts.[6]

Sir Philip Sidney died in 1586, at the age of thirty-one. Two decades later Doctor António Sousa de Macedo was born in Porto, Portugal. He became secretary at the Portuguese Embassy in London and ambassador to Holland, and spent most of his life on complicated diplomatic missions. He nevertheless found time to write several theological and historical treatises, as well as a number of poems. One of them, a long mythological epic, *Ulissipo*, takes up the Greek myth of the foundation of Lisbon by Ulysses and describes the battling forces of a Homeric Jupiter (Zeus), representing the Catholic Trinity, against Pluto (Hades), in the role of the Prince of Darkness, with humankind as their bloody Trojan battleground.[7] As we have seen, the intellectuals of the Iberian peninsula knew Homer mainly through Virgil. Homer's vague shadow floats over Portugal's national epic, Luis de Camões's *Os Lusíadas* (1572), and, to a lesser degree, over Gabriel de Pereira de Castro's *Ulisseia ou Lisboa Edificada* (1636). In both Portugal and Spain, Homer's authority was firmly acknowledged, though his works were mostly unread.

In one short condemnatory paragraph, the erudite (and wonderfully capricious) authors of the *História da Literatura Portuguesa*, A. J. Saraiva and Óscar Lopes, react with displeasure to what they judge to be Sousa de Macedo's pedestrian style: "What is most infuriating about the work," the authors tell us, "is this untenable compromise, surely more for the modern taste than for that of his time, between mythology and a reality described at times as prosaically as possible." As an example of this, they note that in canto 2, Sousa de Macedo enumerates "all agricultural crops, all major botanical and zoological species of the Lisbon region, by their own names, without mythological transposition." Though the index of the *História* lists eight more references to Sousa de Macedo, these are bare citations in various lists of essayists and poets. As far as Saraiva and Lopes are concerned, the author of *Ulissipo* does not deserve to be remembered.[8]

And yet the fourteen cantos of *Ulissipo* merit a more charitable reading. Though the short catalogues of canto 2 do not stand up to the catalogue of ships in book 2 of the *Iliad,* for example, they have a Homeric tone that is not entirely displeasing. Rivers are briefly enumerated with their classical attributes, cities are cited so as to distinguish the one founded by Ulysses from its brethren, a few plants and animals are mentioned, but they are not mere real estate listings. Also, they contain a few memorable lines that perhaps Sidney would not have disowned.

Her face was a beautiful labyrinth,
Where love was given up for lost.[9]

When Alexander Pope began his translation of the *Iliad,* his concern was neither literal faithfulness nor archaeological veracity but a brave attempt to "invent again" what the greatest of poets had invented for the first time: to achieve something close to perfection through an established literary correctness within which a poet's imagination could build its singular designs. For Pope, it was no Muse that inspired Homer but the poet's own creative genius. "Homer," he wrote in his preface, "is universally allowed to have had the greatest invention of any writer whatever. ... It is the invention that in different degrees distinguishes all great geniuses: the utmost stretch of human study, learning, and industry, which masters everything besides, can never attain to this."[10]

Pope was largely self-educated. The son of a Roman Catholic London draper, he spent a difficult childhood afflicted with a tubercular disease of the spine, a recluse in his parents' home in Windsor Forest, a situation that led him in later life to be both suspicious of and greedy for attention. At the age of sixteen, he wrote a series of pastorals in imitation of Theocritus and Virgil, embarking on a lifelong relationship with the ancient authors from whom he would draw both rhetoric and subject matter. In 1715, at the age of twenty-seven, he published the first volume of his translation of the *Iliad*. Pope had imagined his enterprise as a long journey whose end seemed almost unattainable. He had no Greek—no doubt a stumbling block for anyone attempting a translation of Homer—but he worked from the translations of others, namely those of George Chapman, John Ogilby, and Thomas Hobbes, as well as from John Dryden's unfinished *Iliad*, and from Latin versions, which he could only more or less decipher since his Latin was far from perfect. He wrote diligently, constructing the book in the strict form of heroic couplets, elevating the tone when he felt that Homer was being too pedestrian. Every day he would translate thirty or forty verses before getting out of bed, then he would continue to revise them until the evening, when he would read through the finished pages "for the versification only."[11] Before starting he wrote out the sense of each of Homer's lines in prose, and only after grasping the full meaning would he proceed to shape it into verse. And yet, however honed these mechanics, the process itself was never mechanical.

Pope knew his audience. "He supplied exactly what was wanted," wrote Lytton Strachey. "He gave the eighteenth century a Homer after its own heart—a Homer who was the father—not quite of poetry, indeed, but of something much more satisfactory—of what the eighteenth century believed poetry to be; and, very properly, it gave him a fortune in return."[12]

Homer made Pope financially independent. No author had ever earned as much from a translation. The *Iliad*, published in six volumes, brought him £5,320, the *Odyssey* (translated by

Pope in collaboration with William Broome and Elijah Fenton)
£3,500, a total profit of almost £9,000—a fortune in those days.
"Thanks to Homer," Pope said, he could "live and thrive,/indebted
to no prince or peer alive."[13] Although his *Iliad* was met with high
praise from the reading public, the academics were less enthusiastic. Edward Gibbon, who enjoyed the translation, said that
it had "every merit except that of likeness to the original," and
the despotic Master of Trinity College, Cambridge, Richard Bentley, judged it "a pretty poem, Mr Pope, but you must not call it
Homer." Dr. Johnson, however, not the least gifted of readers,
called it "the noblest version of poetry the world has ever seen."
And Henry Fielding, in his amusing *A Journey from This World to
the Next,* imagined seeing Homer in Elysium with the scholarly
Madame Dacier sitting in his lap. "[Homer] asked much after Mr
Pope, and said he was very desirous of seeing him; for that he had
read his *Iliad* in his translation with almost as much delight, as he
believed he had given others in the original."[14]

But some critics disliked what they perceived as Pope's artificiality rather than his artifice, and made fun of his scruples in
rendering Homer's vulgarities vulgar. William Hazlitt argued that
Pope's "chief excellence lay more in diminishing, than in aggran-
dizing objects . . . in describing a row of pins and needles, rather
than the embattled spears of Greeks and Trojans." Leslie Stephen,
in his biography of Pope, saw the problem clearly: "Any style
becomes bad when it dies; when it is used merely as tradition,
and not as the best mode of producing the desired impression.
. . . In such a case, no doubt, the diction becomes a burden, and a
man is apt to fancy himself a poet because he is the slave of the
external form instead of using it as the most familiar instrument."
But that was after Pope had triumphed; it was his successors who
failed to match his achievements.[15]

Pope took every precaution to deflect criticism. "Our author's
work," he wrote of Homer in his preface, "is a wild paradise, where

if we cannot see all the beauties so distinctly as in an ordered garden, it is only because the number of them is infinitely greater." He then pushed as far as he could the botanical metaphor: "It is like a copious nursery, which contains the seeds and first productions of every kind, out of which those who followed him have but selected some particular plants, each according to his fancy, to cultivate and beautify. If some things are too luxuriant, it is owing to the richness of the soil; and if others are not arrived to perfection or maturity, it is only because they are overrun and oppressed by those of a stronger nature." In other words, Homer's perfection cannot be fully transplanted by anyone. "The concept of a definitive text," wrote Jorge Luis Borges in 1932, "is the outcome of either religion or weariness." What we call a definitive translation, therefore, is only one that we have read more times than another. We grow accustomed to Edward FitzGerald or George Chapman, T. E. Lawrence or J. H. Voss, and because we are especially familiar with one of them, believe it to be truer and better than the rest. Pope's version is for most of his readers (for those who enjoy his daring, inspired music) definitive. Almost any example will do to prove his excellence, such as this description from book 23, after Achilles has killed Hector and built a funeral pile for Patroclus. The winds will not rise to feed the flames, and the goddess Iris must deliver Achilles' prayer to the winds Boreas and Zephyr.

Swift as the word she vanish'd from their view;
Swift as the word the winds tumultuous flew;
Forth burst the stormy band with thundering roar,
And heaps on heaps the clouds are tossed before.
To the wide main then stooping from the skies,
The heaving deeps in watery mountains rise:
Troy feels the blast along her shaking walls,
Till on the pile the gather'd tempest falls.[16]

Robert Fagles, whose translations are used throughout this book, has been widely praised for his accuracy and modern ring. In his free-verse version of the *Iliad* of 1990, he paints the same scene in six lines:

Message delivered, off she sped as the winds rose
with a superhuman roar, stampeding clouds before them.
Suddenly reaching the open sea in gale force,
whipping whitecaps under a shrilling killer-squall
they raised the good rich soil of Troy and struck the pyre
and a huge inhuman blaze went howling up the skies.[17]

Our modern ear recognizes Fagles's idiom, from the "Message delivered" to the "killer-squall," and the "inhuman" for the huge blaze is very good; it all rings true. But Pope is not aiming for verisimilitude; rather a natural artificiality punctuated by cadenced rhymes, composing verses with a repetitive beat not unlike today's rap, attempting an art that is "itself unseen, but in the effects, remains," as he had called for in his "Essay on Criticism":

First follow Nature, and your Judgment frame
By her just Standard, which is still the same:
. . . .
Art from that Fund each just Supply provides,
Works without Show, and without Pomp presides.[18]

Pope wrote at the closing (and also at the beginning) of a particular moment in English literature, with certain codes and conventions which he handled better than almost anyone, perhaps because he had invented many of them. "By perpetual practice," wrote Dr. Johnson, "language had in his mind a systematical arrangement; having always the same use for words, he had words so selected and combined as to be ready at his call." Pope's style was never external to him, never mechanical: it only seemed so in the eyes of certain of his readers who either demanded scientific exactness from the poet or had already become attuned to William Wordsworth's cadences, and who therefore felt that Pope's lines were strained and weak and nothing but decorative. William Cowper, a minor poet, said that Pope "Made poetry a mere mechanic art/And ev'ry warbler has his tune by heart." But, as George Steiner wisely maintained, "Pope's detractors have been those who have not read him." That is, read him with his aesthetic credo in mind.[19]

Matthew Arnold certainly had read Pope, and yet in spite of judging him a "prodigious talent" found him wanting as a translator. "Homer," Arnold wrote in 1861, "invariably composes 'with his eye on the object,' whether the object be a moral or a material one: Pope composes with his eye on his style, into which he translates his object, whatever it is."[20] Arnold was a keen reader, an astute critic, a gifted educator, and sometimes a good poet. The son of a Rugby headmaster, he became first a fellow of Oriel College, Oxford, and then inspector of schools, an appointment that allowed him, for thirty-five long years, to observe the conditions of education in England and led to his plea for better educational standards, following the Prussian model (*Schools and Universities on the Continent*, 1868), and to his arguments for a livelier artistic engagement (*Culture and Anarchy*, 1869). Arnold was, above all, a cosmopolitan, impatient with the provincialism and shortsightedness that he found in English intellectual life. But it was perhaps in his discussion of the problems related to Homeric translation that he best demonstrated his critical skills.

Arnold's points of departure are the two main schools of thought regarding translation in general. The first (put forward by the moral philosopher and classicist Francis William Newman, only the better to condemn it) held that "'the reader should, if possible, forget that it is a translation at all, and be lulled into the illusion that he is reading an original work; something original,' (if the translation be in English), 'from an English hand.'" The second, strongly defended by Newman, held that a translator should "'retain every peculiarity of the original, so far as he is able, *with the greater care the more foreign it may happen to be*'; so that it may 'never be forgotten that he is imitating, and imitating in a different material.'" The translator's "'first duty'" "'is a historical one; to be *faithful*.'" Both sides of Newman's argument, Arnold pointed out, would agree as to faithfulness, "but the question at issue between them is, in what faithfulness consists." Arnold reasonably noted that even if Newman were to achieve his purpose and "'retain every peculiarity of his original,'" who would assure him that what he had done adhered to Homer's manner and habit of thought? "The only competent tribunal in this matter"—the Greeks—Arnold pointed out, "are dead."[21]

During Newman's tenure as professor of Latin at University College London, in 1856 he himself produced a translation of the *Iliad*, which was poorly received. But Newman, being not the most congenial of men, must have expected the negative criticisms. The younger brother of Cardinal Newman (canonized as a saint in the Catholic Church in 2019), Francis William described himself as "anti-everything." He was a deist, vegetarian, and anti-vaccinationist, and declared that he "considered a monastery to be like a madhouse." He considered himself a proto-feminist, arguing that "the perfection of the soul lay in its becoming *woman*," and believed in a woman's right to vote, to educate herself, and "to ride astride." He sought to make life rational in all things, including clothing. He wore an alpaca tailcoat in summer, three coats in winter (the outer one green), and in bad weather a rug with a hole cut for his head. When it was muddy, he wore trousers edged with six inches of leather. George Eliot called him "our blessed St. Francis."[22]

Arnold advised any would-be translator to leave aside a number of questions—whether Homer existed, whether he was one or many, whether the Christian doctrine of the Atonement was foreshadowed in Homeric mythology—since, even if it were possible to answer them, they could be of no benefit to the translation. Nor should the translator assume that modern sentiment is applicable to ancient stories: whatever it was that the ancients believed, we must assume that it was something different from what we believe today. The translator of Homer should be four things: rapid in his telling, plain and direct in his expression, plain and direct in his thought, and finally, eminently noble. These qualities, Arnold recognized, were probably "too general to be of much service to anybody," except a future poet who tried his hand at Homer and who would have "(or he cannot succeed) that true sense for his subject, and that disinterested love of it, which are, both of them, so rare in literature, and so precious."[23]

Newman dismissed Arnold's criticisms without really addressing them, using pedantic grammatical quibbles and abstruse semantic principles. He imagined that Arnold was being ironic when he was being reflective, and disrespectful when he was nothing but accurate. That most exacting of critics, A. E. Housman, writing in 1892, had this to say of Arnold's arguments: "But when it comes to literary criticism, heap up in one scale all the literary criticism that the whole nation of professed scholars ever wrote, and drop into the other the thin green volume of Matthew Arnold's *Lectures on Translating Homer*, which has long been out of print because the British public does not care to read it, and the first scale, as Milton says, will straight fly up and kick the beam."[24]

CHAPTER 12

Realms of Gold

Talking it over, we agreed that Blake was no good because he
learnt Italian at over 60 to study Dante, and we knew Dante was
no good because he was so fond of Virgil, and Virgil was no good
because Tennyson ran him, and as for Tennyson—well, Tennyson
goes without saying.

—Samuel Butler, *The Notebooks*, 1912 (posthumous)

For the Romantic poets, it was not in literary straitjackets that
poetry was to be found but in wild inspiration, out in the fresh
air and in the experience of country life. Form should mirror
feeling. John Keats believed that time spent in natural surround-
ings would "strengthen more my reach in Poetry, than would
stopping at home among books, even though I should reach
Homer."[1] Keats, or at least so he said, had come to Homer through
George Chapman's 1598 translation of the *Iliad* in opulent four-
teen-syllable lines. Keats's account of the discovery is justly
famous.

> Much have I travell'd in the realms of gold,
>   And many goodly states & kingdoms seen;
>   Round many western islands have I been
> Which bards in fealty to Apollo hold.
> Oft of one wide expanse had I been told
>   That deep-brow'd Homer ruled as his demesne;
>   Yet did I never breathe its pure serene

Till I heard Chapman speak out loud and bold:
Then felt I like some watcher of the skies
  When a new planet swims into his ken;
Or like stout Cortez when with eagle eyes
  He star'd at the Pacific—and all his men
Look'd at each other with a wild surmise—
  Silent, upon a peak in Darien.[2]

Chapman, in his "Preface to the Reader," had argued that the English tongue was best suited for translating Homer, "Prince of Poets," for "Poesy is the flower of the Sun, and disdains to open to the eye of a candle." This, for the Romantics, felt closer to the notion of the primordial, groundbreaking Homer, the "with-all-skill-enriched Poet" whom no rigid poetic form could truly contain.[3] Attacking Pope to boost Chapman was, they felt, a good way of defending Homer.

William Blake attacked all three, but especially Homer. Blake's relationship to Homer is not easy to understand: Homer was both a poet to be lauded and a name to be reviled; both one of the "Visionary Poets" (Blake ranked him with Virgil, Milton, and Dante) and one of the "superseded" classics; one of the "Inspired Men" society condemned as dangerous outsiders and also a figurehead for the classical past, used by society for defending intellectual crimes such as trading and hoarding, translating and copying, while at the same time despising true creation. "The Classics!" Blake raged. "It is the Classics, & not Goths nor Monks, that Desolate Europe with Wars."[4]

According to Blake, what set Homer "in so high a rank of Art" was his craft in dealing with symbols. Homer, he wrote in about 1820, "addressed to the Imagination, which is Spiritual Sensation, & but mediately to the Understanding or Reason." And yet in Blake's view, Homer's poems had been degraded by readers who found in them contemporary morals. "If Homer's merit," Blake

argued, "was only in these Historical combinations & Moral sentiments he would be no better than *Clarissa*," Samuel Richardson's
huge sentimental novel. And Blake added, beyond appeal: "The
grandest Poetry is Immoral, the Grandest characters Wicked!"
Homer's "Poetry of the Heathen," however, was "Stolen and
Perverted from the Bible, not by Chance but by design, by the
Kings of Persia & their Generals, the Greek Heroes, & lastly by the
Romans." It is as if, for Blake, Homer stood for various different
notions unrelated and unrelatable to one another. Perhaps a clue
to the ambiguous identity Blake lent Homer can be seen in one
of the illustrations he made for Dante's *Commedia*. The eighth
image in the series is a depiction of the "Father of Poetry," as
Dante saw him, crowned in laurel, bearing a sword and attended
by the three other poets from antiquity whom Dante named in
the *Inferno* (Horace, Ovid, and Lucan). Except that instead of giving Homer his name, Blake wrote "Satan" and then partly erased
the caption. (Satan was, for Blake, the true hero of *Paradise Lost*.)[5]

What Blake thought of Pope is clearer. He coupled him with
Dryden, whose poetry he branded "Monotonous Sing Song, Sing
Song from beginning to end."[6] His near contemporary Lord Byron
disagreed. He had read Pope thoroughly and found him a greater
revolutionary than any of Byron's fellow writers and, as a poet, "a
touchstone of taste." "With regard to poetry in general," Byron
wrote to his publisher John Murray on September 17, 1817, "I am
convinced that [we] are all in the wrong, one as much as another;
that we are upon a wrong revolutionary poetical system, or systems, not worth a damn in itself. . . . I am the more confirmed in
this by having lately gone over some of our classics, particularly
Pope, whom I tried in this way . . . and I was really astonished (I
ought not to have been so) and mortified at the ineffable distance
in point of sense, harmony, effect, and even Imagination, passion,
and Invention, between the little Queen Anne's man, and us of
the Lower Empire."[7]

Byron admired Pope's *Iliad*. He had read Homer in the original, and Pope's less than accurate rendering of Homer's Greek did not diminish for him the force of Pope's poetic language. In 1834, John Stuart Mill complained that the classical curriculum in England ignored history and philosophy in favor of philology and poetry, preferring to teach Homer over Plato.[8] Although this was not entirely true (the classical philosophy scholars of Oxford and Cambridge are proof to the contrary), Byron's Greece is indeed that of the *Iliad* and the *Odyssey* rather than that of Socrates and his disciples.

For Shelley too, Greece was Homer. Homer's poems, he wrote in "A Defence of Poetry" in 1821, were "the elements of that social system which is the column upon which all succeeding civilization has reposed. Homer embodied the ideal perfection of his age in human character; nor can we doubt that those who read his verses were awakened to an ambition of becoming like to Achilles, Hector, and Ulysses: the truth and beauty of friendship, patriotism, and persevering devotion to an object, were unveiled to the depths in these immortal creations."[9] Except that, more than Shelley himself, it was his contemporaries who attributed to Shelley and to his fellow poets the ancient features of classical heroes—Shelley as Patroclus, Byron as Achilles—and something of this masquerade must have been felt by Byron when he chose to sail for Greece on July 13, 1823, "to seek in action the redemption he had not found in thought."[10]

Of course, for both Shelley and Byron, Homer's Greece was more than a catalogue of noble examples. Greece represented for Byron an idealized utopian past as well as the betrayed present in which the governments of Europe had allowed a usurper (the Ottoman Empire) to plunder the sacred inheritance.

Oh, thou eternal Homer! I have now
    To paint a siege, wherein more men were slain,

With deadlier engines and a speedier blow,
    Than in thy Greek gazette of that campaign;
And yet, like all men else, I must allow,
    To vie with thee would be about as vain
As for a brook to cope with Ocean's flood;
But still we Moderns equal you in blood;

If not in poetry, at least in fact;
    And fact is truth, the great desideratum!
Of which, howe'er the Muse describes each act,
There should be ne'ertheless a slight substratum.[11]

Susan Sontag, reviewing Simone Weil's "The 'Iliad'; or, The Poem of Force," written at the beginning of World War II, considered the paradoxical relationship between poetic truth and factual truth. "There are certain ages," Sontag wrote, "which do not need truth as much as they need a deepening of the sense of reality, a widening of the imagination. I, for one, do not doubt that the sane view of the world is the true one. But is that what is always wanted, truth? The need for truth is not constant; no more is the need for repose. The truth is balance, but the opposite of truth, which is unbalance, may not be a lie."[12]

Homer's poems addressed both this balance and this unbalance. If Homer had created the poetic model for both in craft and theme, then, Byron believed, it was the modern poet's task to translate these uncertain elements into a contemporary idiom. The subjects of war and travel in the *Iliad* and the *Odyssey* were recast into *Childe Harold's Pilgrimage* (1812) and *Don Juan* (1819–24), in which both heroes have something of Odysseus and something of Achilles in their makeup, and become the privileged witnesses of less-than-heroic Troys. In *Don Juan,* for example, memory of Homer's story serves as a debasing mirror for the Siege of Ismail of 1790, when Russian forces took over the Ottoman stronghold—

a muddled feat which in turn reflects, for Byron, the political tur-
moil of Europe after Napoleon.

> But now, instead of slaying Priam's son,
>> We only can but talk of escalade,
> Bombs, drums, guns, bastions, batteries, bayonets, bullets,
> Hard words, which stick in the soft Muses' gullets.

What was honorable combat in Homer's *Iliad* becomes, in the
morally impoverished early decades of the nineteenth century,
little more than official murder. With a side stab at Wordsworth
in his "Thanksgiving Ode," Byron comments:

> "Carnage" (so Wordsworth tells you) "is God's daughter":
> If *he* speak truth, she is Christ's sister, and
> Just now behaved as in the Holy Land.[13]

The British prime minister William Ewart Gladstone, leader
of the Liberal Party and a keen reader of Homer, became interested in a scientific approach to Homer's epithets, not from a
poetic point of view, as did Byron, but on philological evidence.
For Gladstone, the poems of Homer were to be considered historical documents, a record of "manners and characters, feelings
and tastes, races and countries, principles and institutions." In
regard to "feelings and tastes," and taking the famous image of
the "wine-dark sea" (*oinopos*, "wine-looking"), Gladstone argued
that the ancient Greeks thought of colors in terms of light and
dark, not hues. He did not suggest that Homer was color-blind,
rather that he "operated, in the main, upon a quantitative scale."
Furthermore, for Gladstone, Homer was not a shady figure from
the legendary past but a real presence, an example for nineteenth-
century politicians. In November 1890, shortly after the majority
of Irish MPs refused to ratify Charles Stewart Parnell's leadership

of the Liberal Party, the eighty-year-old Gladstone commented to his biographer, John Morley, "Homer's fellows would have cut a very different figure, and made short work in the committee room last week."[14]

Literary craft was another matter. By and large, Byron's enjoyment of Homer did not prompt him to imitate the master. Only occasionally did Byron pick up a Homeric epithet or simile and make it his own, perhaps because he felt that the popular devices of one age lose both power and familiarity when applied in another. Homer, like Milman Parry's guzlars, used formulas and conventions of various kinds to construct his work which (again, like the guzlars) he manipulated in order to convey, enlarge, contradict, or subvert the meaning, and to lend the conventional poem a personal voice. It is impossible for us, at a distance of almost three millennia, to know how Homer's audience received these devices: whether they looked for faithful adherence to tradition or expected an original twist to the formulas. The linguist Walter J. Ong was skeptical: "The appositeness of the Homeric epithet had been piously and grossly exaggerated."[15]

The Homeric conventions are of various kinds. Some are formulaic phrases, even entire lines of verse, to begin a story or introduce a teller, like the "They lived happily ever after" or the "Once upon a time" of folktales as, for example: "So Proteus said, and his story crushed my heart," or "When young Dawn with her rose-red fingers shone once more," repeated throughout the works.[16] Others are formal epithets (Parry called them "ornamental epithets") that accompany a person or place as a title: "Menelaus the red-haired king" or "the strong-built city of Athens," equivalent to calling Richard Nixon "Tricky Dick" or referring to Chicago as "the windy city."[17] Certain translators (Robert Fitzgerald, for instance) choose not to reproduce these conventions, possibly because they believe that, whereas Homer's listeners might have found the epithets almost inaudible but necessary, a modern audience would judge their repetition trite or tedious. Borges suggested that for the poet to say "divine Patroclus" was simply the conventional correct form of address, just as we say "to go on foot" and not "by foot."[18] But these conventions no longer seem like conventions to us: the "rose-red fingers" of Dawn may strike a new reader as delightfully quirky instead of formally expected. "The tradition," wrote Albert Lord, "feels a sense of meaning in the epithet, and thus a special meaning is imparted to the noun and to the formula." And Lord concluded: "I would even prefer to call it the traditionally intuitive meaning."[19]

Conventions also dictate the description of certain actions, such as the killing of a soldier. When in the *Iliad* the Trojan Erymas is killed by Idomeneus, commander of the Cretan fleet, or Laogonus, son of the Trojan priest Onetor, by Meriones, Idomeneus's second in command, the chronicle of these deaths does not follow an individual course but makes a set pattern that begins with mentioning the point of impact ("under the jaw and ear," "straight through the mouth") and ends with a traditional periphrasis for death ("hateful darkness gripped him," "death's dark cloud closed down around his corpse").[20] These are not intended to be realistic descriptions. Rather, they are the equivalent of other established literary sequences in certain genre fiction, such as describing the crime early in a detective novel, and gathering all the suspects in one room at the end.

Perhaps the best known of these conventions, and the one that has had, for the readers of Homer, the strongest effect, is the extended or epic simile. Unlike an ordinary metaphor that catches qualities in one object which it ascribes to another, thereby creating a new literary space in which what is said and what is implied intermingle and increase, the epic simile places side by side two different actions that do not blend but remain visually separate, one coloring or qualifying the other at length. Of these, there are over two hundred in the *Iliad* alone. In book 16, after the Trojans, led by

Hector, have succeeded in driving the Greeks back to their ships, Patroclus, dressed in Achilles' armor, counterattacks and pushes the Trojans back to their walls. The scene is one of gruesome savagery.

> As ravenous wolves come swooping down on lambs or kids
> to snatch them away from right amidst their flock—all lost
> when a careless shepherd leaves them straggling down the hills
> and quickly spotting a chance the wolf pack picks them off,
> no heart for the fight—so the Achaeans mauled the Trojans.[21]

For Homer and his audience, wolves preying on sheep and the unreliable shepherd-god not paying due attention to his flock were no doubt common and terrifying experiences, and yet the image must have soon become trite through repeated usage. By the time the simile reached the eighteenth century, though wolves continued their ancestral butchery outside the city walls, the image had become more domesticated, and Byron's audience certainly had less direct experience than Homer's of the savagery of wolves. However, it is one of the few formulas that Byron chose to borrow from Homer. The first line of "The Destruction of Sennacherib" echoes the savage image without dwelling on it:

> The Assyrian came down like the wolf on the fold.[22]

The line is powerful, and manages to lend to a stale device a degree of vividness it perhaps never possessed: first we see the Assyrians descending, then our eyes are directed toward the wolf attacking sheep, and we are left to draw our own conclusions.

Sometimes a poet will reverse the process, and lead us upstream from the second element of the comparison to the first, without beginning with "as." This is a famous sonnet by the Argentinian poet Enrique Banchs; the beast in question is not a wolf but a tiger; the simile is the same:

Turning his iridescent side in sinuous step
The tiger passes sleek and smooth as verse
And fierceness polishes the hard and terse
Topaz of his vigorous cold eye.

He stretches the deceitful muscles out,
Malevolent and languid, of his flanks,
And lies down slowly on the dusky banks
Of scattered autumn leaves. Now all about

The jungle slumbers in the silent heat.
Between the silken paws the snub-nosed head,
The still eye fixed impassively ahead

While nervously the tail, with steady beat,
Thrashes a guarded threat against the straight
cluster of nearby branches. So is my hate.[23]

Violence and hatred like a wild beast, a wild beast like violence and hatred: not every reader is convinced by the comparison. In one of his comic poems, the American Ogden Nash poked fun at this poetic device:

What does it mean when we are told
That the Assyrian came down like a wolf on the fold?
In the first place, George Gordon Byron had had enough experience
To know that it probably wasn't just one Assyrian, it was a lot of
  Assyrians.[24]

Nash's joke about "the kind of thing that's being done all the time by poets, from Homer to Tennyson" raises a serious point. No image is solely metaphorical; it elicits from the reader a literal interpretation at the same time as it conjures up a poetic coupling, neither of which is ever exhaustive. As in Dante's multiple levels of reading, the Homeric image is simultaneously a conventional formula, a realistic description, a metaphor, and an analogy. It can also be a single image that stands for something vaster, a sort of metonymy of what Homer wants to describe. For instance, there are no specific descriptions of the various landscapes that Odysseus encounters. Rather, Homer gives us "a welcoming river, a tree, and the mother earth. It is as if Odysseus were entering the house of a bountiful host," wrote the classics scholar Paolo Vivante. "Human need singles out of the general scenery one element, one distinctive landmark which, on that very strength, assumes an independent identity and grows in the imagination. . . . Hence a singular effect: the startling plenitude of what is most familiar."[25]

Madame de Staël, Byron's brilliant contemporary, argued that it was in fact those very images that rendered Homer great, not his ideas, which she found shallow. Against the classic models of the pagan world she set the new world of Christian northern Europe, Germany in particular—ancient form against Romantic feeling. "Homer and the Greek poets," she wrote in 1800, "were remarkable for the splendor and variety of their images, but not for any deep thoughts of their mind. . . . Metaphysics, the art of bringing ideas into widespread use, has much quickened the step of human spirit; but, in the act of making the road shorter, it may at times have stripped it of its more brilliant aspects. Every object presents itself in turn to Homer's gaze; he does not always choose wisely, but he always depicts it in an interesting fashion." In fact, like Pope, she praised above all Homer's inventiveness. For Madame de Staël, Homer was a craftsman, not a thinker, a purveyor of splendid pictures, not of ideas.[26]

CHAPTER 13

Homer as Idea

As learned commentators view
In Homer more than Homer knew.
—Jonathan Swift, *On Poetry*, 1733

In 1744, the year of Pope's death, Giambattista Vico, former professor of rhetoric at the University of Naples and historiographer to King Charles de Bourbon, published the third revised edition of his revolutionary *La scienza nuova* (The New Science). Misunderstood or ignored by his contemporaries, Vico proposed a cyclical theory of history that began with Homer and his poetic knowledge and eventually returned to it, in an ever-ascending spiral. Philosophers in Vico's age offered two conflicting theories of knowledge: the first was based on evidence and argument, "the philosophy of life and existence," while the second was centered on introspection and thought, "the philosophy of the irrational."[1] Vico offered a third possibility: the imagination, an independent power of the mind that he called *fantasia*. Poetic images, such as those created by Homer to tell "true" stories but condemned as lies by Plato, were not "concepts in poetic cloaks." These *universali fantastici*, or "universal images born from the imagination," were to be considered on their own terms. Western philosophy had always seen these images as literary or rhetorical, and because they were not conceptual, they were regarded as "not philosophical." In contrast, Vico took Homer's side against Plato's rationalism and argued for a knowledge he called *sapienza poetica*, "poetic wisdom," whose driving force was memory, the goddess Homer knew as Mnemosyne. "Memory," wrote Vico, "has three different aspects: memory when it remembers things, imagination when it alters or imitates them, and invention when it gives them a new turn or puts them into proper arrangement and relationship. For these reasons, the theological poets called Memory the mother of the Muses."[2] Later, James Joyce was to sum up Vico's notion as "Imagination is the working over of what is remembered."[3]

In book 2 of the *Iliad*, when Homer is about to list the gathering of the Greek armies on the plain outside Troy, he stops his narrative and invokes the Muses, saying that he does not deem himself capable of describing what is to follow. Partly this is the literary device that later, in the Middle Ages, became codified as *excusatio propter infirmitatem* (an apology for one's own shortcomings), partly it is a way of lending verisimilitude to the telling by shifting responsibility: "It is not I who says this, but something greater than I, and therefore it must be true."

> Sing to me now, you Muses who hold the halls of Olympus!
> You are goddesses, you are everywhere, you know all things—
> all we hear is the distant ring of glory, we know nothing—
> who were the captains of Achaea? Who were the kings?
> The mass of troops I could never tally, never name,
> not even if I had ten tongues and ten mouths,
> a tireless voice and the heart inside me bronze,
> never unless you Muses of Olympus, daughters of Zeus
> whose shield is rolling thunder, sing, sing in memory
> all who gathered under Troy.[4]

The Muses can "sing in memory," that is to say, they can speak the truth embedded in memory. It is not the poet who knows, but the daughters of Mnemosyne, notably the Muse Urania, whom Homer calls the muse of divination, and of the knowledge of good and evil (she will later become the muse of astronomy). From this concept, Vico developed the notion that poetic wisdom does not belong to one poet but to a people, and that "there is no authorship to Homer's works in the ordinary sense of the word": "the mind of the Greek people is their author." For Vico, Homer was not a person but "an idea."[5]

Some fifty years later, Friedrich August Wolf, who most probably had not read Vico, developed a similar theory about Homer and his poems. A pious legend has it that this son of a modest schoolteacher was the first student of philology of any German university; in order to discourage him from pursuing what appeared to be a fruitless career, the university authorities warned him that after he had graduated, there would be only a couple of poorly paid openings for a philology professor. Wolf answered that this did not worry him, since he only required one. Indeed, at the age of twenty-four, he became professor of philology at the University of Halle, where he began to develop his Homeric theory. The resulting book, written in a complicated, almost impregnable Latin, was eventually published in 1795 as *Prolegomena ad Homerum*.[6]

At the time, German readers relied on two potent guides to ancient Greek culture. One was Johann Joachim Winckelmann, the respected classical scholar who had risen from a cobbler's son to become one of the most erudite men of his age, and who had summed up the Greek ideal as "a noble naïveté and a calm greatness."[7] The other was Johann Heinrich Voss, whose translations of the *Odyssey* in 1781 and the *Iliad* in 1793 proved that modern German could serve as a powerful medium for epic poetry by employing a pattern of verses of varying lengths (dactylic hexameters) that allowed great freedom of expression and the full use of a rich vocabulary.

Wolf's arguments opposed both the reverential consecration of Winckelmann's Homer and the untouchable nobility of his verse in Voss's rendition, and called for a serious investigation of how books such as the *Iliad* and the *Odyssey* had come into being. With his *Prolegomena,* Wolf gave birth to the new science of classical studies, or *Altertumswissenschaft.*

At about the same time, in France, in the aftermath of the querelle between the anciens and modernes, the brilliant polymath Denis Diderot found in Homer an example of what, in his opinion, should be left behind if enlightened progress was to be made. It was not that Homer did not move him or that he thought the *Iliad* lacked the realism he sought in art. Diderot admitted, for example, that Homer was capable of powerfully conveying the horrors of war: "I enjoyed the sight of crows in Homer gathered around a corpse, tearing the eyes out of its head and flapping their wings with delight." But Homer could be understood as a counterargument to the Enlightenment's view of a world driven by rationality alone, a view put forward, for instance, in Diderot's *D'Alembert's Dream* of 1769. This witty book consists of a series of philosophical dialogues in which Diderot proposes a revised materialist account of human history and animal life, suggesting that emotions, ideas, and thoughts can be explained through biological evidence, without recourse to theology or spirituality, and dismissing all uncritical reverence for the past. Diderot's *Encyclopédie,* in seventeen large volumes of text plus eleven of illustrations, edited in collaboration with Jean Le Rond d'Alembert and published between 1751 and 1772, attempted to define science, art, and craft through rational methods only, and included under innocuous headings dangerous subjects such as religion and systems of government. Under the general entry for "Greek Philosophy," for instance, Diderot amused himself by dismissing Homer as "a theologian, philosopher, and poet" and quoted the unattributed view (which, he admits, "demonstrates a want of both philosophy and taste") that Homer was an author "unlikely to be read much in the future."[8]

Vico had suggested that Homer was the product of the heroic cycle in society's development. For Diderot, Homer belonged to a primitive, superstitious age. For Wolf, Homer's age was merely one of the many that constitute our stratified history. Diderot's arguments were political. Wolf's arguments, even though they led to the same conclusion as Vico's, were strictly historical and philological. According to Wolf, the books we attribute to Homer are the fruit of a long development in which many poets and performers played a part, and he argued that the original source could not ever be retraced, only surmised from much later echoes. For Wolf, the *Iliad* and the *Odyssey* were like archaeological sites, to be dug up and scrutinized in order to establish the different levels of their construction. Consequently, Homer was not the composer of his books but their end product, a colophon added to the voices of generations of bards in order to lend authority and coherence to the text. For Wolf too, Homer was "an idea," but an idea that came to bring closure to, not to set in motion, the creative process.

Wolf's criticism sounded a warning note not only among literary critics but also among theologians. If the unity of the "Bible of the Greeks" could be called into question, why not the Bible itself? If Scripture's purpose was not to tell stories but to tell the truth, following Cicero's prescription for the writing of history, "that it shall not dare say anything false," then not even the Bible was exempt from scientific scrutiny.[9] Johann Wolfgang von Goethe thought that this was going too far—that there was a line to be drawn between the criticism of Homer's writings and the criticism of God's word. "They are now pulling to pieces the five books of Moses," he complained late in life to his friend Johann Peter Eckermann, "and if an annihilating criticism is injurious in anything, it is so in matters of religion; for here everything depends upon faith, to which we cannot return when we have once lost it."[10]

Goethe was very familiar with Wolf and his work. In the summer of 1805, he stopped in Halle and decided to attend one of Wolf's lectures. Wolf's daughter agreed to allow the illustrious visitor into her father's classroom. Goethe then told her that he would not sit among the students but would hide behind a curtain to listen. This curious gesture might have an explanation. Goethe had met Wolf ten years earlier, immediately after reading the newly published *Prolegomena.* He liked the man as much as he disliked the book. To Friedrich Schiller, he wrote that Wolf's *Prolegomena* was "interesting enough, though it sits with me badly. The idea might be good and the effort respectable, if only the gentleman, in order to dress its weak flanks, had not stripped the richest gardens of the Realm of Aesthetics and turned them into boring fortifications."[11] At the same time (he didn't say this to Schiller), Wolf's dismantlement of Homer granted Goethe the right to aspire to the rank of epic poet himself. If, as Wolf argued, Homer did not exist as author, and if the *Iliad* and the *Odyssey* were a ragbag of different compositions, then surely a later poet, with some understanding and talent, might dig in them to find material with which to build new masterpieces. Goethe's unfinished poem "Achilles," begun in 1799, stems from an exploratory reading of Homer in search of ideas for an epic. "These days I was away in order to study the *Iliad*, to see whether between it and the *Odyssey* there might not lie an epic story. I only find tragic material, but is that really true or is it rather I who can't find the epic? The end of Achilles' life and its background allow for an epic handling . . ., but the question arises, Is it right to handle tragic material as if it were at best epic?"[12] Goethe found the project so daring that when writing to Schiller about a visit from Wilhelm von Humboldt, he said that he refrained from mentioning particulars for fear of appearing "too bold."[13] The same reason may have prompted him not to make himself visible at Wolf's lecture.

If Homer, as Wolf maintained, was an idea, a collective noun, a concept, then for Goethe and his contemporaries it was one that changed with every age and with the needs and talents of every age, becoming an emblem of its time. In spite of Wolf's criticism, Homer's ancient Greece was a tempting replacement for their shattered world in the aftermath of the French Revolution, a world in which Germany held together precariously, torn by internal quarrels and enfeebled by religious differences. Johann Gottfried Herder in his histories of European philosophy, Christoph Martin Wieland in his historical novels and imaginary dialogues, Wilhelm Heinse in his utopian fiction, Friedrich Schlegel in his essays on classical antiquity, Karl Philipp Moritz in his guide to ancient mythology, and, above all, Friedrich Hölderlin in every one of his fragmentary books—all, however different their visions, found in Homer and his universe a model for their ideal Germany, where men were noble and brave, and poetry and philosophy their principal activities.[14]

In England, Edmund Burke used Homer as the example of many of his propositions in his *Hints for an Essay on Drama.* "It is natural with men," wrote Burke, echoing his German contemporaries, "when they relate any action with any degree of warmth, to represent the parties to it talking as the occasion requires; and this produces that mixed species of poetry, composed of narrative and dialogue, which is very universal in all languages, and of which Homer is the noblest example in any. This mixed kind of poetry seems also to be most perfect."[15]

For Goethe, Homer as a shifting mirror was the primordial example of the poet who first embodies the truth of his people and then allows himself to embody the truth of future men and women in faraway and inscrutable ages. Artists like Homer, whether they existed in flesh and blood or only as spirit, stood outside time because they were divine beings, intercessors between gods and men. To the poet's craft, Homer's and his own, Goethe lent the word *Schöpfertum*, "creative activity," an act of imaginative generation that sublimates the people's innermost needs and becomes defined through that which their nation wants. As a concept in search of a conceiver, Homer might have uttered the words Goethe lends Christ in another context: "Oh my people, how I yearn for you!"—a god seeking believers.[16] In Goethe's reading, the divine Homer brought for each new generation the possibility of a cultural redemption to which Goethe himself aspired for Germany. Perhaps exaggerating a little this relationship between the two poets, the literary historian E. R. Curtius declared, "The founding hero (*heros ktistes*) of European literature is Homer. Its last universal author is Goethe."[17]

CHAPTER 14

The Eternal Feminine

All the argument is a cuckold and a whore.

—William Shakespeare, *Troilus and Cressida*

Goethe started early in making Homer his own: among the first books he read as a child were, together with the *Arabian Nights* and Fénelon's *Télémaque*, the *Iliad* and the *Odyssey*.[1] By the age of twenty-one, in 1770, he was shamed by Herder, who had befriended the young Goethe in Strasbourg, into perfecting his Greek by reading Homer with the help of a parallel Latin translation. The acquaintance with the original no doubt provided Goethe with the impetus to lend Homer's books to his hero in *The Sorrows of Young Werther,* the sensationally popular novel that Goethe wrote three years later, in less than ninety days. Shortly after arriving in the country village where he will meet for the first time the love of his life (alas, promised to another man), Werther writes to the receiver of his confidences that he longs for no new books, he needs no guidance, he wants no encouragement: all he requires is "a lullaby to cradle me and that I find plenty of in my Homer."[2] Homer provides for Werther (and for the young Goethe, if we may confuse in this instance author and fictional character) not instruction or information, not even a text to meditate upon, but a gratifying spectrum of vicarious emotions, "from sorrow to joy, and from delicious melancholy to violent passion."

The distinction between books that instruct and books that lull is one that Friedrich Schiller was to address more than twenty years later in an essay published in *Die Horen,* the magazine he had founded with Goethe's support. "On Naive and Sentimental Poetry" separates writers into two categories: those who are at one with Nature, depicting it in the truest fashion, and those who, aware of their separation from Nature, long to return to it imaginatively.[3] For Schiller, both Homer and Goethe belonged to the first category, while he himself chose the second. Carl Gustav Jung remarked in 1921 that Schiller's distinction was profounder than it appeared at first glance. What Schiller implied, said Jung, was a distinction not between fundamental classes of poets but between "certain characteristics or qualities of the individual product. Hence it is at once obvious that an introverted poet can, on occasion, be just as naïve as he is sentimental." Schiller, Jung argued, was not concerned with the question of "types" but of "typical mechanisms."[4]

Homer, "as naive poet," Schiller had written, "allows Nature to have unlimited hold over him." For Jung, this meant that Homer unconsciously identified with Nature, creating by analogy an association between the subject poet and his thematic object, lending it his creative power and representing it in a certain way because that is the way it shapes itself within him. "He is himself Nature: Nature creates in him the product."[5] For Schiller, according to Jung, Homer is his own poems.

Goethe's perception of Homer both embraced and expanded Schiller's. He too identified Homer with the Homeric creations, but for Goethe the relationship was not a closed circle. Every reading of the *Iliad* and the *Odyssey* rescued from the mesh something of Homer's gift, freeing the ancient poet, over and over again, from Nature's "unlimited hold." This ongoing exchange regularly bore new fruit, as Goethe's own writings attested. Homer's poems provided the naive (and sentimental) Goethe with copy for his plays, whether for entire conflated plots—Odysseus and the Phaeacians, or Odysseus and Circe, or for his *Nausicaa*, for example—or, more importantly, for the central material of his *Faust, Part Two*.

In April 1827, when Goethe was seventy-eight years old, he decided to include in the fourth volume of the authorized edition of his works (known as *Ausgabe letzter Hand* or ALH) a poetic fragment he called "Helena: A Classical-Romantic Phantasmagoria," subtitled "Intermezzo for *Faust*." Writing to a French editor who was interested in including the fragment in a translated edition of *Faust*, Goethe stressed that it was essential to understand that the two texts bore no resemblance to one another, and that the story of Faust and Helen of Troy was utterly different from that of Faust and Gretchen, which, in another context, he described as a "relationship which came to grief in the chaos of misunderstood learning, middle-class narrow-mindedness, moral disorder and superstitious delusions." A synopsis, written by Goethe a year earlier, explains how *Faust, Part Two* differs from *Faust, Part One*. "The old legend," wrote Goethe, "tells us (and the scene is duly included in the puppet play) that Faust in his lordly arrogance requires Mephistopheles to procure for him the beautiful Helen of Greece, and that Mephistopheles after some demur consents to do so. In our own version, we felt in duty bound not to omit so significant a motif."[6]

Goethe lends a tone of satire to the scene. Commanded by the German Emperor, Mephistopheles conjures up Paris and Helen at the imperial court. The courtiers are divided: the men criticize Paris while the women swoon over his handsome features, and when the men admire Helen, the women make fun of her big feet and pale complexion. Faust, overcome by Helen's beauty, tries to cast Paris aside, but as he does the apparitions vanish and the feast ends in a riot. Faust faints. When he wakes, he demands that Mephistopheles procure Helen for him, and the two set off on a long, fantastical journey to the Kingdom of the Dead. Persephone, moved by an eloquent plea, allows Helen to return to the Land of the Living on condition that she remain in an imaginary palace resembling that of Menelaus in Sparta: there Faust must try to seduce her. Faust succeeds, and a child is born from their union, but the child is killed in an accident, and his death draws Faust and Helen apart. The final acts see Faust back in the Emperor's realm, where as a reward for helping him defeat a rival Faust is given a tract of imperial land almost completely covered by the sea. Faust ends his life blinded by Care for having despoiled and murdered an elderly couple who occupied part of his land. Mephistopheles, however, does not succeed in obtaining his soul, which is taken to heaven by mystical spirits led by the soul of Gretchen.

Helen begins with Homer and, it could be said, ends with Goethe. It is in the *Iliad* that she first appears as the beautiful woman "for whom so many Argives/lost their lives in Troy, far from native land," a land that now seems to her unreal: "There was a world," she wonders, "or was it all a dream?"[7] But like the other women in Homer, Helen is not just a pawn in the war of men. Everything about her is complex, even her beauty, which is never described except through the eyes of her beholders (Anne Carson calls her the "Norma Jeane Baker of Troy").[8] There is a moment of great pathos when the old men of Troy, aloft on a tower while the Greek armies gather outside the walls for what will be yet another bloody battle, realize that everything and everyone might be lost to the enemy and know that they might be spared if Paris's bride is returned to her rightful husband. And then they see Helen moving along the ramparts and say to one another:

Who on earth could blame them? Ah, no wonder
the men of Troy and Argives under arms have suffered
years of agony all for her, for such a woman.
Beauty, terrible beauty![9]

Osip Mandelstam, reflecting on these lines in the twentieth century, wrote in a poem: "If there was no Helen,/What would Troy be to you, Achaean men?"[10]

Even though the protagonists of both the *Iliad* and the *Odyssey* are men, at the core of each poem is an extraordinary woman. In the *Odyssey*, Odysseus's troubled journey would be meaningless without Penelope at the end: she is not waiting idly but supporting his efforts to reach Ithaca with her unraveling of her tapestry, his advances in space counterpoised by her retreating strands in time. In the *Iliad*, Achilles defines the battle as "fighting other soldiers to win their wives as prizes," since the long war hinges on kidnapped Helen, and progresses through the dispute over Chryseis (promised to Agamemnon) and Briseis (promised to Achilles). The action is driven by the fighting men, the justification they give for it lies with the women: the relationship between the two weaves the story into the future. Helen is magically aware of her emblematic role. She says to Paris:

Zeus planted a killing doom within us both,
so even for generations still unborn
we will live in song.[11]

The plural is telling. In a voluminous study of the character of Helen, identifying her as a matriarch who ruled over a fertile Mycenaean kingdom and as a pre-Greek fertility goddess, the historian Bettany Hughes remarks on the color of the cloth Helen is weaving before she climbs to the top of the tower where the old men will see her. As Paris and Menelaus prepare for combat, the goddess Iris, disguised as Hector's sister Laodice, visits Helen in Priam's palace. She finds Helen in the hall, where she is weaving a great purple web of double fold, embroidering on it "many battles of the horse-taming Trojans and the brazen-coated Achaeans." Iris then urges Helen to go to the city gates and witness the battle about to be fought over her. Hughes sees Helen's cloth as a metaphor for poetry, "in which case Helen herself is the poet, pulling together the threads of men's lives, creating her own story, building an epic to be passed on to future generations. In a sense she (not Homer) is the bard, a woman fabricating the world around her," making it live in a web of song.[12]

In the last years of the sixteenth century, Christopher Marlowe, inspired by the early German versions of the Faust story, was the first to dramatize in English, in his *Tragical History of Doctor Faustus*, the legendary encounter between the wizard doctor whose "study fits a mercenary drudge/Who aims at nothing but external trash" and the woman who is the world's paragon of beauty, describing her with the famous lines:

> Was this the face that launch'd a thousand ships,
> And burnt the topless towers of Ilium?
> Sweet Helen, make me immortal with a kiss.

The "thousand ships" belong to the catalogue of the Greek fleet in book 2 of the *Iliad*, the "topless towers" to the elders' watch in book 3 and to the *Aeneid*, book 2: the kiss that makes its receiver "immortal" comes from Helen's power as "deathless goddess," also in the *Iliad*, book 3. She is, as Marlowe interprets Homer's creation, the measure of comparison with all beauty, female or male, whether with the lovely Zenocrate in his *Tamburlaine* or with the handsome Gaveston in *Edward II*.[13]

Marlowe may have been inspired to write the scene in which Helen appears to Dr. Faustus by an episode recorded in one of the lives of the historical Faustus, supposed to be a certain Georg von Helmstadt. When this Faustus lectured on Homer at the University of Erfurt in Germany, where he held an academic post, he made the heroes of the poems appear before his audience as if by magic: Priam, Hector, Ajax, Odysseus, and Agamemnon took the stage, one after the other, and looked at the astounded students, then each "shook his head as if he were still in action on the field before Troy." In the fifteenth century, the inventor Giovanni Fontana from Padua spoiled the fun by suggesting that images such as these could be produced by means of a *lanterna magica*, which projected images painted on glass by the light of a candle.[14]

Two and a half centuries later, Edgar Allan Poe would equate Helen's immortal beauty with the immortality of the ancient world itself, whose knowledge reaches us "from regions which are Holy Land," thereby closing a circle in which Homer's Helen can provide the exhausted intellectual (Faust or Poe) with all that the world of books (including presumably those of Homer) cannot give him.

> Helen, thy beauty is to me
> Like those Nicaean barks of yore
> That gently, o'er a perfumed sea,
> The weary, wayworn wanderer bore
> To his own native shore.[15]

Helen, however, not only grants immortality; she is also an eternal *casus belli*, a tag repeated several times in the *Iliad* (though King Priam magnanimously tells her that he does not blame her but the gods: "They are the ones who brought this war upon me"). When Goethe has her appear in *Faust, Part Two*, she painfully recalls the suffering that has taken place because of her and asks if she is cursed with the dreadful gift of always having men fight for her:

Is it a memory? Has delusion seized my mind?
Was I all that? And am I? And shall I still be
The nightmare image, Helen the cities' bane?[16]

If Gretchen in *Faust, Part One* is the seduced innocent who ends up murdering her baby, then Helen in *Faust, Part Two* is her counterpart, the innocent seducer whose child dies because of her own recklessness. And yet, of all the main characters, only Helen appears condemned to an eternity in which she will always be, as she herself declares, "so much admired and so much censured." Helen is all ambiguity: upon seeing her, Faust cannot decide if this creature, "conjured out of time," is a dream or a memory. All he knows is that nothing but her love will fulfill him, and in fact Faust's only period of contentment is during his time in Helen's arms. Perhaps for Goethe it is this fulfilled love that justifies the decision of saving the "great sinner Faust" in the end. And yet the doctor's salvation is not achieved through Helen's hand. *Faust, Part One* ends with a "voice from above" declaring Gretchen redeemed, and it is Gretchen's spirit who in *Faust, Part Two* leads the doctor's soul to heaven, to the "Eternal Feminine" of the last verses. Helen, the other incarnation of that same "Eternal Feminine," must instead return to Homer's realm: she can appear but not remain visible in Goethe's modern world, which, in spite of its enthusiasm for the ancients, refuses (in Werther's words) "to be guided or encouraged or sent into raptures."[17]

There is yet another version of the "Eternal Feminine," the one incarnated in the character of Penelope. She is traditionally acknowledged to be the archetypal faithful wife: Latin authors from Plautus to Statius mention her as an ideal mate, and Saint Jerome lists her among the examples of pagan chastity.[18] In the *Odyssey*, however, Penelope is not merely the patient wife. Waiting for her husband to return, while not readily accepting a replacement, she casts an eye on the flock of suitors and asserts their merits, not according to their wealth or social standing but as physical creatures. "In order to please Penelope," writes the critic Giulia Sissa, "they have to be on par with Ulysses in showing the might of their bodies."[19] Joyce was aware of this aspect of Penelope when he gave voice to Molly Bloom, who has not had sexual relations with her husband since the death ten years earlier of their son Rudy, who lived for only eleven days. Lying in bed, Molly reviews her previous lovers in a weblike reverie, weaving and unweaving those past affairs in her mind, and finally accepting her husband in the marriage bed once again. Unlike Helen, Molly does not mind "being sent into raptures." On the contrary.

Shortly before his death in 1832, Goethe finished the last section of his autobiography, *Dichtung und Wahrheit* (Poetry and Truth). In it, he hails his century as one fortunate enough to have witnessed the rebirth of Homer. "Happy is that literary age," he wrote, "when great works of art of the past rise to the surface again and become part of our daily dealings, for it is then that they produce a new effect. For us, Homer's sun rose again, and according to the requirements of our age. . . . No longer did we see in those poems a violent and inflated heroic world, but rather the mirrored truth of an essential present, and we tried to make him as much ours as possible."[20]

CHAPTER 15

Homer as Symbol

We are symbols, and inhabit symbols.

—Ralph Waldo Emerson, "The Poet" (1844)

Friedrich Nietzsche had little time for Goethe's views on Homer, which he found "incompatible with that element out of which Dionysian art grows—the orgiastic. Indeed I do not doubt that as a matter of principle, Goethe excluded anything of the sort from the possibilities of the Greek soul. Consequently Goethe did not understand the Greeks." Like Goethe, Nietzsche had read Homer at a very young age. The gifted son of a pastor, he studied in both Bonn and Leipzig and was elected to the chair of classical philosophy at the University of Basel at the age of twenty-five. During his professorship, three years later, he wrote his first great book, *The Birth of Tragedy,* published in 1872, in which he began to outline his theory about the driving forces of Greek culture. But already in 1869, in his inaugural lecture at Basel, he had pronounced the question on Homer that unwittingly echoed Vico's and foreshadowed Jung's: "Has a person been made out of an idea or an idea out of a person?"[1]

For Nietzsche, no one could read Homer's books as Homer wrote them: we read not the stories Homer told but the interpreted versions of those stories. "Why did the whole Greek world exult over combat scenes of the *Iliad*?" he asks in a posthumously published fragment. "I fear that we do not understand these sufficiently in a 'Greek' manner; indeed, that we should shudder if we were ever to understand them 'in Greek.'" What allows for these individual readings is that at the core of ancient Greek culture is a living tension between, on the one hand, a tendency toward order and individual fulfillment (which Nietzsche called "Apollonian") and, on the other, violence and destructive rapture (the "Dionysian"). In this context, Homer was for Nietzsche a creative Apollonian force that wrote his poems "in order to persuade us to continue to live." Homer's gods justify human existence by sharing their lives with us mortals; for his heroes, the greatest pain is therefore to leave this life, especially when one is young. Nietzsche saw Homer as the "total victory of the Apollonian illusion," an illusion that entails believing ourselves worthy of being glorified, and therefore imagining beautiful gods who are our own reflection. In this, he joins Schiller's characterization of Homer as a natural poet. "By means of this mirage of beauty," concludes Nietzsche, "Hellenic 'will' battled with the talent, correlative to the artistic talent, for suffering and the wisdom of suffering, and as a monument to its triumph stands Homer, the naïve artist."[2]

Seventeen years after writing this, in 1889, in Turin, the syphilis from which Nietzsche had suffered for years manifested itself in serious mental disturbances. To the bewilderment of his hosts, Nietzsche locked himself in his room, pounded the piano night and day, pranced about naked singing loudly, and performed autoerotic Dionysian rites. When a local doctor for the insane came to examine him, Nietzsche cried out, "*Pas malade! Pas malade!*" At last his friends persuaded him to leave Turin and return to Basel. In 1900 he died in Weimar, dressed in a white robe and recognizing no one.[3]

Nietzsche's poetical reading of Homer had placed him on the opposite side of Wolf's unsentimental investigations, though both believed that Homer was an abstract noun, a classic concept rather than a historical person. Homer's poems were a different matter. Nietzsche (and perhaps Wolf as well) understood that one of the qualities of a classic is that it elicits from the reader a double sense of witnessed truth: that of poetic artifice and that of experienced reality, the truth of both balance and unbalance discussed by Sontag, or, in Nietzschean terms, that of Apollonian illusion and that of Dionysian struggle.

Sigmund Freud, writing in 1915, some six months after the outbreak of the First World War, suggested that something like this split perception of the world manifested itself in our relationship with death. He did not refer to Nietzsche: his biographer Peter Gay remarked that "Freud treated Nietzsche's writings as texts to be resisted far more than to be studied."[4] Freud did, however, follow Nietzsche in noting that the value we place on life after death was a development of post-Homeric times and, like Nietzsche, quoted in support of his theory the answer Achilles gave to Odysseus in the Underworld. For Odysseus (that is, the living, for whom death is still unimaginable), death is a form of heroic fulfillment. Odysseus tells Achilles that he should not grieve at having died because

> Time was, when you were alive, we Argives
> honored you as a god, and now down here, I see,
> you lord it over the dead in all your power.[5]

But Achilles furiously denies this: he does not believe in the posthumous glory granted by death to its best-beloved. His only concern is life, which he no longer has, and against which he will trade any reward of fame or glory, the pains of life weighed against the pains of death. This counterpoint is apparent throughout the

Iliad: for instance, when Agamemnon is wounded in the arm, his hurt is like that of a woman in labor, the pain of looming death compared to the pains of giving birth. Achilles understands this. And this is the same Achilles who, in the *Iliad,* telling the young son of Priam that he will not spare his life, is suddenly aware that one day he too will die:

> even for me, I tell you,
> death and the strong force of fate are waiting.
> There will come a dawn or sunset or high noon
> when a man will take my life in battle too.[6]

Achilles knows that he is mortal and at the same time refuses to accept the fact as final. Freud argued that, like Achilles, our unconscious "does not believe in its own death; it behaves as if it were immortal. What we call our 'unconscious'—the deepest strata of our minds, made up of instinctual impulses—knows nothing that is negative, and no negation; in it, contradictories coincide. For that reason it does not know its own death, for to that we can give only a negative content. Thus there is nothing instinctual in us which responds to a belief in death." And Freud adds: "This may even be the secret of heroism."[7]

Homer and the ancient world (especially that of the Greek tragedians) provided Freud with a useful vocabulary of what he called "symbols" and lent him key words for the abstract concepts he dealt with in his psychoanalytical investigations. These sometimes took on the concrete shape of art objects, which he enjoyed collecting throughout his life. In his study, first in Vienna, then in London, he kept dozens of Egyptian, Greek, and Roman figurines and pottery, "strewn over every available surface: they stood in serried ranks on bookshelves, thronged table tops and cabinets, and invaded Freud's orderly desk, where he had them under his fond eye as he wrote his letters and composed his papers."[8] It was as if the presence of signs from the past helped him find the words for naming that which the unconscious would not even deny. To one of his patients, he explained that his fondness for the ancient world served as a useful mirror for his practice. "The psychoanalyst, like the archaeologist in his excavations, must uncover layer after layer of the patient's psyche, before coming to the deepest, most valuable treasures."[9] But, as Peter Gay remarked, "this weighty metaphor does not exhaust the significance of this addiction for Freud."[10] Freud found in Homer and his world a constantly changing trove of symbolic readings, which, as his own work proved, reflected the tension between contradictory revelations. As if echoing the dialogue between Andromache and Hector in book 6 of the *Iliad*, Freud wrote, "We recall the old saying, *Si vis pacem, para bellum*. If you want to preserve peace, arm for war." And he concluded, "It would be in keeping with these times to alter it: *Si vis vitam, para mortem*. If you want to endure life, prepare yourself for death."[11]

Freud drew cautious parallels between archaeological discoveries and psychological truths, suggesting symbolic links between, for instance, the memory of disappeared civilizations and the group psychology of certain social upheavals. "If all that is left of the past are the incomplete and blurred memories which we call tradition, this offers an artist a peculiar attraction, for in that case he is free to fill in the gaps in memory according to the desires of his imagination."[12] In the same way, Freud's psychoanalysis (one of his more intelligent disciples argued) confronts us "with the abyss within ourselves" and forces on us "the incredibly difficult task of taming and controlling its chaos."[13]

Carl Gustav Jung tempered what he considered a reductive method in Freud's reading. "Those conscious contents which give us a clue to the unconscious background," Jung wrote, "are incorrectly called symbols by Freud. They are not true symbols, however, since according to his theory they have merely the role of signs or symptoms of the subliminal processes. The true symbol differs from this and should be understood as an expression of an intuitive idea that cannot yet be formulated in any other or better way." For Jung, only certain images, fully denoting an idea in all its sprawling and even contradictory complexity (Plato's metaphors or Christ's parables), are "genuine and true symbols." Homer, who knew this, did not end the *Iliad* with the narrow image of death. Just before the closing verses, he joined the grief of the defeated to the grief of the victors, and conjured up the memorable image of both combined in one, that, as Jung thought, surely cannot yet be formulated in any other or better way.[14]

In 1908, the English poet Rupert Brooke attempted to disclose both the symbolic or "poetic" and the historical or "realistic" readings of Homer in a double sonnet in which he imagined a possible forked ending for the *Iliad*. Though hardly a professional soldier (he died in 1915 not of a gunshot wound but of blood poisoning on his way to the Dardanelles), Brooke is today mainly remembered as a war poet on the strength of the first lines of "The Soldier," written in the year of his death: "If I should die, think only this of me:/That there's some corner of a foreign field/That is for ever England." The *Iliad* was in Brooke's mind during the war, as it was in the minds of his fellow English soldiers, who identified more with Homer's Greek fighters than with his Trojan victims. A few weeks before his death, Brooke wrote in Homeric terms to his friend Violet Asquith: "Do you think *perhaps* . . . they'll make a sortie and meet us on the plains of Troy? It seems to me strategically so possible. . . . Will the sea be polyphloisbic and winedark and unvintageable?" Brooke's Homeric poem, "Menelaus and Helen," reads:

I

Hot through Troy's ruin Menelaus broke
    To Priam's palace, sword in hand, to sate

On that adulterous whore a ten years' hate
And a king's honour. Through red death, and smoke,
And cries, and then by quieter ways he strode,
  Till the still innermost chamber fronted him.
  He swung his sword, and crashed into the dim
Luxurious bower, flaming like a god.

High sat white Helen, lonely and serene.
  He had not remembered that she was so fair,
And that her neck curved down in such a way;
And he felt tired. He flung the sword away,
  And kissed her feet, and knelt before her there,
The perfect Knight before the perfect Queen.

II
So far the poet. How should he behold
  That journey home, the long connubial years?
  He does not tell you how white Helen bears
Child on legitimate child, becomes a scold,
Haggard with virtue. Menelaus bold
  Waxed garrulous, and sacked a hundred Troys
  'Twixt noon and supper. And her golden voice
Got shrill as he grew deafer. And both were old.

Often he wonders why on earth he went
  Troyward, or why poor Paris ever came.
Oft she weeps, gummy-eyed and impotent;
  Her dry shanks twitch at Paris' mumbled name.
So Menelaus nagged; and Helen cried;
And Paris slept on by Scamander side.[15]

The Greek poet Yannis Ritsos imagined the similar double ending of closure and quiet despair for Penelope after her long wait:

It wasn't that she didn't recognize him in the light from the hearth: it
    wasn't
the beggar's rags, the disguise—no. The signs were clear:
the scar on his knee, the pluck, the cunning in his eye. Frightened,
her back against the wall, she searched for an excuse,
a little time, so she wouldn't have to answer,
give herself away. Was it for him, then, that she'd used up twenty
    years,
twenty years of waiting and dreaming, for this miserable
blood-soaked, white-bearded man? She collapsed voiceless into a
    chair,
slowly studied the slaughtered suitors on the floor as though seeing
her own desires dead there. And she said "Welcome,"
hearing her voice sound foreign, distant. In the corner, her loom
covered the ceiling with a trellis of shadows; and all the birds she'd
    woven
with bright red thread in green foliage, now,
on this night of the return, suddenly turned ashen and black,
flying low on the flat sky of her final enduring.[16]

CHAPTER 16

Homer as History

... but where I sought for Ilion's walls,
The quiet sheep feeds, and the tortoise crawls.
—Lord Byron, *Don Juan*, 1819–24

Heinrich Schliemann, an amateur archaeologist who died a decade before Nietzsche, shared Nietzsche's double vision of the *Iliad*, both as invention and as history. Schliemann was less interested in the truth of the person Homer (though Schliemann thought he had indeed existed) than in that of his poems. Schliemann believed that if properly deciphered, Homer's books, poetical inventions though they were, could provide an accurate guide to the physical site of ancient Troy.

According to Schliemann (who also confessed that he was prone to lying and exaggeration), his passion for Homer began in his early childhood, when his father would recite for him at bedtime the adventures of the Homeric heroes. The boy was so enthralled by the stories that one Christmas, when he was ten, he presented his father with the gift of "a badly written Latin essay upon the principal events of the Trojan war and the adventures of Ulysses and Agamemnon."[1] Because of the family's scarce means, the boy was unable to attend college; he was instead apprenticed at the age of fourteen to a village grocer and quickly forgot most of what he had learned at home.

One of the odd characters in Schliemann's village happened to be an apprentice miller, a young man who had once studied the classics but had later become an alcoholic. Rumor had it that he had been expelled from school for bad behavior and that to punish him his father, a Protestant clergyman, had made him learn the miller's trade. In despair, the young man had taken to drink, but he had not forgotten his Homer. One evening, the drunken miller staggered into Schliemann's shop and in front of the astonished boy recited one hundred lines of ancient Greek in resounding rhythmic cadence. Schliemann did not understand a word, but the music of the verses made such an impression on him that he burst into tears and asked the man to repeat them again and again, bribing him with tumblers of brandy. "From that moment on," he later confessed, "I never ceased to pray God that by His grace I might yet have the happiness to learn Greek."[2]

A chest ailment made it impossible for Schliemann to continue working at the grocer's, and in search of new employment, he traveled to Hamburg, where he found a position as a cabin boy on a ship bound for Venezuela. A storm stranded the ship on the Dutch coast, and Schliemann, believing destiny had decreed that he live in Holland, settled down in Amsterdam as a filing clerk. He decided to study languages and learned in quick succession English, French, Dutch, Spanish, Italian, Portuguese, and Russian, but not until 1856, at the age of thirty-four, did he begin to study his beloved Greek. Sometime later, a number of successful business transactions left him with a huge fortune. In his accounts of these adventures, Schliemann does not tell us what those transactions were, but his vast correspondence reveals that he was involved in various unscrupulous dealings: the commerce of saltpeter for gunpowder during the Crimean War, the purchase of gold from the Californian prospectors during the gold rush, the buying and selling of cotton during the American Civil War. A rich man at last, Schliemann was now able to fulfill his dream of visiting ancient Greece and exploring the places described by Homer. In this he was astonishingly successful. In 1873, using the *Iliad* as his travel guide, Schliemann unearthed, beneath the town of Hissarlik in northwestern modern Turkey, the fabled city of Troy—not one but nine strata of Trojan cities.[3]

Contrary to Schliemann's own marvelous account, he did not immediately stumble on the site. From the seventeenth century on, readers had imagined that it was possible to find "Priam's six-gated city," as Shakespeare called it in *Troilus and Cressida*. John Sanderson, Queen Elizabeth I's ambassador, wrote that twice he had unsuccessfully set off in search of Troy, first in 1584 and then in 1591. Throughout the eighteenth and nineteenth centuries, the search continued intermittently. Robert Wood published a book in 1769, *Essay on the Original Genius of Homer*, that, though not proposing an exact location for the city, described the changes in the topography that would probably have taken place since Homer's time (changes which we now know to be correct). Some fifty years later, the armchair archaeologist Charles Maclaren correctly suggested that Troy's location was in Hissarlik, but the first serious diggings of the site were begun by Frank Calvert, a scholarly Englishman who had lived in Turkey all his life. Schliemann, whose sights were at first fixed on another location, finally agreed with Calvert's choice and joined him in the excavations.[4]

Calvert and Schliemann soon had a falling out. Calvert publicly expressed his opinion that there was missing in the site an essential link between two strata, that of the prehistoric occupation of the city and that of the so-called Archaic style of approximately 700 BCE. In other words, there was no evidence of roughly 1200 BCE, the time of the Trojan War itself. Schliemann was furious and accused Calvert of being "a foul fiend . . . a libeller and a liar." A few weeks later, Schliemann was vindicated. On May 31, 1873, he uncovered, in the stratum he had argued was Homer's Troy, a treasure of copper cauldrons full of golden and silver cups and vases, copper lanceheads, and an astonishing collection of gold jewelry: rings, bracelets, earrings, diadems, and one ornate headband. To record the find, Schliemann had his wife photographed in what he called "the Jewels of Helen." Though the jewels now appear to have been dated correctly to the time of Homer's Troy, the "treasure" itself was probably found by Schliemann over various weeks, scattered about in a number of places and then gathered in order to make believe that they were all part of one lot.[5]

Soon afterward, Schliemann smuggled the treasure out of Anatolia. When his theft was discovered, the Ottoman official in charge of overseeing the excavation was put in prison, and the authorities revoked Schliemann's excavation permit. Later, Schliemann handed over to the Ottoman authorities a small part of the treasure, now housed in the Istanbul Archaeological Museum, in exchange for permission to continue to excavate at Troy. The rest of the treasure was acquired in 1881 by the city of Berlin. At the end of the Second World War, when the Red Army entered Berlin, Professor Wilhelm Unverzagt from the German Royal Museums handed over the treasure to the Soviet Art Committee, thus saving it from looting. The objects were then flown to Moscow, where throughout the Cold War the Soviet government denied any knowledge of their whereabouts. Today Russia acknowledges possession of Schliemann's treasure, but refuses to return it, deeming it compensation for the destruction of Russian cities and the looting of Russian museums by the Nazis. This decision was backed in 1998 by a Russian law that prevents the Russian authorities from making any such restitution. In 1996, British and American heirs of Calvert announced they would file a claim to a portion of the Trojan treasure.[6] They were not successful.

Professional archaeologists and academic classicists were enraged by Schliemann's audacity and attempted to dismiss his findings. Matthew Arnold called him "devious." The orientalist Joseph Arthur, Count de Gobineau, said Schliemann was "a charlatan." The archaeologist Ernst Curtius (not to be confused with scholar E. R. Curtius) branded him "a swindler." In these attacks there were at least four issues at play: first, what the academics considered the insolent intrusion of an amateur into their professional field; second, the highly disturbing notion that poetry might not be pure invention, but might instead provide accurate depictions of the material world it portrayed; third, the inevitable conclusion that the *Iliad* and the *Odyssey* might have their origin in days far beyond the heroic age of Greece, in the preclassical and nebulous times outside the reach of the university curriculum. Finally, they questioned the veracity of Schliemann's assumptions, arguing that the ruins he had uncovered were not those of Homer's Troy (which now we know occupy a different stratum, identified as Troy VIIa). "Homer is a poet, Homer is a historian," argues Michael Schmidt. "To insist on the modern separation of those two roles is to impose an anachronism on him."[7]

To Schliemann's daring imagination, these academic quibbles must have sounded like a reproach made to someone who, having unearthed the rabbit hole leading into Wonderland, is told that this was not the actual entrance through which Alice herself descended. But Schliemann persisted. He described the ruins he had uncovered as "Troy, the city besieged by Agamemnon," and the precious objects he had unearthed as "the treasure of King Priam," because, he wrote, they were "called so by the tradition of which Homer is the echo; but as soon as it is proved that Homer and the tradition were wrong, and that Troy's last king was called 'Smith,' I shall at once call him so."[8] Whatever the criticism of the professionals, in the popular eye Schliemann became a hero, the discoverer of a world believed until then to be purely imaginary.

CHAPTER 17

Madame Homer

If [the critic Desmond MacCarthy] sincerely wishes to discover
a great poetess, why does he let himself be fobbed off with a
possible authoress of the *Odyssey*?

I have often been told that Sappho was a woman, and that
Plato and Aristotle placed her with Homer and Archilochus
among the greatest of poets.

—Virginia Woolf, "The Intellectual Status of Women," 1920

Some twenty-five years after Schliemann's discoveries, in 1897,
Samuel Butler published in London a little book called *The
Authoress of the Odyssey: Where and When She Wrote, Who She
Was, the Use She Made of the Iliad, and How the Poem Grew Under
Her Hands.* The son of a clergyman and grandson of a bishop,
Butler had by then tried his hand, mostly with fair success, at
a dozen different activities, from sheep farmer in New Zealand
(which gave him the setting for his utopian fantasy *Erewhon*) to
painter, theologian, poet, scientist, musician, classicist, and novelist (his most celebrated work, *The Way of All Flesh*, was published
posthumously, in 1903). Butler believed that a careful reading of
the *Odyssey* could prove that the author was not an old blind
male bard but a young unmarried woman, and a native of Sicily. He placed her life roughly between 1050 and 1000 BCE and
argued that she had before her while she worked Homer's *Iliad*,
from which, from time to time, "she quoted freely." Butler dismissed Friedrich Wolf's theories of a multilayered authorship,
which he ridiculed as "the nightmares of Homeric extravagance

which German professors have evolved out of their own inner consciousness," but he conceded that two distinct poems, "with widely different aims," had been cobbled together to make the *Odyssey* as we know it. With happy nonchalance, Butler said that he had based his theory on a comment made in passing by the scholar Richard Bentley (the same man who had so scornfully dismissed Pope's translation) that the *Iliad* was written for men and the *Odyssey* for women. Butler denied the notion of an exclusive audience, arguing that the *Odyssey* "was written for any one who would listen to it," but maintained that "if an anonymous book strikes so able a critic as having been written for women, a prima facie case is established for thinking that it was probably written by a woman."[1]

The idea had come to Butler in 1886. He had been writing the libretto and much of the music for a secular oratorio based on the travels of Ulysses, and decided to reread the *Odyssey* in the original, something he had not done for many years. "Fascinated, however, as I at once was by its amazing interest and beauty, I had an ever-present sense of a something wrong, of a something that was eluding me, and of a riddle which I could not read. The more I reflected upon the words, so luminous and so transparent, the more I felt a darkness behind them that I must pierce before I could see the heart of the writer—and this was what I wanted; for art is only interesting in so far as it reveals an artist."[2]

Once certain of his intuition, Butler found in the *Odyssey* the evidence to sustain it. For example, he discovered in the poem mistakes that, he said, "a young woman might easily make, but which a man could hardly fall into." Among these, he listed believing that a ship had a rudder at both ends (book 9), that well-seasoned timber can be cut from a growing tree (book 5), and that a flying hawk could tear its prey while in the air (book 15).[3] He then proceeded to map out carefully the palace of Ulysses to prove that only a woman would know what took place in all quarters of the building, and when certain descriptions presented problems, he argued again that only a woman would have no qualms about "shifting the gates a little" for the purpose of her story. Finally, "When Ulysses and Penelope are in bed ... and are telling their stories to one another, Penelope tells hers first. I believe a male writer would have made Ulysses' story come first and Penelope's second."[4] Butler then considered a problem which scholars have been confronting since the early days of Homeric commentary: Ulysses' description of Ithaca does not correspond exactly to any known Greek island:

> Sunny Ithaca is my home. Atop her stands our seamark,
> Mount Neriton's leafy ridges shimmering in the wind.
> Around her a ring of islands circle side-by-side,
> Dulichion, Same, wooded Zacynthus too, but mine
> lies low and away, the farthest out to sea,
> rearing into the western dusk
> while the others face the east and breaking day.[5]

The topographical references Homer gives us for Ithaca are detailed and vivid, but they do not match the features of the Ithaca we know today. It has often been suggested that Homer, composing his poem somewhere in Asia Minor, simply invented the description of Odysseus's home, which he had never seen, or was misinformed about it. One theory suggests that Ithaca was in fact an island that has now become part of the mainland: the westernmost tip of Cephalonia, known as Paliki. There can be no certainty in any of these suggestions. Butler, however, imagined instead that there was in Homer's time another island called Ithaca, which he located in the area around Trapani in Sicily. Butler chose "the lofty and rugged island of Marettimo" as the most likely candidate.[6]

Classicists and historians received the book in scornful silence or with finger-wagging disapproval. As late as 1956, the American historian Moses I. Finley accused Butler of taking for granted "that not only was the author(ess) of the *Odyssey* a Victorian novelist, but that the values and emotions of the characters in the poem were identical with those of his own time."[7] The criticism is fair. And yet, quirky and unconvincing as Butler's theory might be, it established a precedent for a particular relationship to the classics that would become almost commonplace among writers of the twentieth century. Instead of viewing the work as a hallowed summit readers could never reach and in whose shadow they strove, as Goethe had suggested, Butler proposed a level ground on which they shared a common space that could be entered, inhabited, renamed, and reshaped in an endlessly renewed process. The process itself was, of course, not original, and yet its shameless appropriation had a pleasing cheek about it. But then Butler never lacked self-confidence. He once remarked to his friend William Ballard that when Perseus had come to free Andromeda, the dragon had never felt in better health and spirits, and was looking remarkably well. Ballard said he wished that this fact appeared in the poets. Butler looked at him and observed: "Ballard, I also am 'the poets.'"[8]

Writing in the same ingenious vein, in 1932 T. E. Lawrence imagined Homer, the author of the *Odyssey*, not as a young Sicilian lady but as an old British gentleman.

> A bookworm, no longer young, living from home, a mainlander, city-bred and domestic. Married but not exclusively, a dog-lover, often hungry and thirsty, dark-haired. Fond of poetry, a great if uncritical reader of the *Iliad*, with limited sensuous range but an exact eyesight which gave him all his pictures. A lover of old bric-à-brac, though as muddled an antiquary as Walter Scott. . . . He loved the rural scene as only a citizen can. No farmer, he had learned the points of a good olive tree. He is all adrift when it comes to fighting, and had not seen deaths in battle. He had sailed upon and watched the sea with a palpitant

concern, seafaring being not his trade. As a minor sportsman he had seen wild boars at bay and heard tall yarns of lions . . . Very bookish, this house-bred man. His work smells of the literary coterie, of a writing tradition. His notebooks were stocked with purple passages and he embedded these in his tale wherever they would more or less fit. He, like William Morris, was driven by his age to legend, where he found men living untrammelled under the God-possessed skies. Only, with more verbal felicity than Morris', he had less poetry.[9]

Like Butler and Lawrence, the writers who followed began to establish a companionable relationship with Homer. In the twenty-first century, Margaret Atwood, perhaps with an eye on Butler, took up Homer's account of Odysseus's return and reimagined it from the point of view of Penelope and her maids. In book 22 of the *Odyssey,* after Odysseus shoots Antinous, one of the two leading suitors, and reveals himself to the rest of the astonished men, he begins killing them one by one with the assistance of Telemachus, the swineherd Eumaeus, and the cowherd Philoetius. The goatherd Melanthius tries to arm the surviving suitors but is quickly found out, tortured, and put to death. Odysseus, having run out of arrows, puts on his armor and finishes off the suitors with his sword and spear, while the twelve maids who have slept with them are strung up by their necks with a ship's cable by Telemachus. Emily Wilson has suggested in the introduction to her translation of the *Odyssey* that the choice of hanging over hacking keeps the maids' tainted bodies from polluting the floors of the palace, and prevents the young Telemachus from coming too close to the women's "sexualized bodies." Also, in hanging them, Telemachus proves his incipient manhood by defying his father's instruction to slash them with "long swords" and by belittling the women he will kill.[10] After the massacre, Odysseus purges his halls and court with cleansing fumes.

Atwood found the story unsatisfactory. There are, she said, "two questions that must pose themselves after any close reading of the *Odyssey*: what led to the hanging of the maids, and what was Penelope really up to? The story as told in the *Odyssey* doesn't hold water: there are too many inconsistencies."[11]

Butler thought that these "inconsistencies" were simply due to the fact that Homer was a woman. "All readers," Butler wrote, "will help poets, playwrights and novelists, by making believe a good deal, but we like to know whether we are in the hands of one who will flog us uphill, or who will make as little demand upon us as possible." And in the scene of the killing of the suitors and the hanging of the maids, Butler argued that the former mode prevailed, since in his opinion, the author of the *Odyssey* identified herself here with Penelope (though Butler believed that she depicted herself in the poem as Nausicaa). "She does not care how much she may afflict the reader in his efforts to believe her—the only thing she cares for is her revenge. She must have every one of the suitors killed stone dead, and all the guilty women hanged, and Melanthius first horribly tortured and then cut in pieces. Provided these objects are attained, it is not necessary that the reader should be able to believe, or even follow, all the ins and outs of the processes that lead up to them."[12]

Atwood does not find the mechanics of the scene implausible, only the story itself. For Atwood's Penelope, the killing of the maids is the result of a terrible error. In her version, when Odysseus asks the nurse Eurycleia to choose twelve of the fifty household maids to be sacrificed, the old woman, not knowing Penelope's plot, chooses the twelve faithful ones who pretended, following Penelope's instructions, to be rude to their queen. (In chapter 14 of *The Handmaid's Tale*, Atwood imagines a similar punishment called the "Salvaging," whereby the society of Gilead is saved from the threat posed by the supposed offenders.) Atwood's Penelope imagines for the slaughter a sinister explanation. "What if Eurycleia was aware of my agreement with the maids—of their spying on the Suitors for me, of my orders to them to behave rebelliously? What if she singled them out and had them killed out of resentment at being excluded and the desire to retain her inside position with Odysseus?"[13]

Whichever the cause, the twelve maids killed "as doves or thrushes beating their spread wings/against some snare rigged up in thickets" (as Homer movingly describes them) haunt the reader's imagination, and Atwood's version links their story to contemporary accounts of mass rapes and the attendant ostracism from their own people of women in Bosnia, Rwanda, Darfur, and many other of today's battlefields.[14] Various other contemporary novelists, most notably Pat Barker in her version of the *Iliad*, *The Silence of the Girls*, have taken up the theme of the victimhood of women in Homer's poems.[15] If, as Butler suggested, the author of the *Odyssey* was a woman, she would have no doubt been aware that rape is (like anger, revenge, and plunder) a weapon of war. According to Atwood, the fury of the murdered maids haunts Odysseus like a curse throughout eternity, infecting him with the constant wish "to be anywhere and anyone else."[16] As we have seen, Dante and Tennyson echo that curse.

Readers will never be quite certain whether Butler put forward his authorship proposal in earnest. If he did not, then he had more of a talent to be witty than to recognize the wit of others. After he told William Thackeray's eldest daughter, Lady Ritchie, of his *Odyssey* theory, she responded by announcing that she had one of her own: that the sonnets of Shakespeare had been written by Anne Hathaway. Butler did not get the joke. He repeated the story, shaking his head and muttering, "Poor lady, that was a silly thing to say."[17]

In the years following the publication of Butler's book, though in academic circles the old questions kept being batted about (was Homer a singular or plural author, or was he an author at all?), in fiction and poetry Homer began to be treated as a living author rather than a resident of Olympus, and the legacy of Greece and Rome as common contemporary property to be pilfered at will. If Butler too was "the poets" then the identification worked both ways, and Homer became (in Butler's eyes, at least) a Butler of ancient times, a Butler whose teachings extended up to the present day. "All Greek gentlemen were educated under Homer," wrote John Ruskin in 1865, making Homer the primordial elder of the European tribe. "All Roman gentlemen, by Greek literature. All Italian, and French, and English gentlemen, by Roman literature, and by its principles."[18]

Rudyard Kipling, for whom our understanding of the present is helped by mirroring what we know of the past, believed that it was useful to make these far-fetched associations: to learn from the merits and faults of the Roman Empire to criticize the empire of Queen Victoria, to read in the stories of the Middle Ages how to live better lives in our own times, to find in Horace and Shakespeare models for the present writer's craft. His portrait of Homer illustrates the point clearly:

When 'Omer smote 'is bloomin' lyre
    He'd 'eard men sing by land an' sea;
An' what he thought 'e might require,
    'E went an' took—the same as me!

The market-girls an' fishermen,
    The shepherds an' the sailors, too,
They 'eard old songs turn up again,
    But kep' it quiet—same as you!

They knew 'e stole; 'e knew they knowed.
    They didn't tell, nor make a fuss,
But winked at 'Omer down the road,
    An' 'e winked back—the same as us![19]

The past can be mirrored in the present not only through the lens of gender and political constructs but also through the eye of comedy, identifying in the past elements that strike the present as humorous or ironic. In 1762 the English wine merchant Thomas Bridges published, under the pseudonym of Caustic Barebones, *A Burlesque Translation of Homer in Two Volumes*. By "Homer," Bridges meant the *Iliad*. Bridges's humor proved popular, and his *Homer Travestie* (as the half-title page calls it) ran to several editions, though a reader today will find it hard to be amused by lines such as these:

Come, Mrs. Muse, but, if a maid,
Then come Miss Muse, and lend me aid!
Then thousand jingling verses bring,
That I Achilles' wrath may sing.[20]

This tendency spilled over into the following century. During the reign of Queen Victoria, the accepted norms of social behavior could be undermined through parody by transposing History (with a capital H) onto the stage as burlesque and melodrama. Almost anything was fair game: from Sir Walter Scott's medieval dramas that glorified the notion of chivalry as "the nurse of pure and high affection, the stay of the oppressed, the redresser of grievances, the curb of the power of the tyrant," to the venerable works of Greece and Rome that in the words of Matthew Arnold "make the best that has been thought and known in the world current everywhere."[21]

On June 21, 1819, Thomas John Dibdin, London's most prolific dramatist, who reaped enormous earnings with his burlesques based on Scott's novels, staged "an entirely new Comic, Pathetic, Historic, Anachronasmatic, Ethic, Epic Mélange" called *Melodrama Mad! or, The Siege of Troy*, which was hailed by the press as "the best burlesque we have ever witnessed" and became the hit of the season, thereafter repeatedly requested for royal command performances. Several other writers followed in Dibdin's footsteps, and London saw a succession of Homer-inspired burlesques such as *Telemachus; or, The Island of Calypso* (1834), *The Iliad; or, The Siege of Troy* (1858), *Patient Penelope; or, The Return of Ulysses* (1863), and *Aeneas; or, Dido Done!* (1870). The audience was supposed to know the source texts (or at least be familiar with the titles) and catch the references to contemporary slavery in depictions of ancient Greece, and to the American Civil War in racist jokes mocking the abolitionist rhetoric. The conventions of pantomime were prevalent: for instance, the heroic Ulysses was urged to join his comrades by a chorus of "Cowardy cowardy custard." The multifaceted Homer became a Victorian gentleman and proved, even if through heavy-handed parody, that, as Matthew Arnold hoped, the Greek classics held the answers to many a Victorian quandary.[22]

CHAPTER 18

Ulysses' Travels

Mr Gladstone read Homer for fun, which I thought served him right.

—Winston Churchill, *My Early Life*, 1930

Since Homer was now a man of a thousand faces—a young Sicilian woman, a literary gentleman, an uneducated busker—he could just as easily be an Irishman in exile, and his heroes could fight the daily battles of an ordinary Dublin citizen. They could travel the labyrinthine city from adventure to adventure like a soldier trying to return home or a son in search of his father. They could be our contemporaries, since Homer had foreseen everything, and, as the German poet Durs Grünbein remarked, "the present is wind in the eyes of Homer." They could feel surrounded by an ever-tempting sea that lent its color, wine-dark or "snot-green" (as James Joyce called it), to its poets. They could attempt to be, if not good (Joyce used the German word *gut*), then at least *gutmütig*—decent.[1]

Like Butler, Joyce assumed that he too was "the poets," and at first the young Joyce was of two minds about allowing Homer into their company. To the writer Padraic Colum, the twenty-year-old Irishman declared that he had no interest in Homer, whose epics, he felt, were "outside the tradition of European culture." In his eyes, the only European epic was Dante's *Commedia*. Possibly this extreme view was the result of his Irish Catholic upbringing, since, as we have seen, the Counter-Reformation ideology, with its profound distrust of Greek, lived on strongly in most Catholic countries. Joyce had studied Latin at school: later, when living in Trieste, he picked up a few words of modern Greek but deeply regretted his ignorance of Homer's tongue. To his friend Frank Budgen, a civil servant posted in Zurich, he said, "But just think, isn't that a world I am peculiarly fit to enter?"[2]

Joyce wanted to do more than enter that world: he wished to rebuild it from scratch, on Irish ground and with Irish materials. William Butler Yeats, in an essay written in 1905 that Joyce kept with him in Trieste, had suggested that the time was ripe for a new writer to revisit the ancient world of the *Odyssey*. "I think that we will learn again," he said with visionary wisdom, "how to describe at great length an old man wandering among enchanted islands, his return home at last, his slowly gathering vengeance, a flitting shape of a goddess, and a flight of arrows, and yet to make all these so different things ... become ... the signature or symbol of a mood of the divine imagination."[3] In Yeats's rallying call and Vico's theories, Joyce found confirmation of his intuition. Philological synchronicities bolstered his confidence. The *Odyssey* begins with Odysseus on Calypso's island, Ogygia. Joyce discovered that Ogygia was the name Plutarch had long ago given to Ireland. Although Joyce told Vladimir Nabokov in 1937 that basing his *Ulysses* on Homer's poem was "a whim" and that his collaboration with Stuart Gilbert in preparing a Homeric correspondence to *Ulysses* was "a terrible mistake" (Joyce deleted the Homeric titles of his chapters before *Ulysses* was published in book form), Homer's presence is obvious throughout the novel. Nabokov suggested that a mysterious character who keeps appearing in *Ulysses*, described only as "the man in the brown macintosh" and never clearly identified, might be Joyce himself lurking in his own pages.[4] It might just as well be Homer, come to supervise the renovation of his works.

Following Joyce's dismissal of his inspiration, Nabokov argued that the relationship between the *Odyssey* and *Ulysses* was nothing but fodder for critics. And yet it would be absurd not to recognize the deliberate parallels and homages, quotations and borrowings from Homer in the novel, some with direct reference to his poems, others via Dante and Virgil. In the process of association, however, they all become Joycean, as in the beautiful use of Homeric epithets in Joyce's description of the Citizen Cyclops:

> The figure seated on a large boulder at the foot of a round
> tower was that of a broadshouldered deepchested stronglimbed
> frankeyed redhaired freelyfreckled shaggybearded widemouthed
> largenosed longheaded deepvoiced barekneed brawnyhanded
> hairylegged ruddyfaced sinewyarmed hero.

Joyce manages to be funny and respectful of Homer at the same time, not falling into the kind of parodic imitation that amused A. E. Housman:

> O suitably attired in leather boots
> Head of a traveller, wherefore seeking whom
> Whence by what way how purposed art thou come
> To this well-nightingaled vicinity?[5]

Joyce told Budgen that he was writing a book based on the *Odyssey* and that it would deal with eighteen hours in the life of an "all-round character." He contended that no such person had ever been described. Christ, Hamlet, Faust all lacked the complete experience of life. He dismissed Christ as a bachelor who had never lived with a woman, Hamlet as being only a son, neither husband nor father, and Faust as someone neither young nor old, without home or family, cumbered with Mephistopheles "always hanging round him at his side or heels." There was one, however, who, he thought, might fill the bill. Ulysses was "son to Laertes, father to Telemachus, husband to Penelope, lover of Calypso, companion in arms to the Greek warriors around Troy, and King of Ithaca. He was subjected to many trials, but wisdom and courage came through them all." Furthermore, Joyce reminded Budgen that while Ulysses was a brave soldier on the battlefield, determined to see the fight to the end, he had also been a war dodger who had tried to escape military service by pretending to be mad and plowing his field with an ass and an ox yoked together. He was trapped by the recruiting sergeant, who laid the baby Telemachus in front of the plow—a counterpoint to the story in which Achilles' mother hides him among the women to prevent his joining the army, but he is recognized by Odysseus when the cross-dressing hero chooses, from a number of gifts, a shield and spear instead of jewelry.[6] These things—the shield and the spear—are destined to become symbols. "The tree which made it," says Elizabeth Cook in her lyrical version of the story, "was always meaning to become a spear."[7]

Odysseus is indeed one of the most complex characters in Homer's poems. Adroitly, Emily Wilson, in her 2018 translation of the *Odyssey*, has the first line of the poem read, "Tell me about a complicated man." "Versatile" write Fagles and Robert Fitzgerald; "sage" wrote Pope; "crafty" suggests Richmond Lattimore, lending Odysseus's talent a more positive interpretation.[8] Odysseus is many things. In the *Iliad*, he is a cautious, reasonable warrior. He is also an able diplomat, capable of taking Agamemnon's offer of reconciliation to Achilles, and a master of rhetoric who knows how to play dumb in order to better surprise his audience. He is a wily storyteller. The mystery writer Sarah Caudwell has one of her characters (whom the narrator calls "the crew") note that the more fantastic stories in the *Odyssey*, "the magic and monsters and giants and wizards and impressionable goddesses living alone on islands," are told by Odysseus himself at the fireside of King Alcinous, when invited to sing for his supper by describing his travels. "Under such conditions," the crew suggests, "the most truthful of travellers might embroider a little."[9]

Priam's old counselor Antenor describes Odysseus speaking in public, standing at first stiff and still with his eyes on the ground and then bursting into speech.

> You'd think him a sullen fellow or just plain fool.
> But when he let loose that great voice from his chest
> and the words came piling on like a driving winter blizzard—
> then no man alive could rival Odysseus!

Quoting Antenor's description, the Mexican writer Alfonso Reyes argued that Odysseus's intellectual dexterity rendered him dangerous in the eyes of authority. Reyes recalled a certain well-spoken South American diplomat who told him that whenever he returned to his country, he imagined the dictator-in-office thinking to himself, "I must distrust this man, he knows his grammar."[10]

In the *Odyssey*, Odysseus has become a crafty hero who knows his grammar and can survive by his wits, somewhat similar to the trickster figure in folktales. But he is never maliciously deceitful: his mocking of the Cyclops in book 9, for instance, after he and his men have blinded him and escaped by clinging to the underbelly of the Cyclops's rams as they leave the cave, is fully justified by the monstrous behavior of the creature who violates the duty of *xenia*, respect for strangers.[11] Nor is he ever willingly unfaithful: his true love is Penelope, and if he becomes the lover of Circe and Calypso it is explicitly in spite of himself because as a mortal he cannot resist the advances of a goddess. However, when Princess Nausicaa shows that she is attracted to him, he politely turns her down.

But once the stories of Odysseus traveled to Rome, the nature of the hero changed. There had been Greek antecedents of this other, shadowy Odysseus as far back as 415 BCE, when Euripides depicted him in *The Trojan Women* as a violent, bullying military man. In Rome, "Ulysses" became an unscrupulous, vainglorious character, associated in the Latin mind with the clever Levantine Greeks against whom the Romans had a deep-rooted prejudice. Virgil depicted him as a heartless plunderer, a sort of Greek Moriarty, Sherlock Holmes's nemesis, a master-craftsman of crime.[12] It is in the guise of this third personality that Ulysses enters the literature of Europe. Dante condemns Ulysses, together with his comrade Diomedes, to the Eighth Circle of Hell, in which the Counselors of Fraud, spiritual thieves who advise others to thieve, writhe enveloped in everlasting flames: the rapacious ardor that consumed them from inside now consumes them from the outside, and if in life they used their tongues to make others burn with greed, now the tongues of fire burn them. And it is here that Dante intuitively has Ulysses fulfill Tiresias's prophecy, of which Dante, ignorant of Homer, could not have known. In the Homeric Underworld, the soothsayer Tiresias announces not what will be but what may be: the possibilities of the foreseeable future are always more than one and the outcome depends on the hero's choice. Tiresias tells Odysseus that if he fulfills certain conditions he will reach Ithaca and kill his wife's suitors, but that staying at home may not be his lot. Odysseus, Tiresias warns, will feel the urge to "go forth once more" and undertake one last, fatal journey. The description that Dante gives Ulysses of his final adventure is among the most beautiful verses Dante ever wrote and no English translation does it proper justice. However, more than six centuries later, Alfred, Lord Tennyson, imagined a vigorous, moving version that is not unfaithful to Dante's achievement and which ends thus:

Old age hath yet his honour and his toil;
Death closes all: but something ere the end,
Some work of noble note, may yet be done,
Not unbecoming men that strove with Gods.
The lights begin to twinkle from the rocks:
The long day wanes: the slow moon climbs: the deep
Moans round with many voices. Come, my friends,
'Tis not too late to seek a newer world.
Push off, and sitting well in order smite
The sounding furrows; for my purpose holds
To sail beyond the sunset, and the baths
Of all the western stars, until I die.
It may be that the gulfs will wash us down:
It may be we shall touch the Happy Isles,
And see the great Achilles, whom we knew.
Though much is taken, much abides; and though
We are not now that strength which in old days
Moved earth and heaven; that which we are, we are;
One equal temper of heroic hearts,
Made weak by time and fate, but strong in will
To strive, to seek, to find, and not to yield.[13]

Tennyson, steeped in the classics at Cambridge, takes Dante's condemned king back to his Homeric source. Ulysses, who "cannot rest from travel," must relinquish his role as the rogue too clever for his own good and again assume the identity of a hero. "I am become a name," he says, summing up his long journey from the soldier-survivor who called himself "Nobody" to the returned king anxious to sail once more. "Among the many things that Ulysses has been," wrote Mario Vargas Llosa, "there is one constant in Western literature: the fascination with human beings who do away with limits, who, instead of bowing to the servitude of what is possible, endeavor, against all logic, to seek the impossible."[14] This is true not only in Western literatures. In Turkey, in the first half of the twentieth century, the Turkish novelist Yasar Kemal saw in the people of his native Anatolia human beings who also would not bow to servitude of what is possible and who imagine for themselves deeds beyond the limits that have arbitrarily been decreed for them. Commenting on his best-known novel, *Memed, My Hawk*, Kemal explained that his inspirations were the popular singers of his country, "the Turkish and Kurdish Homers of my time." And Kemal added: "My conception of the novel is closer to Homer than to anyone else."[15]

In a long poetic version of the *Odyssey* by the Greek novelist Nikos Kazantzakis, Odysseus becomes a bleaker version of his Tennysonian counterpart. He is a wanderer in search of self-knowledge, a chameleon figure who is (the line is Tennyson's) "a part of all that I have met." He is a king, a soldier, a lover, the unhappy founder of a utopian community in Africa, but he is never successful in his enterprises. And yet, for this Odysseus, failure is less important than experience. Like that other man of many parts, Frankenstein's monster, who ends his days in the icy waste of the Arctic, Kazantzakis's Odysseus is washed up on the icy waste of Antarctica, and his last words echo Dante's in the *Commedia*:

> Then flesh dissolved, glances congealed, the heart's pulse stopped,
> and the great mind leapt to the peak of its holy freedom,
> fluttered with empty wings, then upright through the air
> soared high and freed itself from its last cage, its freedom.
> All things like frail mist scattered till but one brave cry
> for a brief moment hung in the calm benighted waters:
> "Forward, my lads, sail on, for Death's breeze blows in a fair wind!"[16]

A South American contemporary of Tennyson, the Argentinian José Hernández, composed in 1872 an epic poem whose hero,

Martín Fierro, is an Odyssean gaucho, an army dodger, as Odysseus had tried to be. Fierro is accompanied in his adventures by Sergeant Cruz, who, like Odysseus's friend Diomedes when faced with the brave Glaucus in the *Iliad,* refuses to fight Fierro and becomes his intimate friend. Fierro's morals are less those of the Homeric king of Ithaca than of the scoundrel in Virgil or the sinner in Dante. Fierro's world is ruled by cunning and violence, as proclaimed in the lessons taught by a cynical old gaucho, El Viejo Vizcacha ("Old Badger," a sort of South American Nestor). For example, Old Badger advises:

> Become a friend of the judge
> Don't give him reason to complain,
> And when he loses his temper
> You should meekly bow your head,
> Because it's always good to have
> A post against which to scratch your back.[17]

Joyce's version of the king of Ithaca, the Dublin Jew Leopold Bloom, occupies a middle ground, neither that of the Tennyson hero nor that of Dante's adventurer. Being of partial Jewish descent, Bloom is endemically an exile, both inside and outside the Irish fold, a condition Joyce himself, as an Irish artist, experienced. But Bloom's Jewishness brings him close to another Ulysses, the Wandering Jew of medieval legend. Between 1902 and 1903, Victor Bérard, one of the most original of French classicists, published two massive volumes of scholarship under the title *The Phoenicians and the Odyssey,* suggesting that Homer's poem had Semitic roots and that all its geographical names were actual places that could be revealed by finding an equivalent Hebrew word.[18] For instance, Homer calls Circe's island both Nesos Kirkes and Aiaia. Aiaia means nothing in Greek but in Hebrew it means "Island of the She-Hawk," which in Greek translates as Nesos

Kirkes. For Bérard, Homer was Greek, but since the Phoenicians were the best sailors of the ancient world, he made his seafaring Odysseus a Phoenician, that is to say, Semitic. Without distinguishing between the various Semitic people, Joyce helped himself to Bérard's theory to justify his conception of Ulysses-Bloom as a milder version of the Wandering Jew (as Buck Mulligan calls him in the novel), whose name in the Middle Ages is Cartaphilus or Ahasuerus. Joyce had read Eugène Sue's potboiler version, *Le juif errant,* before leaving Ireland in 1904 and was familiar with the story. According to the legend, as Christ paused by his door carrying the Cross to Calvary, Ahasuerus (or Cartaphilus) cried out to him, "Walk faster!" To which Christ replied, "I will go, but you will walk until I come again!" The curse echoes that of Poseidon, who condemns Odysseus to wander "time and again off course."[19]

Joyce's *Ulysses* is not an interpretation of Homer, neither is it a retelling, even less a pastiche. Certain chapters, such as the Wandering Rocks (chapter 10), are in Homer merely a geographical location; other episodes chosen by Joyce run through the entire *Odyssey,* such as the chapters that Joyce devotes to Telemachus (chapters 1–3), Penelope (18), and Ithaca (17); others can be read as separate chapters both in *Ulysses* and in the *Odyssey,* such as the episodes of the Sirens (chapter 11), the Laestrygonians (8), and the Lotus Eaters (5). If anything, Joyce's *Ulysses* is a parallel *Odyssey,* existing on a different spatial and temporal plane.

Dr. Johnson, writing in 1765, argued, "The Pythagorean scale of numbers was at once discovered to be perfect; but the poems of Homer we yet know not to transcend the common limits of human intelligence, but by remarking, that nation after nation, and century after century, has been able to do little more than transpose his incidents, new-name his characters, and paraphrase his sentiments. The reverence due to writings that have long subsisted arises therefore not from any credulous confidence in the superior wisdom of past ages, or gloomy persuasion of the degeneracy of mankind, but is the consequence of acknowledged and indubitable positions, that what has been longest known has been most considered, and what is most considered is best understood."[20] Joyce did more than acknowledge Homer's position: he reimagined the story of the primordial journey undertaken by every individual, in every age. His coupling was less between Ulysses and Bloom than between Homer and Joyce himself, less between the creations than between the creators. Other writers made Homer theirs through translation, transposition, projection. Joyce did it by starting again.

CHAPTER 19

Homer Through the Looking-Glass

No ancient poem is on the subject of soap-bubbles.
—Lewis Carroll, *Symbolic Logic*, 1895

In the years preceding the Second World War, in France, the theater was perhaps the most popular form of entertainment, and Homer's poems served as explicit, even dangerous cautionary fables for the plots. Jean Giraudoux—the official spokesman for French culture in the French Ministry of Foreign Affairs, a darling of the fascist periodical *Je suis partout,* and a lover of German *Kultur*—made frequent use of Homer's stories in his plays. During the war his political position was ambiguous, but after the war he was regarded as a patriot, and his work was included, for instance, in an anthology of Resistance literature, *La patrie se fait tous les jours* (The Nation Is Made Every Day) of 1947. His two-act play *La guerre de Troie n'aura pas lieu* (The Trojan War Will Not Take Place, sometimes translated as "Tiger at the Gates") is one of the best-known French dramas of the time. It was written in 1935, the year Hitler promulgated the anti-Jewish laws in Nuremberg and the fascist Croix-de-Feu organization celebrated its eighth anniversary in France. The play was not the author's favorite. Giraudoux had conceived it as a prelude to the *Iliad,* set in a remote age "when the characters have not yet entered the realm of legend," and for a specific audience (that of Louis Jouvet's Théâtre de l'Athénée in Paris), who supposedly knew the classics.[1]

"The Trojan War will not take place," says Andromache to Cassandra as the curtain rises. Hector has convinced Paris that Helen should be returned to her husband. But King Priam and the old poet Demokos argue that this "incarnation of beauty" must be kept in Troy. The Greek embassy arrives, led by Ulysses and Oiax, and Hector attempts to negotiate Helen's return. An insulting remark by Oiax serves as an excuse for Demokos to incite the populace to attack the Greeks. Furious, Hector kills the old poet, who, before dying, accuses Oiax of the deed. Oiax is then murdered by the populace. Cassandra's last words are "The Trojan poet is dead.... Now the Greek poet can begin."[2] Demokos leaves the stage to Homer. Giraudoux's play stops where the *Iliad* starts.

"I wanted to write a tragedy," said Giraudoux. "Most of the characters, we know, are destined to be killed, not in my play but in the course of history, and therefore a sort of shadow hovers over them."[3] The menacing shadow is incarnated in the constant presence onstage of Cassandra, aware of the inevitable catastrophe. Giraudoux's characters are not Homer's. Priam and Hecuba are not the united couple of the *Iliad* but hold opposing views on the imminent crisis. Hecuba is a sharp-tongued, level-headed crone, dead set against the war, Priam a proud and senile warmonger, dazzled by Helen, his son Paris's prize catch. Helen is a complex figure in whom certain critics saw an image of the absurdity of fate, and whose indefinable beauty arouses the lust of the Council of Elders, a crowd of arrogant, greedy old men that includes Demokos. Paris is a young prig, Ajax (renamed Oiax) a bullying fool. Giraudoux conceived Ulysses as a diplomat with evil intentions, a smooth talker, someone much more dangerous than the pompous Demokos: early audiences, surprisingly, saw him as a philosopher-warrior, a man of measured words and goodwill.

Hector is among the most humane of the play's characters, torn between hatred of the war and a taste for violence, darkly aware that his own fate is part of a greater design which he is incapable of conceiving.

In spite of its seamless construction, *La guerre de Troie n'aura pas lieu* remains for some critics unconvincing, and even efforts such as Harold Pinter's remarkable 1982 adaptation for the National Theatre in London during the Falklands War seemed to lack dramatic power. Giraudoux had proposed to write "the affirmation of a horrible link between humankind and a destiny greater than human destiny itself." In this he failed, perhaps because, as the novelist Marguerite Yourcenar remarked, "His characters, rather than myths, are caricatures of myths." Doris Lessing once noted that "myth does not mean something untrue, but a concentration of truth." It may be that in Giraudoux the myths appear too diffuse, too diluted.[4]

In 1990, Derek Walcott attempted the opposite procedure. His reimagined *Odyssey* in a Caribbean setting is a concentration of endless readings of Homer's Odyseus. In his Nobel Prize acceptance speech, Walcott denied that his *Omeros* was an epic in the strict sense of the word; it was rather a collection of epic fragments arranged in three-line stanzas that echo Dante's terza rima in the *Commedia.* Its idiom is a mixture of contemporary English and Creole, and though its characters bear the names of Homer's heroes, they are also the names that slave owners commonly gave to the black population of the islands: Philoctete, Helen, Achille, Hector. The *Odyssey* begins in medias res, when Odysseus is already halfway through his travels; likewise, *Omeros* begins halfway through the *Odyssey,* with the first line of book 11 ("Now down we came to the ship") which becomes, in Walcott's idiom: "This is how, one sunrise, we cut down them canoes." (Already Ezra Pound had chosen the same device: the first of his *Cantos* starts: "And then we went down to the ship . . .")[5]

In *Omeros,* the visit to the Underworld becomes a dream voyage to Africa, the land of the protagonist's roots, where a vision of the past shows him his ancestors being captured by the slavers. The visitor is not Ulysses/Odysseus (Walcott uses both names) but Achille, victim of sunstroke, whose rage at witnessing the ancient abduction is like that of his namesake after the death of Patroclus, burning with hatred toward Patroclus's murderer. Toward the slavers, he feels "the same/mania that, in the arrows of drizzle, he felt for Hector," and toward the enslaved, a terrible grief:

> Warm ashes made his skull white
> over eyes sore as embers, over a skin charred as coal, the core of his
>   toothless
> mouth, groaning to the firelight,
>
> was like a felled cedar's whose sorrow surrounds its bole.
> One hand clawed the pile of ashes, the other fist thudded on
> the drum of his chest, the ribs were like a caved-in canoe
>
> that rots for years under the changing leaves of an almond,
> while the boys who played war in it become grown men who
> work, marry, and die, until their own sons in turn
>
> rock the rotted hulk, or race in it, pretending to row,
> as Achille had done in the manchineel grove as a boy.[6]

If Walcott's Achille is a blend of several Homeric heroes, his bard is a blend of several poets: Homer certainly, but also Joyce, another who became blind in his old age, now incarnated in a blind West Indian veteran who spends his days singing to himself in the shade of a pharmacy near the beach, his khaki dog on a leash:

the blind man sat on his crate after the pirogues
set out, muttering the dark language of the blind,
gnarled hands on his stick, his ears as sharp as the dog's.

Sometimes he would sing and the scraps blew on the wind
when her beads rubbed their rosary. Old St Omere.
He claimed he'd sailed round the world. "Monsieur Seven Seas"

they christened him, from a cod-liver-oil label
with its wriggling swordfish. But his words were not clear.
They were Greek to her. Or old African babble.

To the Homeric characters in *Omeros*, Greek is as foreign as the tongues of Africa; and Africa, for Walcott, is an Ithaca to which Ulysses/Odysseus will never return. Read after Joyce's novel, Homer's *Odyssey* is not only a poem of homecoming but also one of everlasting exile.[7]

Of course, the shadow of the homecoming, of the expected and longed-for return, is constantly present in *Omeros* as it is in *Ulysses* and in the *Odyssey*, and even in Marcel Proust's *À la recherche du temps perdu*, with Marcel as Odysseus lost in the sea of time, forced to perform the ancient Greek rites of *nekuia*, by which ghosts were called up and questioned about the future.[8] In fact, the *Odyssey* can be read as the endless story of a return which the Greeks call *nostos*, a journey that can be achieved only through its repeated telling in dialogue with the living and the dead, a story that exists in prerequisite form even before the adventures begin.

Fifteen years before *Omeros* was published, Italo Calvino perceptively noted that the *Odyssey* is a collection of numerous *Odysseys* fitted one into another like Chinese boxes. It begins with Telemachus's search for a story that does not yet exist, the story that will, at the end of the poem, become the *Odyssey*.

First, in Menelaus's account to Telemachus, the Old Man of the Sea begins the telling at the point where Odysseus himself begins it, on Calypso's island. When he stops, Homer resumes the story and follows his hero until he reaches the court of the Phaeacians. Here the blind bard Demodocus sings to his audience (of which Odysseus, as we have seen, is part) a couple of Odysseus's own adventures: Odysseus weeps and, picking up the narrative, tells how he reached the Underworld and how the ghost of Tiresias revealed to him what would happen next. As Calvino points out, the story of Odysseus's return is the real story of the *Odyssey*, a story which, throughout his adventures, Odysseus must not forget.[9]

The Alexandrian poet Constantine Cavafy, who died in 1933, also understood that Odysseus's nostos is the prerequisite of the *Odyssey*. Cavafy was an inheritor of the Hellenistic tradition, someone who read Homer as if able to discard its innumerable layers of post-Homeric exegeses and reach down to the source. In Cavafy's writing, Odysseus and Achilles are neither modern nor fabled figures. When, for example, he writes, "Our efforts are like those of the Trojans," he is able to convince the reader that his experience is indeed firsthand and that the Trojan suffering is alive in his presence. The metaphor is clear, and does not read as a metaphor.

> Yet we're sure to fail. Up there,
> high on the walls, the dirge has already begun.
> They're mourning the memory, the aura of our days.
> Priam and Hecuba mourn for us bitterly.[10]

Ithaca, Cavafy reminds us, is not only the point of arrival but also, we often forget, that of departure: it has created the distance between the exile and the return. The length and intensity of the journey back increase the value of the remote final goal.

Laistrygonians, Cyclops,
wild Poseidon—you won't encounter them
unless you bring them along inside your soul,
unless your soul sets them up in front of you.

. . . .
Ithaka gave you the marvelous journey.
Without her you wouldn't have set out.
She has nothing left to give you now.

And if you find her poor, Ithaka won't have fooled you.
Wise as you will have become, so full of experience,
you'll have understood by then what these Ithakas mean.[11]

Ithaca, the island Odysseus cherishes in his memory, has allowed the *Odyssey* to run its course. Opposed to this Ithaca is the anonymous port in Cavafy's poem "The City," a starting point that was unthinkingly left behind, a nameless Ithaca abandoned because it seemed unsatisfactory, unrewarding, and which therefore offers Odysseus no adventures, no experience, nothing but the difficulties without the journey.

You won't find a new country, won't find another shore.
This city will always pursue you.
You'll walk the same streets, grow old
in the same neighborhoods, turn gray in these same houses.
You'll always end up in this city. Don't hope for things elsewhere:
there's no ship for you, there's no road.
Now that you've wasted your life here, in this small corner,
you've destroyed it everywhere in the world.[12]

Like Ithaca in the *Odyssey*, Troy in the *Iliad* is both a city and an emblem for the story of a war whose beginning and end are not chronicled in the poem: less than seven weeks are accounted for in the seemingly everlasting conflict, providing in its fragmented nature a useful mirror for our own anguished centuries. In our imagination, Ithaca stands for the home to which we cannot but long to return, Troy for the fortress outside whose walls we fight our unending battles. "Homer," writes Jonathan Shay in his book on combat trauma, "shows us that returning veterans face a characteristic peril, a risk of dying from the obsession to know the complete and final truth of what they and the enemy did and suffered in their war and why."[13]

The 1981 novel *Famous Last Words* by the Canadian writer Timothy Findley takes place on this eternal battlefield. It tells the story of a group of men and women lost in a nightmare place that evokes Cavafy's nameless city, through which they all obediently move without understanding the purpose or destination of their movements. The setting is the Second World War; the narrator, Hugh Selwyn Mauberley, the poet-hero invented by Ezra Pound for his collection of semi-autobiographical poems published in 1920. "I didn't know quite how to tell this story," Findley confessed, "until I realized that if I were Homer, I'd have recognized this wasn't just the story of men and women—but of men and women and the gods to whom they are obedient—and told best through the evocation of icons. So what I must do is transpose this story, which is history, into another key—which is mythology."[14]

Findley's chosen mythological model is the *Iliad*. For Findley, every one of our wars (whether between the Allies and the Germans, democracy and fascism, the upper and the lower classes) is also a war between Greeks and Trojans, a symbolic struggle which in the eye of its literate chronicler dissolves into particular stories of singular men and women struggling under the whims and passions of a pantheon of mad gods. In this complex roman à clef, Mauberley is Homer, commissioned to turn historical characters from gossip-column subjects into mythological icons.

Mrs. Simpson is a half-willing Helen, yoked to a dithering Paris (the weakling Edward VIII) and fated to be rescued by various brutal or righteous Agamemnons and Menelauses. Hera and Zeus are Churchill and Hitler, Athena is Ezra Pound, the murderous Achilles is the Nazi Harry Reinhardt, who, instead of a telltale vulnerable heel, sports alligator shoes, and who (a new twist in the story) will kill his creator by plunging a pickax into Mauberley's eye, rendering him as blind as tradition depicts Homer.

Findley's Homer is neither conventionally good nor just. He is an admirer of absolute power, someone willing to collaborate in the setting up of a puppet government in which the Duke and the Duchess of Windsor are to play king and queen; willing to take part in a cabal that, under the code name "Penelope," waits for the right moment to unleash its evil plan on the world; willing to forsake his writing for a cheap plot of parodic characters. Mauberley is the iconic transgressor: political, sexual, and artistic. He has (like Pound himself) allied himself with the Fascists; he is sexually ambiguous; his literary ambition "to describe the beautiful" is stubbornly opposed to the current "roar of bombast and rhetoric." Mauberley is a hungry, haunted, burrowing creature at odds with the world and with himself. "What power-hungry people do," Findley once said, "can be embraced very generally by my use of the term 'fascist,' because I think that's what fascism is: all power-hungry people can touch the rest of the people where they are hungry to be powerful too, but no, they can never be powerful without the powerful iconic people doing things for them, and in their name."[15] In other words, the power-hungry heroes of Troy can never be powerful without the gods tugging at their strings.

On the walls of one of the rooms of the Grand Elysium Hotel (the name that, in modern mythology, Greta Garbo's celebrated film gives to besieged Troy) Mauberley writes out the story of his life: "All I have written here is true," his confession states, "except the lies."[16] Mauberley's story (like Homer's) will be read and judged by others who will come after him and then will be left to crumble into dust like the walls of the hotel itself. "This is the way the world ends," Eliot had written in "The Hollow Men," "Not with a bang but a whimper"—a line that Pound repeated in his "Canto 74" and then added: "To build the city of Dioce whose terraces are the colour of stars."[17] Dioce was a Medan king who, after being made ruler by the people because of his fair judgments, built a visionary city that was meant to be an earthly paradise. Pound, an admirer of Mussolini, imagined that the Italian dictator would create, like Dioce, an ideal state after the cataclysm of the war. The future world imagined by Findley's Mauberley is like this Diocean Troy, first destroyed by the Greeks and later resurrected in the Rome of Aeneas, of Augustus, of the Renaissance, and finally (according to Fascist ideology) in the Rome of Mussolini, whose triumph Pound-Mauberley wished for and whose threat is very much present. In Mauberley's words on the final page of Findley's novel:

Imagine something mysterious rises to the surface on a summer afternoon—shows itself and is gone before it can be identified. . . . By the end of the afternoon, the shape—whatever it was—can barely be remembered. No one can be made to state it was absolutely thus and so. Nothing can be conjured of its size. In the end the sighting is rejected, becoming something only dimly thought on: dreadful but unreal. . . . Thus, whatever rose towards the light is left to sink unnamed: a shape that passes slowly through a dream.

Waking, all we remember is the awesome presence, while a shadow lying dormant in the twilight whispers from the other side of reason: I am here. I wait.[18]

CHAPTER 20

The Shield of Achilles

A story should have a beginning, a middle, and an end . . . but not necessarily in that order.

—Jean-Luc Godard

In book 16 of the *Iliad* we learn that Patroclus borrows Achilles' armor in order to lead the Achaean army into battle. Ignoring his friend's warning not to drive the enemy too far back, Patroclus advances until he reaches the walls of Troy. There he is stunned and disarmed by Apollo himself, once again showing how the gods unfairly mingle in human affairs. Taking advantage of Apollo's intervention, the Trojan Euphorbus wounds Patroclus, after which Hector kills him and strips Achilles' armor from the body. Hearing that his beloved Patroclus is dead, Achilles returns to the fray in a passionate rage. To protect him, Achilles' mother, the goddess Thetis, asks the smithy god Hephaestus to forge armor and a new shield for her son. The shield forged by Hephaestus turns out to be a marvel, large as a man, a worldly circle protecting its chosen carrier.

Homer's description of the shield is the first known example of ekphrasis, a classic rhetorical device that describes in detail a work of art, allowing the reader to visualize the object kinetically, the eye following the written words as it would when examining the features of the three-dimensional work depicted. Achilles' new shield is nothing less than a depiction of the universe: earth, sea, and sky. Homer carefully notes the wrought details: starting from the center and moving outward in five circles, one after the other, the shield shows at its core the earth, the sea, and the sky with its sun, moon, and stars. Then follows the depiction of life in two cities, the first illustrated with everyday scenes, a wedding and a lawsuit, the second a siege and a battle. Other scenes show further aspects of life in the four seasons: a field being plowed, a harvest being reaped, a vineyard with workers and children, a herd of cattle being attacked by lions, sheep kept in a farm, and finally a festive space where young couples are courting and dancing. The framing and last circle is the great river Ocean, encircling the world. This is the entire universe in movement, displayed before our eyes in a succession of words that act, in modern terms, as a concatenation of stills from a film projected onto the screen of our mind.

In 1937 Sergei Eisenstein noted an affinity between filmic montage and the imagistic sequencing Homer employed in the *Iliad.* In a series of jottings for an essay he never completed, Eisenstein quotes twice from Alexander Pushkin's *Notes on Popular Drama* the observation that "theater was born on the public square." For Eisenstein, theater was the precursor of film, and the earliest public square was the atrium in which the blind bard Demodocus sang about the exploits of Odysseus without knowing that Odysseus himself was in the audience, listening and weeping at the memories. Eisenstein was claiming blood ties with Homer, and the shield of Achilles in the *Iliad* might be considered a proto-film. As the film historian Joanna Paul noted, "certain premodern societies understand visually in a way that can be equated to cinema." It might be said that Homer's poetry anachronistically exemplifies the seventh art.[1]

Every age reimagines the classics in its own proper idiom, whether (in very broad terms) the idiom of translation in the eighteenth century or that of critical reassessment in the nineteenth, or that of modernist experimentation in the early twentieth. In 1954, the Italian novelist Alberto Moravia noted that in the postwar world, Homer was conceived as "pure popular spectacle," which, in contemporary terms, meant film. In Moravia's novel *Il Disprezzo* (Contempt) the writer Riccardo Molteni is hired to compose a screenplay based on the *Odyssey* and draws the director and the producer into a discussion to define the approach the film should take. Molteni would like to follow "a literal interpretation of the norm" so the classical spirit of poetry in Homer will prevail, and suggests that the character of Homer's Ulysses should be based on Dante's depiction of him in the *Commedia*. "In the *Odyssey*, as you know, there's masses of poetry.... All that is needed is to translate it into the film." The director however would like to make a film that concentrates on the relationship between the hero and his wife, "a film about the psychological relationship between Ulysses and Penelope. I intend to make a film about a man who loves his wife and is not loved back." The producer wants simply a showy epic, a film that will display all the fantastic, mythological, and erotic elements of the *Odyssey*, "in other words, a spectacular story, that's what Homer wanted to do." Molteni translates his vision of several episodes of the *Odyssey* into film versions he has seen: Ulysses spying on Nausicaa becomes the peepshow "Beauties in the Bath," the Cyclops is *King Kong*, Circe is Antinéa in Wilhelm Pabst's 1932 film *The Mistress of Atlantis*.[2] A film based on Homer seeks its vocabulary not in the Greek epics but in other films, as Jean-Luc Godard understood when in 1963 he adapted Moravia's novel to the screen under the title *Le Mépris*, with Brigitte Bardot and Michel Piccoli, and director Fritz Lang as himself, hired to adapt the *Odyssey* to the screen. Godard translated Moravia's novel into, among other things, a consideration of how one might use Homer to make a purely cinematographic work of art.

Homer had been a source of inspiration from the very first silent films. The earliest adaptation of a Homeric theme, though not taken from Homer, was a one-minute-long French film, *The Judgment of Paris* (1902). It was followed by a three-and-a-half-minute production, *The Island of Calypso* (also distributed under the titles *Ulysses and the Giant Polyphemus* and *The Mysterious Island*) vaguely based on book 5 of the *Odyssey* and directed by one of the first and most inventive film directors, Georges Meliès, who also played the part of Ulysses. In Italy, a long association of film and the Homeric poems began with a half-hour version of the *Iliad* titled *The Fall of Troy* (1911), directed by Giovanni Pastrone and Luigi Romano Borgnetto. The character of Homer himself introduced the story of Paris, Helen, and Menelaus, which featured over eight hundred actors in what was judged the most ambitious project ever attempted in the world of cinema. The critics were ecstatic. "This spectacular and very interesting film demonstrates, from the dramatic point of view, to what heights the art of cinema can reach. The sets embrace a real city and throughout the film an enchanting depth of perspective is maintained, through which an entire army of citizens and soldiers can be seen swarming in dense ranks. In the scenes of the destruction of Troy, one realizes that one is facing an incomparable production of great beauty and multiple artistic merits."[3] In 1924, Bavaria Films in Germany produced a four-hour silent film, *Helena*, released in two parts, *The Rape of Helen* and *The Fall of Troy*, directed by Manfred Noa and featuring thousands of extras.

The condescending term "sword-and-sandal films" or "peplum" (a Latin word for the ancient Greek garment, the *peplos*) was introduced by French critics in the 1960s to describe not only films with Homeric themes but also all those set in other ancient times, including the biblical extravaganzas from the fifties and sixties such as *Quo Vadis* and *Spartacus*. "Peplum epics," writes the film historian Peter Bondanella, "reject any neorealist interest in historical accuracy, or even any postrealist interest in psychological depth." These modern versions of the ancient classics are, Bondanella says, "neo-mythological."[4]

Certain films with Homeric subjects, choosing to be faithful less to Homer than to the Homeric notions of struggle and travel, succeed precisely because they steer away from literal interpretations. *O Brother, Where Art Thou?*, directed by the Coen brothers and released in 2000, takes from the *Odyssey* merely the name of the protagonist (played by George Clooney) and the story of a troubled journey home. The film is set in rural Mississippi in the thirties, and follows three escaped convicts searching for hidden treasure while a sheriff relentlessly pursues them. On their way they encounter three modern-day sirens who drug them with corn whiskey, a southern blind Tiresias driving a handcar on a railway, and a Cyclops in the shape of a one-eyed Bible salesman. Mr. Lund, a blind radio station manager, plays the role of Homer.

In 1995, the Greek filmmaker Theo Angelopoulos released his version of the *Odyssey* titled *Ulysses' Gaze*, starring Harvey Keitel as the Ulysses character and scripted among others by Tonino Guerra, an Italian poet who had worked with Michelangelo Antonioni, Federico Fellini, and Andrei Tarkovsky. The plot traces the voyage of a modern-day Ulysses. A successful Greek filmmaker, played by Keitel, returns to Greece after a long absence to attend a screening of one of his earlier films. After the screening is disrupted by a local dispute, the filmmaker takes a taxi from Greece to Albania, supposedly in search of three undeveloped reels of film shot by the Manaki brothers, a film that might predate the first film shot in the Balkans. The filmmaker revisits his memories as he crosses the present-day Balkan landscapes. He travels by train, in a barge that carries a statue of Lenin (the Cyclops), and by rowboat, meeting all manner of people along the way. Finally he arrives in Sarajevo, a city under siege, where he encounters the curator of an underground cinema archive who had attempted to develop the missing reels before the war. In a fog that protects Sarajevo civilians from hidden snipers, the filmmaker explores the city with the curator's family until, at the edge of the river, they come upon a group of soldiers, and the family is brutally executed. In Angelopoulos's version of the *Odyssey*, the suitors are innocent civilians and Ulysses is nothing more than a helpless witness, like the film's audience. In his contribution to an anthology film, *Lumière and Company*, made while he was working on *Ulysses' Gaze*, Angelopoulos had a bewildered Ulysses stare silently at the camera and ask in an intertitle: "In which foreign country have I arrived?" For Angelopoulos's Ulysses, in both these films, every country is a foreign country, and Ulysses is condemned always to be a homeless refugee.

In the weeks after the outbreak of World War II, W. H. Auden attended the screening of a Nazi propaganda film in Manhattan showing the invasion of Poland. When Poles appeared on the screen, some of the German audience yelled, "Kill them!" For Auden, this was a momentous event that filled him "with a sense of evil that was irresistible by any secular power," like something in a hopeless, heartless fairy tale. "The transformation of a crowd of feelings into a community is effected by translating the former into words which embody the latter," Auden wrote. "The poem itself is a linguistic society."[5] Perhaps this is what Homer had wanted to do with the evil of war: depict it as a bloody landscape of words.

Years later, in the midst of the Korean War, Auden remembered that "sense of evil" and depicted it as a primordial, infantile, ravished world where Achilles is nothing but "a ragged urchin."

A ragged urchin, aimless and alone,
    Loitered about that vacancy; a bird
Flew up to safety from his well-aimed stone:
    That girls are raped, that two boys knife a third,
    Were axioms to him, who'd never heard

Of any world where promises were kept,
Or one could weep because another wept.[6]

Some fourteen years after the end of World War II, in 1959, the British Broadcasting Company (BBC) in London commissioned the poet Christopher Logue to write a poem for broadcast based on the *Iliad*. Logue chose to write his own version of the struggle between Achilles and the murderous River Scamander in book 21 of the *Iliad*. This was the start (at least the official start) of Logue's lifelong relationship with Homer's poem. Logue worked assiduously on his versions, now called collectively *War Music*. After the first draft for the BBC, Logue kept writing his *Iliad* "five days a week for between three and four hours a day, after which I am done in," he explained in an interview in 1994. "I am a persnickety writer. If I were a film director, I would be a twenty-five-take man, driving the actors and the crew mad." The madness would be worth it: George Steiner called *War Music* "Homer re-experienced." Henry Miller wrote to Lawrence Durrell in 1962: "Just stumbled on Chris Logue's extraordinary rendition of Book 16 of the *Iliad*. I can't get over it. If only Homer were anywhere near as good."[7]

Logue died in 2011 at the age of eighty-five, his great work unfinished. He spoke of *War Music* as "an account of Homer's *Iliad*": "When talking about *War Music* or *Kings* [another section] to myself, I call them my 'Homer poems.' But in public I call them 'an account,' a word I chose because it has a neutral, police-file air to it." *War Music* has also been called "an adaptation," "a translation," "a rendering," "a reading," "a rewriting." It is all those things, but mainly it is a poetic masterpiece in its own right. At first, Logue met the BBC's proposal with much doubt, but at last he consented to it, and the earliest effort, after the broadcast, was published in *Encounter* magazine later that year. "When all is said and done," Logue said, "my Homer poem remains easily identifiable as a work dependent on the *Iliad*. There is no deception. How can there be? As Virgil said, it is easier to rob Hercules of his club than Homer of a single line. But I think I know how to make the *Iliad*'s voices come alive and how to keep the action on the move. It is a legitimate hope, though it may be in vain."

Among the papers Logue left behind, his editor Christopher Reid found a note, typed and pasted onto a page outlining the hopeful plan for further sections of the poem. It read: "At the end of Book 18, Homer describes the creation in Heaven of a new shield.... The new shield's face is covered with designs that show the world as Homer knew it. This passage will be extended. The pictures on the shield will reflect our world." Logue's wish to be a film director had not gone away.

Our world, Logue's world, is a world of images. Ancient Greece was certainly a world of images as well, but the images were constrained to the decoration of palaces and temples and everyday objects, and were not part of the commercial and political vocabulary of today that takes its grammar and language from advertising. Few images survive from before the fifth century BCE until around the time of the Peloponnesian War (431–404 BCE), but even after that time, Greek society was not permeated by an all-present iconography as it is today.[8] The Greeks used their own eyes to see. Today, photography, film, and video have replaced our direct visual apprehension of the world, and our experience is to a great extent mediated or taken over by the eye of the camera. The pictures of Achilles' shield correspond to the iconographic possibilities of Homer's time; Logue decided to extend the range of such depictions not only thematically (as he did in the published version of *War Music* in which he refers to wars of the nineteenth and twentieth centuries, to rockets launched from Cape Canaveral, to contemporary colloquialisms, etc.) but stylistically (the cinematic medium apparent throughout the poem).

Conscious of the importance of Homer's depicting the world on Achilles' shield, Logue used film techniques throughout his poem to do the same: montages, wide shots, flashbacks, and close-ups, so the reader is made to witness the action as if on a screen, the time of the narrative dependent on Logue's camera and not on the flicking of pages. "Picture the east Aegean sea by night," is the first line of *War Music*. "Now look along the beach . . ." The reader then follows the scene as Logue swivels his camera from a fixed position, in a panning motion similar to that of an audience turning their heads to accompany the lens's movement. Next, a flashback, and we are made to see what has taken place earlier: "And we move ten days back."[9]

Homer's extended metaphors also become cinematic: "See sheep in Spain: the royal flock / Taking five days to pass you as they wind / White from their winter pasture." And then: "Muter than these / But with as irresistible a flow / The army left its lines." Or this Terrence Malik-like patchwork of seemingly disconnected takes:

> Consider planes at touchdown—how they poise;
> Or palms beneath a numbered hurricane;
> Or birds wheeled sideways over windswept heights;
> Or burly salmon challenging a weir;
> Right-angled, dreamy fliers, as they ride
> The instep of a dying wave, or trace
> Diagonals on snowdrops.
>
> Quick cuts like these may give
> Some definition to the mind's wild eye
> That follow-spots Achilles' sacred pair.

The ear must accompany the eye:

> The noise they make while fighting is so loud
> That what you see is like a silent film.[10]

"Poetry is not a silent art," Logue said. "The poem must perform, unaided, in its reader's head." Which reflects back to Pope, who, perhaps thinking of his own *Iliad*, wrote that a poem must be "Something whose truth convinced at sight we find,/That gives us back the image of our mind."[11]

CHAPTER 21

The Never-Ending War

Rumsfeld: I liked what you said earlier, sir. A war on terror. That's
    good. That's vague.
Cheney: It's good.
Rumsfeld: That way we can do anything.
—David Hare, *Stuff Happens*, 2006

If, as Calvino suggests, there exists a story that is the *Odyssey*'s
implicit prelude, then the *Iliad* too may suggest such a primordial narrative: the tacit and archetypal story of war. In September
2004, over the course of three evenings, almost three thousand
people filled the largest theater space in the Rome Auditorium to
listen to a dramatized reading of the *Iliad* which the Italian novelist Alessandro Baricco had published the previous year. Baricco,
author of the best-selling novel *Silk,* lent to the various characters
of Homer's poem a stage and a voice to tell the Siege of Troy. In a
postscript to the published text, Baricco insisted that these were
not ordinary times in which to read the *Iliad* but, as so often,
times of war, large and small, which bring in their wake the whole
warrior array, from murder and torture to proclamations of good
intent and acts of heroism. In these times of war (the war in Iraq
had been launched a year earlier), said Baricco, to read the *Iliad* in
public is a trifle, but not just any trifle. "To say it clearly, I mean
that the *Iliad* is a story of war, without care and without measure.
It was composed in praise of a warring humanity, and it did it in

such a memorable way that it should last throughout eternity and reach the last descendant of our last descendants, still singing the solemn beauty and the irredeemable emotion that war once was and always will be. In school, perhaps, the story is told differently. But at its heart lies this: the *Iliad* is a monument to war."[1]

Baricco gives several reasons for his definition. First, the compassion with which Homer has transmitted the arguments of the defeated. In a story written from the point of view of the victors, Homer reminds us that what remains most vivid, above all, is the humanity of the Trojans: Priam, Hector, Paris, even minor characters such as Pandarus (killed by Diomedes) and Sarpedon (killed by Patroclus). The Greek soldiers are the barbarous invaders who will raid the city and go home with the loot; the Trojans are the civilized city dwellers with palaces and well-kept roads. And the reasonable voices we hear are not from the Greek soldiers or the men of Troy but from the women: Andromache, Helen, Hecuba. Isn't it astonishing, asks Baricco, that in a male warrior society such as that of the Greeks, Homer decided to preserve so strongly the voices of women and their desire for peace? Baricco points out that the women are Scheherazades: they know that as long as they continue to speak, war does not take place. Even the men must realize that Achilles delays his entry in the war by staying with the women, and that all the time they are arguing about how to fight, they are not fighting. When Achilles and the other men finally enter into battle, they do so blindly, fanatically devoted to their duty. But before that happens comes the long and slow time of women. "Words," says Baricco, "are a weapon with which they manage to freeze the war."[2]

There is one minor character in the *Iliad* who appears early on, using, as do Baricco's women, words as weapons, furiously disparaging the war, and then disappearing forever. His name is Thersites, "the ugliest man who ever came to Troy./Bandy-legged he was, with one foot clubbed,/both shoulders humped together, curving over/his caved-in chest, and bobbing above them/his skull warped to a point,/sprouting clumps of scraggly, woolly hair." Thersites berates the kings and their armies, especially Agamemnon and Achilles.

> Still moaning and groaning, mighty Atrides—why now?
> What are you panting after now? Your shelters packed
> with the lion's share of bronze, plenty of women too,
> crowding your lodges. Best of the lot, the beauties
> we hand you first, whenever we take some stronghold.
> Or still more gold you're wanting? More ransom a son
> of the stallion-breaking Trojans might just fetch from Troy?—
> though I or another hero drags him back in chains . . .
> Or a young woman, is it?—to spread and couple,
> to bed down for yourself apart from all the troops?
> How shameful for you, the high and mighty commander,
> to lead the sons of Achaea into bloody slaughter!
> *Sons?* No, my soft friends, wretched excuses—
> women, not men of Achaea! Home we go in our ships!
> Abandon him here in Troy to wallow in all his prizes—
> he'll see if the likes of us have propped him up or not.
> Look—now it's Achilles, a greater man he disgraces,
> seizes and keeps his prize, tears her away himself.
> But no gall in Achilles. Achilles lets it go.
> If not, Atrides, that outrage would have been your last!

Odysseus doesn't let him continue and threatens to grab him, strip him, and whip him, howling, naked, back to the ships. With that, he cracks his scepter over Thersites' back and shoulders, making a bloody welt, and leaving the deformed creature "stunned with pain,/blinking like some idiot."[3]

The Polish poet Zbigniew Herbert, puzzled by the appearance of such a character in a poem where nothing can be considered trivial, wondered whether Thersites was a vociferous representative of one of the conquered people, perhaps a Minoan prince stripped of his power by the Greeks.[4] In any case, here is a voice opposing the war, denouncing the looting and the greed, and questioning the slaughter. (Luiz de Camões has a similar figure oppose the departure of Vasco da Gama's expedition of conquest in *Os Lusíadas,* an anonymous dissenter known in Portuguese literature as "o Velho de Restelo," "The Old Man of Restelo.")[5]

Reading through the *Iliad,* Baricco says that it occurred to him that our infatuation with the beauty of war has not waned: if war is hell, however atrocious this might sound, it is a beautiful hell. War in our time, from international conflicts to inner-city gang wars, though cursed and abominated, is far from being considered an absolute evil. Adam Nicolson, in his enlightening book *The Mighty Dead,* convincingly compares the ethics of Homer's warriors to the street gangs of the twenty-first century. "When the law is no good," Nicolson writes, "the only justice that makes sense is retaliatory, and that is the governing ethic of the Greeks in the *Iliad.* It is the dark heart of the gang on the beach, where *personal affronts attack identity,* where *counterstrikes tend to be excessive,* where *minor slights are interpreted as major blows to character,* where warriors *rely on the honor that accrues to those who demonstrate prowess in disputes,* where *honor is accumulated much like real capital and bringing someone down for what he did to you raises your worth in the eyes of your peers,* where *intolerance earns respect* and *strength is protective.* Every one of those phrases in italics," says Nicolson, "is used by Jacobs and Wright to describe life in the murderous slums of St. Louis, Missouri; every one also describes the world of the *Iliad.*"[6]

Carlos Fuentes, the great Mexican novelist, who died in 2012, left an unfinished novel, *Achilles; or, The Guerrillero and the Assassin,* published posthumously by his widow, Silvia Lemus. In Fuentes' archives, Lemus found a paper dated 2003 that described three novels he wanted to write. He managed to write only two before his death, *Diana; or, The Solitary Huntress* and *Achilles*. In his notes, Fuentes explains that the event that led him to write *Achilles* was the murder of Carlos Pizarro Leongómez, a charismatic guerrilla leader who gave up the armed fight and presented himself as a candidate for the presidency of Colombia, before being murdered by a *sicario* (hired killer) on board an Avianca flight in 1990. The press described Pizarro as "the handsomest dead guerrillero since Che Guevara."[7] Fuentes imagined Pizarro as Achilles and other characters in the roles of Diomedes and Castor. The theft of Athena's sacred statue becomes in Fuentes's novel the theft of the sword of Simón Bolívar by the guerrilleros. The violence of the guerrilla war was for Fuentes foreshadowed in the *Iliad*.

This gang-like aspect of the heroic wars that Homer captures so vividly lies in the gory details of brutality and victimhood, not in an all-seeing authorial eye. Homer places us in the middle of the battlefield, but the picture is a kaleidoscopic image made up of endless moving parts. Centuries later, this piecemeal procedure would be employed by Stendhal, who has his hero, Fabrice, witness the Battle of Waterloo from an inside corner of the field, the horrible point of view of a witness of the bloody details: "What seemed horrible to him was a horse, all bloody, struggling on the plowed earth, with its feet in its own entrails; it wanted to follow the others: the blood flowed in the mud. . . . A very ugly spectacle awaited the new soldier there; a cavalry soldier, a handsome young man five feet ten inches tall, was having his leg cut off at the thigh. Fabrice closed his eyes and drank four glasses of brandy in quick succession." Witnessing these horrors, Fabrice comes to realize that he is finally a true soldier. "Ah! The fire of the battle at last! he said to himself. I've seen the fire! he repeated with satisfaction. I'm a true military man at last."[8]

Stendhal's relationship with Homer began early on, when he was only eighteen years old. "This morning, reading the end of the

Odyssey," he wrote in his journal, "it occurred to me that Penelope would be a superb subject for a tragedy."[9] He then sketched out a *cento,* a poem-collage made from lines of other poems; in Stendhal's case, passages from Homer translated into French verse. Later, and more importantly, the older Stendhal learned from Homer how to depict war in all its teeming complexity by focusing on particular snippets.

Other writers followed in Stendhal's Homeric footsteps. Tolstoy learned the technique from Stendhal and employed it in chapter 19 of *War and Peace* to portray the confusion of the Battle of Borodino, but he avoided depicting the battle through the eyes of a classic heroic figure. "The ancients have left us model heroic poems, in which the heroes furnish the whole interest of the story," Tolstoy wrote, "and we are still unable to accustom ourselves to the fact that for our epoch histories of that kind are meaningless."[10] Tolstoy had read the *Iliad* as a boy on his family estate, in the Russian translation by Nikolay Gnedich, which remains unchallenged even today, and in his mid-twenties he returned to the poem with enthusiasm. In 1870, Tolstoy wrote to his wife that he intended to learn Greek in order to read Homer in the original. "Without false modesty," he would later say of his *War and Peace,* "it is like the *Iliad.*"[11]

Homer was read in Russia since at least the Byzantine era, and Byzantine hagiographies included brief quotations of Homer. By the end of the sixteenth century, the frescoes in the cathedrals of the Kremlin featured, among the Christian saints, an image of Homer as forerunner of the biblical prophets.[12] Dostoyevsky approved. "Homer," wrote the author of *Crime and Punishment,* "can find his parallel only in Christ. . . . In the *Iliad* Homer presented all the ancient world with an organization for both its spiritual and earthly life with absolutely the same force as Christ was to exercise regarding the new."[13] The leaders of the October Revolution agreed with Dostoyevsky, and in order to wipe out this outmoded relic of a deposed world, in 1921 they closed down all university departments of classical philology.[14]

In the twentieth century, writing about the Vietnam War, Tim O'Brien listed the terms that define the complex paradox of war itself. "War is hell, but that's not the half of it, because war is also mystery and terror and adventure and courage and discovery and holiness and pity and despair and lying and love."[15]

We must accept that war is also love, and our only escape from its malevolent attraction (and this is Baricco's moving proposal) is to create an alternative beauty that may compete with our longing for war, something built day after day by thousands and thousands of common people. If we do this, says Baricco, we will succeed in keeping Achilles away from the homicidal fighting: not through fear or horror, but by tempting him with a different kind of beauty, more dazzling than the one that attracts him now, and infinitely less violent. This, then, is the *Iliad*'s necessary prelude.

Baricco's hopeful argument has a long and venerable opposition, dating back almost to the time of Homer himself. For Heraclitus, war was not an undesirable attraction but the combatant energy that held the world together, and he reproached Homer for not lending the warring impulse sufficient encouragement. "Homer should be turned out of the literary canon and whipped. He was wrong in saying: 'Would that strife might perish from among gods and men!' He did not see that he was praying for the destruction of the universe, for, if his prayer were heard, all things would pass away." Furthermore, Heraclitus argued, "We must know that war is what is common to all beings, and that it is driven by justice; therefore, everything is born from and made necessary through discord."[16]

Dante considered this vigorous notion from a different point of view. Since the goal of law is the common good, Dante reasoned, and this cannot be obtained through injustice, any war undertaken "for the common good" must be just. In Dante's eyes,

Rome's conquest of the world was just, since it must have been effected "not through violence but through law."[17] In our day, those who speak of "necessary losses" and "collateral damage" follow the same argument.

Baricco lays his finger on a terrible paradox. We know that the murderous violence of war is abominable, and yet something in us loves the spectacle. Homer's description of the putting to death of the goatherd Melanthius forces the reader to see every prurient detail:

> They hauled him out through the doorway, into the court,
> lopped his nose and ears with a ruthless knife,
> tore his genitals out for the dogs to eat raw
> and in manic fury hacked off hands and feet.

And when Odysseus and Telemachus attack the treacherous suitors, Homer compares the vengeful king and his son to eagles swooping on small birds that cringe under the clouds:

> The eagles plunge in fury, rip their lives out—hopeless,
> never a chance of flight or rescue—and people love the sport.[18]

"People love the sport." Writing in 1939 on the notion of force in the *Iliad,* Simone Weil argued that the prevailing feeling throughout the poem is one of bitterness, "the only justifiable bitterness, for it springs from the subjections of the human spirit to force, that is, in the last analysis, to matter. This subjection is the common lot, although each spirit will bear it differently, in proportion to its own virtue. No one in the *Iliad* is spared by it, as no one on earth is. No one who succumbs to it is by virtue of this fact regarded with contempt. Whoever, within his own soul and in human relations, escapes the domination of force, is loved but loved sorrowfully, because of the threat of destruction that constantly hangs over him." Only someone who has suffered through war, injustice, misfortune, someone who has learned how far "the domination of force" extends "and knows how not to respect it, is capable," according to Weil, "of love and justice."[19] Perhaps this is what Dante had in mind.

To educate soldiers to the paradox of war, in the first year of the Second World War the poet and critic Herbert Read compiled an anthology, *The Knapsack,* small enough to be packed into a kit. Three extracts from Chapman's Homer begin his selection: the invocation to Ares from his translation of *The Battle of the Frogs and Mice,* Agamemnon taking up arms in book 11 of the *Iliad,* and the forging of Achilles' shield in book 18. Read explained that he was guided in his choice by both a wish to avoid the "sustained tone of moral seriousness" and a "certain abstractness" in the idealism of other war anthologies, as well as by a desire to show "the dialectic of life, the contradictions on which we have to meditate if we are to construct a workable philosophy." "In war," Read argued, "and in the daily struggle of everyday life, it is a workable philosophy that each man has to construct for himself if he is to preserve a serene mind." The wish for a "serene mind" occurs in the invocation to Ares in the *Battle of the Frogs and Mice.* In 1982, Charles Simic wrote "My Weariness of Epic Proportions," a poem that gave voice to that wish:

I like it when
Achilles
Gets killed
And even his buddy Patroclus—
And that hothead Hector—
And the whole Greek and Trojan
Jeunesse dorée
Are more or less
Expertly slaughtered

So there's finally
Peace and quiet
(The gods having momentarily
Shut up)
One can hear
A bird sing
And a daughter ask her mother
Whether she can go to the well
And of course she can
By that lovely little path
That winds through
The olive orchard.[20]

On one hand, we cannot deny the benevolent ideals that sometimes lead to war, the heroism and altruism with which it is sometimes fought, and the freedom from oppression that is sometimes its consequence. With the excuse of best intentions, Homer lovingly describes the sword piercing the flesh, the spurting blood, the broken teeth, the marrow oozing from the severed bones, and Ajax speaks of "the joy of war" and Paris strides into battle "exultant, laughing aloud." On the other, the slaughter, the destruction, the suffering of every kind brought on by war cannot be defended and, doubtless, Homer loathed war. "Scourge of cities," "lying, two-faced," he calls the war god Ares. And Zeus himself speaks of "the horrid works of war." Pity and mourning, and a plea for compassion, are never far from the battlefield. It is not by chance that supplications (first of the priest of Apollo, Chryses, for his daughter taken by Agamemnon, and last of King Priam for the body of his son Hector) begin and end the *Iliad*.[21]

The extraordinary power of the *Iliad* comes from the fact that it holds the tension between these two truths. Émile Zola, writing from the perspective of nineteenth-century realism, refused Homer any such subtlety. "In his books, the heroes are nothing but gang bosses. There, women are raped, people are duped, they insult one another for months, they cut one another's throats, they drag around the corpses of their enemies. Read the novels of Fenimore Cooper about the Indians, and you'll see the similarities."[22] Zola was mistaken: Homer is never merely descriptive and certainly never commonplace. It is easy for a modern reader to confuse the use of conventional epithets with conventional descriptions, but the fact that the epithets themselves are fixed by convention does not mean that they are synonymous: Homer knew sixty-odd ways to say "So-and-So died" and they are all different.

War, Homer explicitly tells us, has its place in the universe, and he goes on to show us, particularly in the *Iliad* but also the *Odyssey,* how fully he understood our ambiguous relationship to violence, our desire for it and our hatred of it, the beauty we ascribe to it and the horror it makes us feel, so that when faced with it we are forced to look both ways. Two examples from the *Iliad* will illustrate the point.

Book 6 begins with the Greek and Trojan forces battling on the plain of Troy, between the rivers Simois and Xanthus. One of the Trojans called Adrestus (there are three of that name) is caught alive by Menelaus after his horses have bolted and he is hurled to earth from his chariot. Menelaus rises over him, "his spear's long shadow looming," and Adrestus hugs his captor's knees and begs Menelaus to spare him in return for a rich ransom. Adrestus's pleas move the king, but just as he is about to hand Adrestus back to an aide to be taken as prisoner to the ships, Agamemnon appears and chides him for his weakness. Menelaus, Helen's husband, we must remember, is the injured party; Agamemnon, though supreme commander of the Greek army, is only Menelaus's brother. And Agamemnon says:

> Why such concern for enemies? I suppose you got
> such tender loving care at home from the Trojans.

Ah would to god not one of them could escape
his sudden plunging death beneath our hands!
No baby boy still in his mother's belly,
not even he escape—all Ilium blotted out,
no tears for their lives, no markers for their graves!

Goaded by his brother, Menelaus shoves Adrestus with his fist,
and Agamemnon stabs the fallen man "in the flank/and back."
Adrestus falls down dead, face up, and Agamemnon "dug a heel
in his heaving chest/and wrenched the ash spear out."[23]

A second example. Almost at the end of the *Iliad,* the angry
Achilles pursues Hector outside the walls of Troy. Both are soldiers, both have blood on their hands, both have loved ones who
have been killed, both believe that their cause is just. One is
Greek, the other Trojan, but at this point their allegiances hardly
matter. Now they are two men intent on killing one another. They
run past the city walls and past the double springs of the river
Scamander. And at this point, Homer breaks off his description
of the fighting and pauses to remind us of what war obliterates:

And here, close to the springs, lie washing-pools
scooped out in the hollow rocks and broad and smooth
where the wives of Troy and all their lovely daughters
would wash their glistening robes in the old days,
the days of peace before the sons of Achaea came . . .
Past these they raced.[24]

The scene of war, says Homer, is never only that of war: it is
never only that of men acting out in the present the events of the
day. It is always the scene of the past as well, a display of what
men secretly once were, revealed now in their ultimate moments.
Confronting them with the imminence of violent death, war also
confronts them with the memory of days of peace, of the happiness

that life can, and should, grant us. War is both things: the experience of an awful present and the ghost of a beloved past.

War is also the approved experience of unthinkable violence and the allowance for unrestrained slaughter, for war is sweeter (*glukus*, says Homer, "sugary-sweet") than any return home.

> Each Achaean's heart [was]
> mad for war and struggle. Now, suddenly,
> battle thrilled them more than the journey home,
> than sailing hollow ships to their dear native land.[25]

After Hector has killed Patroclus, and his death has plunged Achilles into a state of crazed despair, the ghost of Patroclus appears to Achilles and, with the knowledge of the future that comes to the dead, tells his friend that he too will soon die. He asks that their ashes might be mingled in a single urn so they can be together in death as they were in life.

> Never bury my bones apart from yours, Achilles,
> let them lie together . . .
> just as we grew up together in your house.[26]

Achilles, mad with sorrow, tries to embrace the ghost of his friend, but his arms pass through the phantom body. (Virgil and Dante will reproduce this scene with their own heroes encountering beloved unembraceable dead.) With a shriek, the ghost of Patroclus vanishes, and Achilles wakes up to daylight. Later, by Patroclus's funeral pyre, Achilles cuts off a lock of his hair, which he had planned to offer to the river Spercheios on his return home, and places it in the hand of his dead friend. Then, in the presence of his army, Achilles performs the bloody sacrifice that entails the slaughter of sheep and cattle, of Patroclus's favorite horses, of two of his beloved dogs, and of twelve Trojan boys whom he captured.

He set two-handled jars of honey and oil beside him,
leaned them against the bier—and then with wild zeal
slung the bodies of four massive stallions onto the pyre
and gave a wrenching groan. And the dead lord Patroclus
had fed nine dogs at table—he slit the throats of two,
threw them onto the pyre and then a dozen brave sons
of the proud Trojans he hacked to pieces with his bronze . . .[27]

However, Homer does not leave things here. After the gods have prevented Achilles from desecrating Hector's body, Achilles meets Priam in the scene previously described, the old man seeing his son's youth in the person of his murderer, Achilles seeing his aged father in the father of his enemy. The mutual recognition bears nobility. Agreeing to let old Priam have the remains of Hector, Achilles instructs the serving women first to "bathe and anoint the body" so that the father will not see the corpse of his son in a shameful state. Then Achilles lifts Hector up in his own arms and lays him down on a bier, and as he does this he calls to his beloved Patroclus, whose murder he sought to avenge by the killing of Hector, and addresses the ghost of his friend:

Feel no anger at me, Patroclus, if you learn—
even there in the House of Death—I let his father
have Prince Hector back. He gave me worthy ransom
and you shall have your share from me, as always,
your fitting, lordly share.[28]

Priam's supplication to Achilles to allow him to bury the body of his son fulfills not just a traditional obligation or a sentimental act of mourning. It takes place so that a circle might be closed, and so that those who have suffered might be comforted. In the Underworld, when Odysseus meets the unfortunate Elpenor, who was killed just before they left Circe's island and left unburied, his ghost addresses its old captain with these words:

> My lord, remember me, I beg you! Don't sail off
> and desert me, left behind unwept, unburied, don't,
> or my curse may draw god's fury on your head.
> No, burn me in full armor, all my harness,
> heap my mound by the churning gray surf—
> a man whose luck ran out—
> so even men to come will learn my story.[29]

This is, in essence, what allows war to acquire a redemptory sense: the knowledge that the dead can help us remember injustice. From Priam's plea to have the body of his son restored and Elpenor's to have his body cremated, to today's demands that war graves be opened in Latin America, Bosnia, Spain, and dozens of other places, our healthy impulse is to restore to the dead their rightful role as memorials in their own names. In this way, as Homer knew, we can simultaneously both loudly abominate their loss and lovingly honor their sacrifice.

Shortly before his death in 1955, the American poet Wallace Stevens wrote this Homeric definition of war:

> War has no haunt except the heart,
> Which envy haunts, and hate, and fear,
> And malice, and ambition, near
>
> The haunt of love.[30]

CHAPTER 22

Everyman

Solomon saith: "There is no new thing upon the earth. So
that as Plato had an imagination, that all knowledge was but
remembrance, so Solomon giveth his sentence, that all novelty is
but oblivion."

—Francis Bacon, *Essays* (used as epigraph to Jorge Luis Borges,
"The Immortal")

In 1949, in Buenos Aires, Jorge Luis Borges published a short story
called "The Immortal," later included in the volume *The Aleph*,
and inspired perhaps by his reading of Rudyard Kipling's *Kim* and
H. G. Wells's *The Country of the Blind*. Borges considered "The
Immortal" his homage to Homer.

The story begins in London. In the early days of June 1929,
the Princess of Lucinge receives at her London address the six
volumes of the first edition of Pope's *Iliad*, from the antiquarian
bookseller Joseph Cartaphilus of Smyrna. The man, she says, had
singularly vague features and spoke several languages badly. Later
she heard that he had died at sea, on board the *Zeus*, and that he
had been buried on the island of Ios. In the *Iliad*'s last volume she
finds a manuscript written in a Latinized English.[1]

The manuscript tells the story of a Roman tribune stationed
in Thebes who one sleepless night witnesses the arrival of a rider
coming from the East. The man, bloodied and exhausted, falls
from his horse and asks the name of the city's river; the tribune
tells him it is called the Egypt. The rider explains that the river

for which he searches is another, a secret river at the edge of the world that purifies men of death, and on whose farthest shore rises the City of the Immortals. The man dies, and the tribune is filled with the desire to find the city. At the head of two hundred men, he sets out in search of it. The lands they cross are wild and strange; the men mutiny; the tribune escapes after being shot with an arrow. Feverish, he wanders in the desert; when he wakes, he finds himself, hands tied, in a stone niche carved out of the slope of a mountain. At the foot of the mountain is a brackish stream; beyond it rises the City of the Immortals. There are other niches on the slope and in the valley, as well as shallow holes in the sand; from these he sees gray naked men emerge into the sunlight. The tribune guesses that these are the Troglodytes, a tribe that lacks speech and eats serpents. Devoured by thirst, the tribune throws himself down the slope and drinks from the stream. Before losing consciousness, he inexplicably repeats a few Greek words:

> And men who lived in Zelea under the foot of Ida,
> a wealthy clan that drank the Aesepus' dark waters.[2]

After many days and nights he manages to cut his bonds and shamefully begs or steals his first ration of serpent's meat. The desire to enter the City of the Immortals continues to haunt him. One day, he decides to escape the Troglodytes at the time when most of them leave their holes to look toward the West, without even noticing the sunset. At midnight he reaches the city and sees with relief ("because man so abominates novelty and the desert") that one of the Troglodytes has followed him.

But the City of the Immortals, built on a sort of plateau, shows no points of entrance, no stairs or gates. The fierce sun forces him to take refuge in a cave. Here he finds a well and a flight of steps that leads into the lower darkness; the tribune descends and loses himself in a labyrinth of identical galleries and chambers. After many attempts, he emerges into the city itself and sees, looming ahead, a palace of many shapes and heights. He feels that this building is older than man, older than the earth itself, and that its age suits the labors of immortal craftsmen. He thinks, "This palace was built by the gods." Then he explores it, and corrects himself: "The gods who built this are dead." He notices its peculiarities and pronounces, "The gods who built this were mad." The tribune realizes that the city is not a labyrinth like the one he was lost in underground. "A labyrinth is a house built to confuse men; its architecture, rich in symmetries, is subject to this purpose." The architecture of the palace lacks any purpose whatsoever: corridors lead nowhere, windows are unreachable, doors lead to wells, staircases run upside down. Horrified, he escapes. When he comes out of the cave, he finds the Troglodyte lying at the entrance, tracing incomprehensible signs in the sand. The tribune feels that the creature has been waiting for him; that night, on the way back to the Troglodyte's village, he decides to teach him a few words. The Troglodyte reminds him of the dog Argos in the *Odyssey*; he decides to give him the dog's name. Day after day, the tribune attempts to teach Argos to speak. First months, then years pass, unsuccessfully. At last, one evening, it starts to rain. The entire tribe, in ecstasy, greets the falling water. The tribune calls to Argos, who has begun to whimper. Suddenly, as if discovering something lost and forgotten long ago, the Troglodyte utters a few words: "Argos, dog of Ulysses." And then, still not looking at the tribune, he quotes a line by Homer, "a dog on piles of dung from mules and cattle." The tribune asks him what he knows of the *Odyssey*. Because the Troglodyte's Greek is poor, he must repeat the question. "Very little," the Troglodyte answers. "Less than the poorest bard. Eleven hundred years must have gone by since I composed it."

That night the truth is revealed to him. The Troglodytes are the Immortals, the brackish stream the river sought by the rider.

As to the famous city, the Immortals had destroyed it nine centuries ago, and from its ruins they had built the senseless city the tribune had seen "as a parody or an inversion, and also as a temple to the irrational gods who govern the world and of whom we know nothing, except that they are not like men." That was the last physical endeavor of the Immortals. Judging all enterprise fruitless, they decided to live in thought only, in pure speculation. After building the city, they forgot about it and went to dwell in the caves.

Homer tells the tribune the story of his old age, and of the voyage he undertook, like that of Ulysses, to discover the land of men who ignore the sea and don't eat salt. He lived for a century in the City of the Immortals, and when they tore it down he advised them to build the other one, as he had sung *The Battle of the Frogs and Mice* after singing the Trojan War. "It was like a god creating first the cosmos and afterward chaos."

The tribune realizes that drinking from the stream has made him immortal too, and sadly reflects that being immortal is a banal thing: with the exception of man, every creature enjoys immortality because it ignores death. The divine, terrible, incomprehensible thing is to know that you are immortal. The slightest thought is the beginning or the end of an invisible design; an evil act may be performed so that in the future good may come of it. Given an infinite time, every action is just, but also indifferent: there are no moral or intellectual merits. Homer composed the *Odyssey*; after an endless number of years, the impossibility would be not to compose, even once, the *Odyssey*. Lewis Carroll summed up this dizzying notion in the second volume of *Sylvie and Bruno*. "The day must come," he wrote, "when every possible *book* will be written. For the number of *words* is finite." And he added, "Instead of saying '*what* book shall I write?' an author will ask himself '*which* book shall I write?'"[3] For the Immortals, therefore, everything must take place again, nothing can happen only once, nothing is precarious. The tribune and Homer part company at the gates of Tangiers: they do not say farewell.

The tribune recalls some of his further adventures: taking part in the Battle of Stamford Bridge in 1066 (although he cannot remember on which side he fought); working as a scribe in Bulaq who copied out the story of Sindbad; playing chess in a Samarkand prison; and studying astrology in Bikaner and Bohemia. In 1714, in Aberdeen, he subscribed to Pope's translation of the *Iliad*, which he read with great delight; in 1729 he discussed the poem with a professor of rhetoric called Giambattista (probably Giambattista Vico). "Borges' conception," wrote the Italian essayist Claudio Magris, "revolves around a circular obsession, around the universal identity of all things, around the enumeration that constantly accumulates and multiplies in order to discover there the presence of the unique, and of what is always the same, in order to proclaim the indifference of individual life and the vanity of all judgment."[4]

Borges ends the story by noting that on October 4, 1921, the ship taking the tribune to Bombay stopped on the Eritrean coast; on the outskirts of the port he tasted the water from a clear stream: as he rose, a thorn pierced the back of his hand. The pain made him realize that once again he was mortal. That night he slept until dawn.

The story offers two conclusions. The second concerns a commentary on the published manuscript (by a certain Dr. Cordovero) attempting to prove that the text is apocryphal and attributing it to the pen of the antiquarian Joseph Cartaphilus; a postscript, dated 1950, finds such allegations inadmissible. The first conclusion, by the tribune himself, addresses the uncanny tone of the narrative. The events he has described, he says, seem fantastic because they belong, in fact, to two different men. A Roman tribune would not refer, as he does in the beginning, to the Theban river as Egypt. Homer, however, would: in the *Odyssey*, he invariably says "Egypt" instead of "Nile." The words the tribune utters after drinking the immortal waters belong to the *Iliad*, book 2, lines 935–36. The particular mention of the transcription of Sindbad's adventures and of the reading of Pope's *Iliad* are moving details, but not if said by a Roman tribune; spoken by Homer, however, how extraordinary to discover that he has copied out the story of another Ulysses and that he has read, in a barbarian tongue, his own *Iliad*! When the end approaches, the narrator says, no images remain in his mind, only words, and it is not surprising that time should have mingled the words which represented one man with those uttered by another. The manuscript concludes with this confession: "I have been Homer; soon, I shall be Nobody, like Ulysses; soon, I shall be every man, I shall be dead."

Homer is a cipher. Since he has no proven identity and his books reveal no obvious clues to their composition, he can bear, like his *Iliad* and his *Odyssey*, an infinity of readings. Homer may be what we mean by the vast word *antiquity*—a vicious circle that assumes the definition of what it seeks to define—or what we mean by the word *poetry,* or by *humanity.* Homer may stand for that obscure early time of our common histories of which we have a few magnificent artifacts but no true knowledge of how those artifacts were understood or felt. It is impossible to guess what sense Homer and his contemporaries might have had of the notion of a shared immortality, of every human being living out a segment of an endless human life in which, given enough time, as Borges suggests, each one will do and feel what everyone else has done or felt.

The translator Robert Fitzgerald, asked why we should care about an old work in a "dead language that no one reads," optimistically answered: "I love the future myself and expect everything of it: better artists than Homer, better works of art than the *Odyssey.* The prospect of looking back at our planet from the moon seems to me to promise a marvelous enlargement of our views. But let us hold fast to what is good, hoping that if we do anything as good those who come after us will pay us the same compliment."[5]

The chronology we have invented for ourselves prompts us to imagine that our world and our own selves evolve in time, and that there is progress of feeling and imagination as there is development of technology and invention. We see ourselves as better than our ancestors, those savages of the Bronze Age who, though they wrought fine cups and bangles and sang beautiful songs, massacred one another in horrible wars, possessed slaves and raped women, ate without forks, and conceived gods who threw thunderbolts. It is difficult for us to imagine that such a long time ago we already had words to name our most bewildering experiences and our deepest and most obscure emotions. The phantom figure we call Homer exists somewhere in the dark distance, like the ruins of a building whose shape and purpose we cannot make out. And yet here and there, in his books, lie perhaps the inklings of an answer.

Hector, attempting to explain to Andromache why he must fight, acknowledges however that

> in my heart and soul I also know this well:
> the day will come when sacred Troy must die,
> Priam must die and all his people with him,
> Priam who hurls the strong ash spear.

To which Achilles unwittingly responds:

> One and the same lot for the man who hangs back
> and the man who battles hard. The same honor waits
> for the coward and the brave. They both go down to Death,
> the fighter who shirks, the one who works to exhaustion.[6]

The communality of death, the arbitrary dealings of fate, are notions general enough for us to indulge in the commonplace that they are shared by all humankind and belong to all places and all times. For the reader of Homer, however, at a distance of two and a half millennia, certain details in the poems render them magically singular, distill them into something intimately familiar, make them ours: Athena, knowing that Odysseus has suffered endlessly for ten long years, heartlessly saying to his son that "it's light work for a willing god to save a mortal/even half the world away"; Achilles the warrior cursing war after the death of Patroclus; the monstrous Cyclops tenderly placing each suckling lamb under its dam; the dog Argos dying of heartbreak on seeing his master return after such a long absence; Odysseus and Penelope in bed, telling each other their stories, husband and wife unable to fall asleep till all is told; Andromache glancing back, again and again, at Hector departing for battle; Priam and Achilles eating together and admiring, one the young man's beauty, the other, the old man's nobility.[7] Homer's poems are not only a "compendium of plot devices" told over and over since the dawn of language to our present day, but a shifting mirror of the totality of human experience.[8] How astonishing that, in a language we no longer know precisely how to pronounce, a poet or various poets whose faces and characters we cannot conceive, who lived in a society of whose customs and beliefs we have but a vague idea, described for us our own lives today, with every secret happiness and every hidden sin.

Heraclitus the Grammarian, in commentaries on Homer that we know under the title *Homeric Problems*, notes: "From the very first age of life, the foolishness of infants just beginning to learn is nurtured on the teaching given in [Homer's] school. One might almost say that his poems are our baby clothes, and we nourish our minds by draughts of his milk. He stands at our side as we each grow up and shares our youth as we gradually come to manhood; when we mature, his presence within us is at its prime; and even in old age, we never weary of him. When we stop, we thirst to begin him again. In a word, the only end of Homer for human beings is the end of life itself."[9]

NOTES

INTRODUCTION

1. See Deborah Steiner, "Soundings of the Lyre: Performing Homer in Archaic Greece," in *Performing Homer: The Voyage of Ulysses from Epic to Opera*, ed. Wendy Heller and Eleanora Stoppino (London: Routledge 2020), 3–17: "It is hard to imagine that a composer would create works as complex and tightly structured as the two Homeric poems unless they could be delivered in their entirety, over a series of successive days. Only a period of sanctioned leisure, such as religious festivals afford, would guarantee a public with the necessary time to spare" (5).

2. Friedrich Nietzsche, "Homer and Classical Philology" (Inaugural Address Delivered at Bâle University, 28 of May 1869), trans. J. M. Kennedy, Project Gutenberg, https://www.gutenberg.org/files/18188/18188-h/18188-h.htm.

3. Gustave Flaubert, "Dictionnaire des idées reçues," in Flaubert, *Bouvard et Pécuchet* (Paris: Editions du Point du Jour, 1947), 381.

4. See Marius Kociejowski, *The Serpent Coiled in Naples* (London: Haus Publishing, 2022), 5.

5. See André Gide, *Oscar Wilde: In Memoriam* (Paris: Mercure de France, 1910), 49.

6. Quoted in Isobel Hurst, *Victorian Women Writers and the Classics* (Oxford: Oxford University Press, 2006), 7.

7. Claude Sintes, ed., *Bibliothèque idéale des Odyssées: d'Homère à Fortunat* (Paris: Belles Lettres, 2022), 19.

8. Quoted in Henry Solly, *These Eighty Years; or, The Story of an Unfinished Life*, vol. 2 (London: Simpkin Marshall, 1893), 81.

9. Virginia Woolf, "On Not Knowing Greek," in Woolf, *The Common Reader: First Series* (London: Vintage, 2003), 23.

10. Emanuel Geibel, "Kriegslied," in Geibel, *Werke*, vol. 2 (Stuttgart: Verlag der J. G. Cotta'schen Buchhandlung, 1883), 243; Simone de Beauvoir, *La Femme rompue* (Paris: Gallimard, 1967), 29.

11. *The Iliad of Homer*, trans. T. S. Brandreth, 2 vols. (London: W. Pickering, 1846), 1:126.

12. "Mucho más que libros," *Semana* online, June 4, 2001, Bogotá.

13. Claude Lévi-Strauss, *The Raw and the Cooked*, trans. J. and D. Weightman (New York: Harper and Row, 1969), 12.

14. Homer, *The Iliad*, 24.594–99, 610, 613–20, trans. Robert Fagles (London: Penguin, 1990).

ONE. A LIFE OF HOMER?

1. See J. A. Davidson, "The Homeric Question," in *A Companion to Homer*, ed. Alan Wace and Frank H. Stubbings (London: Macmillan, 1962), 236; Mostafa El-Abbadi, *The Life and Fate of the Ancient Library of Alexandria* (Paris: Unesco, 1990), 54.

2. Herodotus, *The Histories*, 2.117, ed. A. R. Burn (London: Penguin, 1954), 172; Thucydides, *The Peloponnesian War*, 2.41.4, trans. Martin Hammond (Oxford: Oxford World's Classics), 93; for Aeschylus see Mario Telò, "Tastes of Homer: Matro's Gastroaesthetic Tour Through Epic," in *Taste and the Ancient Senses*, ed. Kelli C. Rudolph (London: Routledge, 2017), 73n11.

3. See Froma I. Zeitlin, "Visions and Revisions of Homer," in *Being Greek Under Rome*, ed. Simon Goldhill (Cambridge: Cambridge University Press, 2001), 97.

4. Walter J. Ong, *Orality and Literacy* (London: Routledge, 2002), 140.

5. Herodotus, *The Histories*, 5.58, p. 361; Homer, *The Iliad*, 6.198–99, trans. Robert Fagles (London: Penguin, 1990).

6. On papyrus see Bruce Heiden, "The Placement of Book Divisions in the *Iliad*," *Journal of Hellenic Studies* 118 (1998): 58–81, and Minna Skafte Jensen, "Dividing Homer: When and How Were the *Iliad* and the *Odyssey* Divided into Songs?" in *Symbolae Osloenses* 74, no. 1 (1999), 5–35; on the statue see M. A. Levy, "Inschriften aus Abydos in Aegypten," in Levy, *Phönizische Studien* (Breslau: Schletter, 1870), 14–35; on the division into books see Jean Irigoin, "Homère, l'écriture et le livre," *Europe* no. 865 (2001): 8–18. A contrary argument is given by Bruce Heiden in "The Placement of Book Divisions in the *Iliad*."

7. Thomas Heywood, *The Hierarchy of the Blessed Angells: Their Names, Orders and Offices; The Fall of Lucifer with His Angells* [1635] (New York: Da Capo, 1973), 207; Miguel de Cervantes Saavedra, *El Ingenioso Hidalgo Don Quijote de la Mancha*, book 2, chap. 74 (Madrid: Real Academia Española, 2015), 1335.

8. "Hymn to Delian Apollo," in *The Homeric Hymns*, trans. Jules Cashford (London: Penguin, 2003), 175.

9. [Thomas Blackwell], *An Enquiry into the Life and Writings of Homer*, 2nd ed. (London: J. Oswald, 1736), 112.

10. Herodotus (attrib.), *The Life of Homer*, trans. Kenneth H. R. MacKenzie, in *The Odyssey of Homer*, trans. Theodore Alois Buckley (London: Henry G. Bohn, 1851), xxxi.

11. John Milton, *Paradise Regained*, 4.259, in *Complete Poems and Major Prose*, ed. Marritt Y. Hughes (Indianapolis: Odyssey Press, 1957), 289; Herodotus (attrib.), *Life of Homer*.

12. For issues relating to Heraclitus and the tradition of the riddle and Homer's death, see G. S. Kirk, "The Michigan Alcidamas-Papyrus; Heraclitus Fr. 56D; The Riddle of the Lice," *Classical Quarterly* 44, nos. 3–4 (July–October 1950): 149–67; Pausanias, *Guide to Greece*, 24.3, trans. Peter Levi (London: Penguin, 1979), 57–58; Graf Pasch van Krienen, *Abdruck seiner italienischen Beschreibung des Griechischen Archipelagus mit Ammerkungen und einer Abhandlung uber den Verfasser und seine Auffindung des Grabes Homer's auf Ios* (Halle: G. Schwetschkescher Verlag, 1860), 147–50.

13. Herodotus (attrib.), *Life of Homer*, xxx.

14. On gesture in performance see Marcel Jousse, "Homère gestualisait ses récitations," in *L'Anthropologie du geste* (Paris: Gallimard, 1974), 1:269; see Ralph Rosen, "Aristophanes' *Frogs* and the *Contest of Homer and Hesiod*," *Transactions of the American Philological Society* 134 (2004): 295–322; N. J. Richardson, "The Contest of Homer and Hesiod and Alcidamas' Mouseion," *Classical Quarterly* 31, no. 1 (1981): 1–10; Homer, *The Odyssey*, 8.51–89, 302–410, 552–84; 1.178, trans. Robert Fagles (London: Penguin, 1996).

15. Pausanias, *Guide to Greece*, 1.2.3, pp. 13–14; Homer, *Odyssey*, 8.87; T. E. Lawrence, "Translator's Note," in *The Odyssey of Homer*, trans. T. E. Shaw (Colonel T. E. Lawrence) (Oxford: Oxford University Press, 1956), iii.

16. Albert B. Lord, *The Singer of Tales* (Cambridge: Harvard University Press, 1981), 19–29.

17. Albert B. Lord, *The Singer Resumes the Tale*, ed. Mary Louise Lord (Ithaca, N.Y.: Cornell University Press, 1995), 23.

18. Plato, *Ion*, trans. Lane Cooper, in *The Collected Dialogues of Plato, Including the Letters*, ed. Edith Hamilton and Huntington Cairns (Princeton: Princeton University Press, 1963), 216, 210.

19. Derek Walcott, "Reflections on *Omeros*," cited in Gregson Davis, "The Poetics of Derek Walcott: Intertextual Perspectives," *South Atlantic Quarterly* 96, no. 2 (Spring 1997): 240.

20. See Margalit Finkelberg, "Homer at the Panathenaia: Some Possible Scenarios," in *The Winnowing Oar: New Perspectives in Homeric Studies*, ed. Christos Tsagalis and Andreas Markantonatos (Berlin: De Gruyter, 2017), 29–42; Claude Mossé, *La Grèce archaïque d'Homère à Eschyle* (Paris: Éditions du Seuil, 1984), 145.

21. Thomas De Quincey, "Homer and the Homeridae," in *The Works of Thomas De Quincey*, vol. 13: *Articles from Blackwood's Edinburgh Magazine*

and the Encyclopaedia Britannica, 1841–2, ed. Grevel Lindop and John Whale (London: Pickering and Chatto, 2021), 18; J. G. Riewald, *Beerbohm's Literary Characters* (London: Allen Lane, 1977), 31.

22. See J. M. Foley, *Homer's Traditional Art* (University Park: Penn State University Press, 1999), 51–58.

23. Ismail Kadare, *Dosja H* (Tirana: Nëntori, 1989); *Le dossier H* (Paris: Albin Michel, 1989, rev. 1996); *The File on H*, trans. David Bellos from the French (Edinburgh: Canongate, 2007).

24. Gilbert Murray, *Five Stages of Greek Religion*, 3rd ed. (New York: Doubleday, 1951), 65.

25. Strabo, *Geography*, 1.2.9, trans. H. L. Jones (London: William Heinemann, 1960), 73; N. J. Richardson, "Homeric Professors in the Age of the Sophists," *Proceedings of the Cambridge Philological Society* n.s., no. 21 (1975): 65–81; A. A. Long, "Stoic Reading of Homer," in *Homer's Ancient Readers: The Hermeneutics of Greek Epic's Earliest Exegetes*, ed. Robert Lamberton and John J. Keaney (Princeton: Princeton University Press, 1992), 43; Aristotle, *Metaphysics*, 1.2.6–15, trans. Hugh Tredennik, ed. G. C. Armstrong (London: William Heinemann, 1930); Bernard Le Bovier de Fontenelle, *Dialogues des morts*, in *Oeuvres de Fontenelle*, vol. 2, ed. G. Depping (Paris: Bélin, 1818), 181.

26. Paul Veyne, *Les Grecs ont-ils cru à leurs mythes?* (Paris: Éditions du Seuil, 1992), 55.

27. Quoted in André Laks and Glenn Most, *Early Greek Philosophers*, vol. 3 (Cambridge: Harvard University Press, 2016), 29.

28. Plutarch, "Alcibiades," in *Plutarch's Lives*, vol. 1, the Dryden translation, ed. and rev. Arthur Hugh Clough (New York: Random House, 1992), 262.

TWO. AMONG THE PHILOSOPHERS

1. Plato, *Republic*, 10.595a–b, trans. Paul Shorey, in *The Collected Dialogues of Plato, Including the Letters*, ed. Edith Hamilton and Huntington Cairns (Princeton: Princeton University Press, 1963), 819–20; Aldous Huxley, *Brave New World* (London: Chatto & Windus, 1932), 260.

2. Rachel Posner, "He Wants to Save Classics from Whiteness," *New York Times*, February 2, 2021.

3. Katy Waldman, "Mary Beard Keeps History on the Move," *New Yorker*, May 16, 2021.

4. Plato, *Republic*, 10.600d, p. 825; Plato, *The Lesser Hippias*, 10.370b, trans. Benjamin Jowett, in *The Collected Dialogues of Plato*, 214.

5. Miguel de Cervantes Saavedra, *El Ingenioso Hidalgo Don Quijote de la Mancha*, book 1, chap. 6 (Madrid: Real Academia Española, 2015), 89.

6. Plato, *Republic* 10.607c–d, p. 832; 9.592a–b, p. 819.

7. Aristotle, *Poetics*, 4.1449a9, trans. Samuel Henry Butcher (New York: Walter J. Black, 1943), 17.

8. Robert Lamberton, "Introduction," in *Homer's Ancient Readers: The Hermeneutics of Greek Epic's Earliest Exegetes*, ed. Robert Lamberton and John J. Keaney (Princeton: Princeton University Press, 1992), xii–xiii.

9. Cicero, *On the Orator: Book 3. On Fate. Stoic Paradoxes. Divisions of Oratory* 3.137–38, trans. H. Rackham (Cambridge: Harvard University Press, 1942), 109.

10. Jean-Pierre Vernat, *Mythe et societé en Grèce ancienne* (Paris: François Maspero, 1981), 212; John Milton, *Areopagitica: A Speech of Mr. John Milton* [1644] (Oxford: Clarendon, 1894), 7.

11. See Strabo, *Geography*, 13.1.45, trans. H. L. Jones (London: William Heinemann, 1960), 91.

12. Translation courtesy of Ruth Padel. The tomb is now believed to contain the remains of at least three adults; see Livia Gerson, "Researchers Are Unraveling the Mystery of the Ancient Greek Tomb of 'Nestor's Cup,'" *Smithsonian Magazine*, October 8, 2021, https://www.smithsonianmag.com/smart-news/nestors-cup-tomb-reveals-new-secrets-180978839/.

13. Homer, *The Iliad*, 11.747–53, trans. Robert Fagles (London: Penguin, 1990).

THREE. VIRGIL

1. See J. Irgoin, "Les éditions des poètes à Alexandrie," in *Sciences exactes et sciences appliquées à Alexandrie* (IIIe siècle av. J.-C.–Ier siècle ap. J.-C.), ed. Gilbert Argoud et Jean-Yves Guillaumin (Saint-Étienne: Publ. de l'Université de Saint-Étienne, 1998), 408–10.

2. See Gregory Nagy, "Response: Aristarchean Questions: Gregory Nagy on Richard Janko on Morris and Powell," *Bryn Mawr Classical Review* 7, no. 14 (1998), available at https://bmcr.brynmawr.edu/1998/1998.07.14/.

3. See Tomas Hägg, *The Novel in Antiquity* (Berkeley: University of California Press, 1983), 110.

4. Longinus, *On the Sublime*, 9.13, trans. Stephen Halliwell, W. Hamilton Fyfe, Doreen C. Innes, and W. Rhys Roberts, rev. Donald A. Russell (Cambridge: Harvard University Press, 1995), 195; Porphyry, *Essay on the Cave of the Nymphs*, quoted in Robert Lamberton, "The Neoplatonists and the Spiritualization of Homer," in *Homer's Ancient Readers: The Hermeneutics of Greek Epic's Earliest Exegetes*, ed. Robert Lamberton and John J. Keaney (Princeton: Princeton University Press, 1992), 129; Boethius, *The Consolation of Philosophy*, 1.4, trans. W. V. Cooper (London: Dent, 1902), 16.

5. See Horace, *Epistles* II: 1, "To Augustus," in *Satires. Epistles. The Art of Poetry*, trans. H. Rushton Fairclough (Cambridge: Harvard University Press, 1926), 403; Pliny attributes this remark to his friend Atilius: "To Novius Maximus" [II: 14], in Pliny the Younger, *Letters*, vol. 1: *Books 1–7*, trans. Betty Radice (Cambridge: Harvard University Press, 1969), 125; Horace, *Epistles* II: 1, "To Augustus"; *Epistles* I: 2, "To Lollius Maximus," 263.

6. Quintilian, *The Orator's Education*, vol. 4: *Book 10*, ed. and trans. Donald A. Russell (Cambridge: Harvard University Press, 1970), 303; Homer, *The Iliad*, 2.931–32, trans. Robert Fagles (London: Penguin, 1990).

7. Quoted in Peter Levi, *Virgil: His Life and Times* (London: Duckworth, 1998), 22.

8. See Manuel Sanz Morales, *Mitógrafos griegos* (Madrid: Akal, 2002), 80.

9. Dante, *De Monarchia*, in *Le opere di Dante*, vol. 1, 5:5, ed. Pier Giorgio Ricci (Milan: Mondadori, 1965), 109, citing Aristotle, *Nicomachean Ethics*, 7.1.1145a–21; Virgil, *The Aeneid: A New Verse Translation*, 6.847–53, trans. C. Day Lewis (New York: Oxford University Press, 1952), 116.

10. Hermann Broch, *Der Tod des Vergil* [1945] (Zurich: Rhein Verlag, 1958), 392.

11. Levi, *Virgil: His Life and Times*, 43.

12. Virgil, *Aeneid*, 1:283–84, p. 18; Homer, *Iliad*, 20.210–11; among the early writers were Stesichorus of Sicily in the sixth century BCE and Hellanicus of Lesbos in the fifth century BCE: see Friedrich Solmsen, "Aeneas Founded Rome with Odysseus," *Harvard Studies in Classical Philology* 90 (1986): 93–110; Naevius, "The Punic War or the Song of the Punic War," in *Remains of Old Latin*, vol. 2: *Livius Andronicus. Naevius. Pacuvius. Accius*, trans. E. H. Warmington (Cambridge: Harvard University Press, 1936), 57; Lucretius, *On the Nature of Things*, trans. H. A. J. Munro (New York: Washington Square Press, 1965), v.

13. Lewis Carroll, "What the Tortoise Said to Achilles," *Mind* (April 1895), in *The Complete Works of Lewis Carroll* (London: Nonesuch Press, 1922), 1230; David Malouf, *Ransom* (London: Chatto and Windus, 2009), 5–6.

14. *The Iliads of Homer, Prince of Poets, Never Before in Any Language Truly Translated, Done According to the Greek by George Chapman* (London: George Newnes, 1904), 26; Tickell quoted in *Homer in English*, ed. George Steiner (London: Penguin, 1996), 107; Alexander Pope, *The Iliad and the Odyssey of Homer*, ed. the Revd. H. F. Cary (New York: George Routledge and Sons, 1872), 14; Dunbar quoted in *Homer in English*, 192; *Iliad*, 2 vols., trans. A. T. Murray (1924; Cambridge: Harvard University Press, 2001), 13; *The Iliad: The Story of Achilles*, trans. W. H. D. Rouse (London: Thomas Nelson and Sons, 1938), 1; H. D. F. Kitto, *The Greeks* (London: Penguin, 1951), 45; *The Iliad of Homer*, trans. Richmond Latti-

more (Chicago: University of Chicago Press, 1991), 27; Robert Lowell, *Imitations* (London: Faber and Faber, 1962), xix; Homer, *The Iliad*, trans. Robert Fagles, 77.

15. Juan de Mena, *La Ilíada de Homero*, edición crítica de las *Sumas de la Yliada de Omero* y del original latino reconstruìdo, acompañada de un glosario latino-romance, por T. González Rolán, María F. del Barrio Vega y A. López Fonseca (Madrid: Ediciones Clásicas, 1996), 1; Homer, *Ilias*, in der Übertragung von Johann Heinrich Voss (Munich: Artemis & Winkler, 1957), 1; Homère, *Iliade*, traduction de Leconte de Lisle (Paris: Profrance, 1998), 1; Haroldo do Campos, *Homero, Ilíada*, introdução e organização Trajano Vieira (São Paulo: Editora Arx, 2001), 1.

16. Juan Valera y Alcalá Galiano, "Cartas dirigidas al Sr. D. Francisco de Paula Canalejas," *Revista Ibérica* 3, no. 4 (1862): 305.

17. Frédéric Gros, *Pourquoi la guerre?* (Paris: Albin Michel, 2023), 135.

18. Homer, *The Odyssey*, 11.555–58, trans. Robert Fagles (London: Penguin, 1996).

19. Nancy Sherman, *Stoic Warriors: The Ancient Philosophy Behind the Military Mind* (Oxford: Oxford University Press, 2005), 66. In Buddhist terms, this is similar to *nekkhamma*, defined in the Pali-English Dictionary as "giving up the world & leading a holy life, renunciation of, or emancipation from worldliness, freedom from lust, craving & desires, dispassionateness" (http://dsal.uchicago.edu/cgi-bin/philologic/getobject.pl?c.2:1:692.pali). Stendhal, *La Chartreuse de Parme* book 2, chap. 18 (Paris: Le Divan, 1927), 110.

20. Giacomo Leopardi, *Zibaldone di pensieri*, vol. 1, sect. 289 (Milan: Mondadori, 1997), 290.

21. Virgil, *Aeneid* 12.837–39, p. 285.

FOUR. CHRISTIAN HOMER

1. See Jean Steinmann, *Saint Jérôme* (Paris: Éditions du Cerf, 1958), 133; and Steinmann, *Saint Jerome and His Times*, trans. Ronald Matthews (Notre Dame, Ind.: Fides, 1959).

2. Saint Jerome, "Letter to Eustochium on Guarding Virginity," in *The Collected Works of Erasmus*, vol. 61: *Patristic Scholarship: The Edition of St Jerome*, ed., trans., and annot. James F. Brady and John C. Olin (Toronto: University of Toronto Press, 1992), 174. The biblical citation is Matthew 6:21.

3. Saint Jerome, "Letter to Magnus, Roman Orator," in *The Collected Works of Erasmus*, vol. 61, 202; Erasmus, "Life of Jerome," in *The Collected Works of Erasmus*, vol. 61, 56.

4. Saint Augustine, *Confessions* 1:13–14, trans. R. S. Pine-Coffin (London: Penguin, 1961), p. 35.

5. See Possidius, *The Life of Saint Augustine*, xxxi, trans. Herbert T. Weiskotten (Merchantville, N.J.: Evolution Publishing, 2008), 57.

6. Horace, *Epistles* I: 2, "To Lollius Maximus," in Horace, *Satires. Epistles. The Art of Poetry*, trans. H. Rushton Fairclough (Cambridge: Harvard University Press, 1926), 263, 267.

7. Saint Augustine, *The City of God*, 1:1:3, trans. Henry Bettenson (London: Penguin, 1972), 5.

8. St Augustine, *Confessions*, 1:13, 16, pp. 32–36.

9. Heinrich Heine, *Werke und Briefe in zehn Bänden*, Herausgegeben von Hans Kaufmann, Textrevision und Erläuterungen von Gotthard Erler, vol. 2 (Berlin: Aufbau Verlag, 1972), 449.

FIVE. OTHER HOMERS

1. See James J. O'Donnell, *Cassiodorus* (Berkeley: University of California Press, 1979), 131–77.

2. For the number forty thousand, see Seneca, "On the Tranquility of Mind," in *Moral Essays*, vol. 2, trans. John W. Basore (Cambridge: Harvard University Press, 1932), 247; for seventy thousand, see Isidore of Seville, *The Etymologies of Isidore of Seville*, ed. Stephen A. Barney et al. (Cambridge: Cambridge University Press, 2006), 139.

3. Edward Gibbon, *The Decline and Fall of the Roman Empire*, vol. 3 (New York: Random House, 1983), 53. The earlier information on the Royal College is also to be found in Gibbon, on the same page.

4. Michael Psellus, *Fourteen Byzantine Rulers: The "Chronographia" of Michael Psellus* book 6, trans. E. R. A. Sewter (London: Penguin, 1966), 185.

5. William V. Harris, *Ancient Literacy* (Cambridge: Harvard University Press, 1989), 296, 304.

6. J. M. Wallace-Hadrill, *The Barbarian West: 400–1000*, rev. ed. (Malden, Mass.: Blackwell, 1996), 16–17.

7. See Armando Petrucci, "La concezione cristiana del libro fra VI e VII secolo," in *Libri e lettori nel medioevo: Guida storica e critica*, ed. Guglielmo Cavallo (Rome: Laterza, 1989), 3–5.

8. See *Venetus Marcianus: Facsimile of the Codex* (Boston: Archaeological Institute of America, 1902), 11–15; Ian James, "Introduction" to Quintus of Smyrna, *The Trojan Epic: Posthomerica* (Baltimore: Johns Hopkins University Press, 2004), xiii. Tiresias's prophecy is in Homer, *Odyssey* 11.138–43.

9. See *The Trojan War: The Chronicles of Dictys of Crete and Dares the Phrygian*, trans. R. M. Frazer, Fr. (Bloomington: Indiana University Press, 1966), 3.

10. See Ronald T. Ridley, *The Historical Observations of Jacob Perizonius* (Rome: Bardi Editore, 1988).

11. Benoît de Sainte-Maure, *Le Roman de Troie*, Prologue, ll. 135–40, extraits du manuscrit Milan, Bibliothèque ambrosienne, D55, édités, présentés et traduits par Emmanuèle Baumgartner et Françoise Vieillard (Paris: Letters Gothiques, Librairie Générale Française, 1998), 8–9.

12. Binduccio dello Scelto, *Storia di Troia*, ed. Gabriele Ricci (Parma: Fondazione Pietro Bembo/Ugo Guanda Editore, 2004).

13. *Merugud Uilix maic Leirtis*, ed. Robert T. Meyer, in *Medieval and Modern Irish Studies*, vol. 17 (Dublin: Dublin Institute for Advanced Studies, 1958), xv, 8.

14. John Lydgate, *The Troy Book*, [1412–20], ed. Robert R. Edwards (Kalamazoo: Western Michigan University Press, 1998), 1–26; Geoffrey Chaucer, *Troilus and Criseyde* [ca. 1385], in *Complete Works*, ed. Walter W. Skeat (Oxford: Oxford University Press, 1912), 153; Charles Muscatine, *Chaucer and the French Tradition* (Berkeley: University of California Press, 1957), 154. See also the discussion of Criseyde in Muriel Bowden, *A Reader's Guide to Geoffrey Chaucer* (London: Thames and Hudson, 1965), 178.

15. Marion Turner, *Chaucer: A European Life* (Princeton: Princeton University Press, 2019), 330.

16. Robert Henryson, *The Testament of Cresseid* [ca. 1500], ll. 558–60, ed. Denton Fox (London: Nelson, 1968), 82; William Caxton, *Recuyell of the Historyes of Troye* [1474], ed. H. O. Sommer, 2 vols. (London: D. Nutt, 1894), 1:xiv.

17. Ben Jonson, "To the Memory of My Beloved, the Author, Mr. William Shakespeare," in Jonson, *Complete Works*, ed. John Jowett et al. (Oxford: Oxford University Press, 2015), xvi; John Dryden, *Troilus and Cressida; or, Truth Found Too Late, a Tragedy* (London: Abel Swall & Jacob Tonson, 1679), sig. A4v.

18. William Shakespeare, *Troilus and Cressida*, ed. David Bevington (London: Bloomsbury, 2015), 5.2.140–49.

SIX. HOMER IN ISLAM

1. See Lakhdar Souami, "Présentation," in Jâhiz, *Le cadi et la mouche: Anthologie du Livre des Animaux* (Paris: Sindbad, 1988), 29–31.

2. The story is told by the tenth-century scholar Ibn al-Nadim in his *al-Fihrist*, quoted in Johannes Pedersen, *The Arabic Book*, trans. Geoffrey French (Princeton: Princeton University Press, 1984), 113.

3. Pedersen, *The Arabic Book*, 113.

4. See G. Strohmaier, "Homer in Baghdad," *Byzantinoslavica* 41 (1980): 196–200.

5. Quoted in Dimitri Gutas, *Greek Thought, Arabic Culture: The Graeco-Arabic Translation Movement in Baghdad and Early 'Abbasid Society (2nd–4th/8th–10th Centuries)* (London: Routledge, 1998), 140.

6. Ismail M. Dahiyat, *Avicenna's Commentary on the Poetics of Aristotle* (Leiden: Brill, 1974), 76.

7. The "deathbed meditations" are associated with the *wasaya*, or "testament," genre in Islamic medieval literature: see Juan Vernet, *Lo que Europa debe al Islam de España* (Barcelona: El Acantilado, 1999), 257; on biographies see Jörg Kraemer, "Arabische Homerverse," *Zeitschrift der Deutschen Morgenländischen Gesellschaft* 106, no. 2 (1956): 259–316.

8. See Patricia Crone, *Medieval Islamic Political Thought* (Edinburgh: Edinburgh University Press, 2004), 177–81.

9. See Robert Irwin, *Night and Horses and the Desert: An Anthology of Classical Arabic Literature* (London: Allen Lane, 1999), 116, 154, 365; *The Subtle Ruse: The Book of Arabic Wisdom and Guile*, trans. René R. Khawam (London: East-West Publications, 1976), 206.

10. See A. I. Sabra, "The Appropriation and Subsequent Naturalisation of Greek Science in Medieval Islam: A Preliminary Statement," *History of Science* 25 (1987), quoted in Crone, *Medieval Islamic Political Thought*, 245.

11. Wilhelm Grimm, "Die Sage von Polyphem," quoted in William Hansen, *Ariadne's Thread: A Guide to International Tales Found in Classical Literature* (Ithaca: Cornell University Press, 2002), 291; see Donald K. Fry, "Polyphemus in Iceland," in *The Fourteenth Century, Acta IV* (1977), quoted by Hermann Pálsson, "Egils Saga Einhenda ok Ásmundar Berserkjabana," in *Dictionary of the Middle Ages*, vol. 4, ed. Joseph R. Strayer (New York: Scribner's, 1984), 402.

12. Andrew Lang, *Homer and the Epic* (London: Longmans, Green, 1893), 225.

13. See F. Gabrieli, "The Transmission of Learning and Literary Influences to Western Europe," in *The Cambridge History of Islam* (Cambridge: Cambridge University Press, 1977), 851–89.

14. Juan de Mena, "Proemio," in *La Ilíada de Homero*, edición crítica de las *Sumas de la Yliada de Omero* y del original latino reconstruido, acompañada de un glosario latino-romance, por T. González Rolán, María F. del Barrio Vega y A. López Fonseca (Madrid: Ediciones Clásicas, 1996), 147.

SEVEN. DANTE

1. Mussato quoted in E. R. Curtius, *Europäische Literatur und Lateinisches Mittelalter* (Bern: A. Francke AG, 1948), 222–23; Francesco Petrarca, *Letters on Familiar Matters (Familiarum rerum libri)*, vol. 2: *Books IX–XVI*, trans. Aldo S. Bernardo (New York: Italic Press, 2003), 69.

2. See Bruce Louden, Homer's "Odyssey" and the Near East (Cambridge: Cambridge University Press, 2011); Dennis Ronald McDonald suggests a parallel between the Odyssey and the apocryphal Acts of Andrew in Christianizing Homer: The "Odyssey," Plato, and "The Acts of Andrew" (New York: Oxford University Press, 1994).

3. Dante Alighieri, Inferno, 4:80–99, in Dante, La Divina Commedia, 3 vols., ed. Anna Maria Chiavacci Leonardi (Milan: Mondadori, 2016).

4. Homer, The Iliad 1.232, trans. Robert Fagles (London: Penguin, 1990).

5. Marcus Aurelius quoted in Robin Lane Fox, Pagans and Christians in the Mediterranean World from the Second Century AD to the Conversion of Constantine (New York: Knopf, 1986), 123.

6. Seneca, "On the Shortness of Life," in The Stoic Philosophy of Seneca, trans. Moses Hadas (New York: Doubleday, 1958), 67.

7. Albertino Mussato, Historia Augusta de gestis Henrici VII, quoted in Pétrarque, La vie solitaire, préface de Nicholas Mann, introduction, traduction et notes de Christophe Carraud (Grenoble: Jérôme Millon, 1999), 12; Francesco Petrarca, Secretum meum, in Petrarca, Prose, ed. Guido Martellotti et al. (Milan: R. Ricciardi, 1955), 22–218.

8. Dante, Paradiso 2:7–9.

9. Homer, The Iliad 1.1; Homer, The Odyssey, 1.1, trans Robert Fagles (London: Penguin, 1996); Virgil, The Aeneid: A New Verse Translation 1.8, trans. C. Day Lewis (Oxford: Oxford University Press, 1952), 11; Dante, Inferno 2:7–9.

10. G. K. Chesterton, "Tricks of Memory," in Chesterton, The Glass Walking Stick and Other Essays (London: Methuen, 1955), 142.

11. Dante, Purgatorio 22:108, in Dante, La Divina Commedia; see Jean-Christophe Saladin, La Bataille du grec à la Renaissance, 2nd ed. (Paris: Belles Lettres, 2000), 41.

12. Petrarca, Letters on Familiar Matters 18:2, pp. 45–46; see Jacob Burckhardt, The Civilization of the Renaissance in Italy, trans. S. G. C. Middlemore (New York: Random House, 1954), 187.

13. George Steiner, "Homer in English Translation," in The Cambridge Companion to Homer, ed. Robert Louis Fowler (New York: Cambridge University Press, 2004), 365.

14. See Miguel Asín Palacios, Dante y el islam (Pamplona y Nacarra: Urgoiti Editores, 2007), 13–20.

EIGHT. HOMER IN HELL

1. Homer, The Odyssey 10.539–41, 550–52, trans. Robert Fagles (London: Penguin, 1996).

2. Homer, *Odyssey* 10.553–95; 24.13–14.

3. Pindar, fragment 129, in *Works*, ed. J. E. Sandys (Cambridge: Harvard University Press and William Heinemann, 1972), 381; Homer, *Odyssey* 11.555–58.

4. Homer, *Odyssey* 11.43–48.

5. Homer, *Odyssey* 11.723–26.

6. Jean le Fèvre was the first to use the expression *danse macabré* [sic] in 1376, in his poem *Le respit de la mort*. See Paul Binski, *Medieval Death: Ritual and Representation* (Ithaca: Cornell University Press, 1996), 156; see Hellmut Rosenfeld, *Der mittelalteriche Totentanz* (Vienna: Böhlau Verlag, 1954), 100.

7. Homer, *Iliad* 6.171–75.

8. Philip Larkin, "The Trees" (1974), in *The Complete Poems of Philip Larkin* (London: Faber & Faber, 2012); Alice Oswald, *Memorial* (London: Faber & Faber, 2011), 73.

9. Elizabeth Cook, *Achilles* (London: Methuen, 2001), 5.

10. Virgil, *Aeneid* 6.306–14, trans. C. Day Lewis (Oxford: Oxford University Press, 1952) (italics mine).

11. Dante Alighieri, *Inferno* 3:112–14, in Dante, *La Divina Commedia*, 3 vols., ed. Anna Maria Chiavacci Leonardi (Milan: Mondadori, 2016).

12. André Malraux, *La voie royale* (Paris: Bernard Grasset, 1930), 182.

13. John Milton, *Paradise Lost* (1667), 1.302–4, in *Paradise Lost and Other Poems* (New York: New American Library, 1961); Paul Verlaine, "Chanson d'Automne," in Verlaine, *Poèmes saturniens* (Paris: Alphonse Lemerre, 1866), 26.

14. Gerard Manley Hopkins, "Spring and Fall," in *Poems of Gerard Manley Hopkins*, ed. Robert Bridges (London: Humphrey Milford, 1918), 51.

15. Dante Alighieri, "Epistola XIII a Can'grande della Scala," *Le opere di Dante*, ed. M. Barbi et al. (Milan: Società Dantesca Italiana, 1921–22), 856; Ecclesiastes 1:4, King James Version.

16. Percy Bysshe Shelley, "Ode to Naples," in Shelley, *The Complete Poems* (New York: Random House, 1994), 122.

17. For the first observation, see Erich Auerbach, *Dante als Dichter der irdischen Welt* (Berlin: De Gruyter, 1969), 231; for the second, see C. S. Singleton, trans., "Introduction," in Dante, *The Divine Comedy* (London: Routledge and Kegan Paul, 1971–75), 51.

NINE. GREEK VERSUS LATIN

1. Dante Alighieri, *Inferno*, 4:76–78, 39, in Dante, *La Divina Commedia*, 3 vols., ed. Anna Maria Chiavacci Leonardi (Milan: Mondadori, 2016).

2. See Robert Kirkbride, *Architecture and Memory: The Renaissance Studioli of Federico da Montefeltro* (New York: Columbia University Press, 2008). 111.

3. See Ingrid Rowland, "The Vatican Stanze," in *The Cambridge Companion to Raphael*, ed. Marcia Hall (Cambridge: Cambridge University Press, 2005), 108.

4. See Susy Marcon and Marino Zorzi, eds., *Aldo Manuzio e l'ambiente veneziano, 1494–1515* (Venice: Il Cardo, 1994), 209–10.

5. Vespasiano da Bisticci, *Vite di uomini illustri del secolo xv*, ed. Paolo d'Ancona and Erhard Aeschlimann (Milan: U. Hoepli, 1951), 75.

6. Leonardo Bruni, "The Study of Literature," sect. 20 in *Humanist Educational Treatises*, ed. and trans. Craig W. Kallendorf (Cambridge: Harvard University Press, 2002), 56.

7. Battista Guarino, "A Program of Teaching and Learning," sect. 19 in *Humanist Educational Treatises*, 283; Aeneas Silvius Piccolimini, "The Education of Boys," sect. 33 in *Humanist Educational Treatises*, 87; Scaliger quoted in Anthony Grafton, "Renaissance Readers," in *Homer's Ancient Readers: The Hermeneutics of Greek Epic's Earliest Exegetes*, ed. Robert Lamberton and John J. Keaney (Princeton: Princeton University Press, 1992), 150.

8. See Francisco Bethencourt, "A fundação," in *História das Inquisições: Portugal, Espanha e Itália, séculos XV–XIX* (São Paulo: Companhia das Letras, 2000), 17–34.

9. See J. N. D. Kelly, *The Oxford Dictionary of Popes* (Oxford: Oxford University Press, 1988), 262.

10. Jean-Christophe Saladin provides a breakdown of these terms by author in *La bataille du grec à la Renaissance*, 2nd ed. (Paris: Belles Lettres, 2000), 119.

11. *Opus Epistolarum Des. Erasmi Roterdami*, ed. P. S. Allen and H. M. Allen, vol. 1: *1484–1514* (Oxford: Clarendon, 1906), 90; Schade quoted in Saladin, *La Bataille du grec à la Renaissance*, 240–47.

12. See Li Sher-shiueh, "Translating Homer and His Epics in Late Imperial China: Christian Missionaries' Perspective," *Asia Pacific Translation and Intercultural Studies* 1, no. 2 (2014): 83–106.

13. See Takero Oji, "The Study of Homer in Japan," *Hikaku Bungaku: Journal of Comparative Literature* 22 (1997): 17–27.

14. See Brother Anthony of Taizé, "Modern Poetry in Korea: An Introduction," *Manoa* 27, no. 2 (2015): xiii–xix.

15. Fraseri quoted in Günay Uslu, *Homer, Troy and the Turks: Heritage and Identity in the Late Ottoman Empire, 1870–1915* (Amsterdam: Amsterdam University Press, 2017), 159; Ahmed Tanpinar, *Histoire de la littérature turque du XIX siècle*, trans. into French by Ferda Fidan, Valérie Gay-Aksoy, Gül Mete-Yuva, and Catherine Erikan (Paris: Actes Sud, 2012), 41.

16. See Neil Kent, *The Soul of the North: A Social, Architectural and Cultural History of the Nordic Countries, 1700–1940* (London: Reaktion, 2000), 190.

17. Oliver Goldsmith, *The Vicar of Wakefield* (1766) (New York: Dutton, 1951), 140.

18. Valera quoted in Henry Kamen, *The Disinherited: The Exiles Who Created Spanish Culture* (London: Penguin/Allen Lane, 2007), 275. I have slightly revised the translation.

19. See Isaías Lerner, "Prólogo," in Pedro Mexía, *Silva de varia lección* (Madrid: Editorial Castalia, 2003), 11–25.

20. Francisco de Quevedo, *Las zahúrdas de Platón*, quoted in Raimundo Lida, *Prosas de Quevedo* (Barcelona: Editorial Crítica, 1980), 77; Francisco de Quevedo, *Defensa de Epicuro contra la común opinión* (Madrid: Clásicos del pensamiento, Tecnos, 1986), 13.

21. See Octavio Paz, *Sor Juana Inés de la Cruz, o Las trampas de la fe* (Mexico DF: Fondo de Cultura Económica, 1998), 252; Sor Juana Inés de la Cruz, "El Sueño," in *Antología poética*, selección e introducción de José Miguel Oviedo (Madrid: Alianza, 2004), 181.

22. Francis Bacon, "The Wisdom of the Ancients" (1619), in *Bacon's Essays*, ed. Alexander Spiers (Boston: Little, Brown, 1884), 318.

23. Ralph Waldo Emerson, "Journal N, 1842," in Emerson, *Selected Journals, 1841–1877*, ed. Lawrence Rosenwald (Cambridge: Library of America, Harvard University Press, 1984), 137.

TEN. ANCIENTS VERSUS MODERNS

1. Michel de Montaigne, *Les essais de Michel de Montaigne*, 2:36, ed. V.-L. Saulnier (Paris: Presses Universitaires de France, 1965), 753.

2. See Bon-Joseph Dacier, *Notice historique sur la vie et les ouvrages de M. de Villoison* (Paris: Imprimerie Impériale, 1806), 13–15.

3. Charles Perrault, *Parallèle des anciens et des modernes* (1688–97) (Geneva: Slatkine, 1971), 39–40; Homer, *The Iliad* 11.656, trans. Robert Fagles (London: Penguin, 1990); Princess Nausicaa, daughter of King Alcinous, in Homer, *The Odyssey* 6.70–73, trans. Robert Fagles (London: Penguin, 1996).

4. Charles-Augustin Sainte-Beuve, *Réflexions sur les lettres* (Paris: Plon, 1941), 98.

5. Noémi Hepp, *Homère en France au XVII siècle* (Paris: Librairie C. Klincksieck, 1968), 67.

6. Pierre de Ronsard, "Je veus lire en trois jours l'Iliade d'Homère," in *Second livre des Amours*, in *Oeuvres complètes*, vol. 1. (Paris: P. Jannet, 1857), 413.

7. *Histoire de l'Académie Royale des Inscriptions et Belles Lettres*, vol. 7 (Paris: Imprimerie Nationale, 1716), 376–77.

8. Jean Racine, "Remarques sur l'*Odysée*," in *Oeuvres complètes*, vol. 2 (Paris: Gallimard, 1950), 804.

9. Louis Racine, *Mémoires contenant quelques particularités sur la vie et les ouvrages de Jean Racine* (Paris: Laplace, Sanchez, 1870), 5.

10. Thomas Aquinas, *Summa Theologica*, 1–2, q. 109 a. 6 (New York: Benziger Brothers, 1947), 1:1127.

11. Blaise Pascal, *Pensées*, 2:14:11 (Paris: Imprimerie d'Auguste Delalain, 1820), 351.

12. Homer, *Iliad* 6.580–84.

13. Jean Racine, *Andromaque* 1.1, in *Oeuvres de J. Racine*, vol. 2, ed. Paul Mesnard (Paris: Librairie Hachette, 1923), 46.

14. See Jean-Pierre Vernant, "Catégories de l'agent et de l'action en Grèce ancienne," in Vernant, *Religions, histoires, raisons* (Paris: François Maspero, 1979), 88–89, 90–91.

15. Homer, *Odyssey* 12.278, 332, 334, 336.

16. Aldous Huxley, "Tragedy and the Whole Truth," in Huxley, *The Complete Essays*, vol. 3: *1930–35*, ed. Robert S. Baker and James Sexton (Chicago: Ivan R. Dee, 2001), 51–52.

17. Racine, *Andromaque*, 5.3, p. 121.

18. Homer, *Odyssey* 5.436–38, 476–77, 490–97.

19. Migrant quoted in Francisco Cantú, "Has Any One of Us Wept?" *New York Review of Books*, January 17, 1992.

20. Racine, "Remarques sur l'*Odysée*," 763.

21. Anne Dacier, *Des causes de la corruption du goût* (1714) (Geneva: Sladkine, 1970).

22. See Hayden Vernon, "Roald Dahl Books Rewritten to Remove Language Deemed Offensive," *The Guardian*, February 18, 2023; Sarah Shaffi and Lucy Knight, "Roald Dahl Publisher Announces Unaltered 16-Book 'Classics Collection,'" *The Guardian*, February 24, 2023.

23. See Patricia Ward, "'Quietism,'" in *The Cambridge Dictionary of Christian Theology*, ed. Ian McFarland et al. (Cambridge: Cambridge University Press, 2011), 425–26; François Fénelon, *Explication des maximes des saints*, in Fénelon, *Oeuvres*, 2 vols. (Paris: Gallimard, 1983–97), vol. 1.

24. François Fénelon, *Les aventures de Télémaque*, in *Oeuvres*, vol. 2. See also Henk Hillenaar, "Le projet didactique de Fénelon auteur de *Télémaque*: enjeux et perspectives," in Nadia Minerva, *Documents pour l'histoire du français langue étrangère ou seconde: "Les aventures de Télémaque": Trois siècles d'enseignement*

du française, 8–12 (Open Edition Journals, https://journals.openedition.org/dhfles/1478. See James Herbert Davis, Jr., *Fénelon* (Boston: Twayne, 1979), 12–13.

25. Montesquieu, *Lettres persanes*, 36, ed. Laurent Versini (Paris: GF-Flammarion, 1995), 125.

26. Baron Frédéric-Melchior Grimm, "Lettre du 1er juin 1757," in *Correspondance littéraire*, vol. 2 (1820) (Paris: Mercure de France, 2001), 125.

ELEVEN. HOMER AS POETRY

1. All information on the painting is taken from Simon Schama, *Rembrandt's Eyes* (New York: Knopf, 1999), 584.

2. Plutarch, "Alexander," in *Plutarch's Lives*, vol. 2, the Dryden translation, ed. and rev. Arthur Hugh Clough (New York: Random House, 1992), 144.

3. Schama, *Rembrandt's Eyes*, 594.

4. Schama, *Rembrandt's Eyes*, 577.

5. Michael Schmidt, *The First Poets: Lives of the Ancient Greek Poets* (New York: Knopf, 2005), 40.

6. Sir Philip Sidney, *The Defence of Poesy*, in *The Renaissance in England*, ed. H. E. Rowlands and H. Baker (Lexington, Mass.: D. C. Heath, 1954), 608 (written 1581; first printed 1595); Sir Francis Bacon, *The Advancement of Learning* (1605), ed. Michael Kiernan (Oxford: Oxford University Press, 2000), 74; T. S. Eliot, "Poetry in the Eighteenth Century," in *The Pelican Guide to English Literature*, vol. 4, ed. Boris Ford (London: Penguin, 1962), 271.

7. See Jaume Bartrolí, *Lisboa: La ciudad que navega* (Barcelona: Ecos, 2013), 16.

8. A. J. Saraiva and Óscar Lopes, *História da Literatura Portuguesa* (Porto: Porto Editora, 2017), 372.

9. António de Sousa de Macedo, *Ulyssippo: Poema heroico*, 2.82 (1638) (Lisbon: Typographia Sollandianas, 1848), 43.

10. Alexander Pope, "Preface," in *The Iliad and the Odyssey of Homer*, ed. the Revd. H. F. Cary (New York: George Routledge and Sons, 1872), 3.

11. Pope, "Preface," 3.

12. Lytton Strachey, *Pope: The Leslie Stephen Lecture for 1925* (Cambridge: Cambridge University Press, 1925), 9.

13. Broome translated eight books of the *Odyssey* and the notes to the complete text, Fenton four, and Pope the remaining twelve. Pope tried to conceal the extent of the collaboration but was eventually found out. See George Fraser, *Alexander Pope* (London: Routledge, 1978), 52. On Pope's profit, see Strachey, *Pope*, 9; Alexander Pope, "The Second Epistle of the Second Book of Horace: Imitated by Mr. Pope," in *The Twickenham Edition of the Poems of Alexander Pope*, vol. 4, ed. J. Butt et al. (1939–69) (London: Routledge, 2001), 169.

14. Edward Gibbon, *Memoirs of My Life*, ed. Henry Marley (London: Routledge, 1891), 57; Bentley quoted in Samuel Johnson, "Pope," in *Lives of the English Poets* (1779–81), vol. 2 (Oxford: Oxford University Press, 1912), 256; Johnson, "Pope," 255; Henry Fielding, *A Journey from This World to the Next* (1743), in *The Complete Works of Henry Fielding, Esq. with an Essay on the Life, Genius and Achievement of the Author*, vol. 2 (London: William Heinemann, 1903), 603.

15. William Hazlitt, *"Lectures on English Poets" and "The Spirit of the Age"* (London: Dent, 1922), 71; Leslie Stephen, *Pope* (London: Macmillan, 1909), 69.

16. Pope, "Preface," 3; Jorge Luis Borges, "Las versiones homéricas," in Borges, *Discusión* (Buenos Aires: Manuel Gleizer, 1932), 106; Pope, *Iliad* 23, in *The Iliad and the Odyssey of Homer*, 273. (This edition does not have line numbers.)

17. Homer, *The Iliad* 23.243–48, trans. Robert Fagles (London: Penguin, 1990).

18. Alexander Pope, "An Essay on Criticism," ll. 68–69, 74–75, in *The Poems of Alexander Pope*, ed. John Butt (London: Methuen, 1963), 146.

19. Johnson, "Pope," 321; William Cowper, *Table Talk*, 1:656 (London: John Sharpe, 1825), 23; *Homer in English*, ed. George Steiner (London: Penguin, 1996), 76.

20. Matthew Arnold, *On Translating Homer: Three Lectures* (London: Longman, Green, Longman, and Roberts, 1861), 18, 21.

21. Arnold, *On Translating Homer*, 2–3, 4.

22. Newman quoted in I. Giberne Sieveking, *Memoir and Letters of Francis W. Newman* (London: Kegan Paul, Trench, Trubner, 1909), 26; Newman quoted in Wilfrid Meynell, *Cardinal Newman: A Monograph* (London: John Sinkins, 1890), 5; Eliot quoted in Richard Garnett, "Newman, Francis William," in *The Encyclopaedia Britannica*, ed. Hugh Chisholm, 11th ed., vol. 19 (Cambridge: Cambridge University Press, 1911), 516–17.

23. Arnold, *On Translating Homer*, 176.

24. A. E. Housman, "Introductory Lecture" (1892), in *The Name and Nature of Poetry and Other Selected Prose*, ed. John Carter (Cambridge: Cambridge University Press, 1961), 24–25.

TWELVE. REALMS OF GOLD

1. John Keats, "Letter to Benjamin Bailey," July 18, 1818, in *The Complete Works of John Keats*, vol. 4, ed. H. Buxton Forman (Glasgow: Gowars and Gray, 1901), 144.

2. John Keats, "On First Looking into Chapman's Homer," in *The Poems of John Keats*, vol. 1 (London: Chatto and Windus, 1924), 24.

3. George Chapman, *The Iliads of Homer, Prince of Poets, Never Before in Any Language Truly Translated, Done According to the Greek* (1598) (London: George Newnes, 1904), p. lxxxvii.

4. William Blake, "On Virgil," in *The Complete Writings of William Blake*, ed. Geoffrey Keynes (Oxford: Oxford University Press, 1957), 411, 778–94; William Blake, "Preface," in *Milton: A Poem in 2 Books to Justify the Ways of God to Man*, in *The Complete Poems*, ed. Alicia Ostriker (London: Penguin, 1977), 513; William Blake, "On Homer's Poetry," in *The Complete Writings of William Blake*, 778.

5. William Blake, "Letter to the Rvd. Dr. Trusler, 23 August 1799," in *The Poetry and Prose of William Blake*, ed. David V. Erdman (Garden City, N.Y.: Doubleday, 1965), 677; William Blake, "On Boyd," "On Dante," in *The Complete Writings of William Blake*, 460, 785; for the image, see William Blake, *The Illuminated Blake*, ed. David V. Erdman (Garden City, N.Y.: Doubleday, 1974) (the poets are named in Dante, *Inferno* 4:88–90); Blake, "On Boyd," 460.

6. William Blake, "Public Address," in *The Poetry and Prose of William Blake*, 600.

7. Lord Byron, "Letter to Octavius Gilchrist, 15 September 1821," "Letter to John Murray, 17 September 1817," in *Byron: A Self-Portrait: Letters and Diaries, 1798–1824*, ed. Peter Quennell (Oxford: Oxford University Press, 1990), 655, 419.

8. John Stuart Mill, "Notes on Some of the More Popular Dialogues of Plato," in *The Collected Works of John Stuart Mill*, ed. J. M. Robson, vol. 11 (Toronto: University of Toronto Press, 1978), 35.

9. Percy Bysshe Shelley, "A Defence of Poetry," in Shelley, *Essays and Letters*, ed. Ernest Rhys (London: Walter Scott, 1886), 11.

10. Herbert Read, *Byron* (London: Longmans, Green, 1951), 33.

11. Lord Byron, *Don Juan*, 7.633–44, ed. T. G. Steffan, E. Steffan, and W. W. Pratt (London: Penguin, 2004), 315.

12. Susan Sontag, "Simone Weil," review of Simone Weil, *Selected Essays*, trans. Richard Rees, *New York Review of Books*, February 1, 1963. This passage is also quoted in Adam Nicolson, *The Mighty Dead: Why Homer Matters* (London: William Collins, 2014).

13. Byron, *Don Juan*, 7.621–24, p. 314; 8.70–72, p. 319.

14. William Ewart Gladstone, *Homeric Synchronism: An Enquiry into the Time & Place of Homer* (London: Macmillan, 1876), 9–10; William Ewart Gladstone, "Aoidos, section I," in Gladstone, *Studies on Homer and the Homeric Age* (Oxford: Oxford University Press, 1858), 487; John Morley, *The Life of William Ewart Gladstone*, vol. 3 (London: Macmillan, 1903), 340.

15. Walter J. Ong, *Orality and Literacy* (London: Routledge, 2002), 21.

16. Homer, *The Odyssey* 4.605; 2.1, trans. Robert Fagles (London: Penguin, 1996).

17. Milman Parry, "The Homeric Gloss: A Study in Word-Sense," *Transactions and Proceedings of the American Philological Association* 59 (1928): 235.

18. Jorge Luis Borges, "Las versiones homéricas," in Borges, *Discusión* (Buenos Aires: Manuel Gleizer, 1932), 96.

19. Albert B. Lord, *The Singer of Tales* (Cambridge: Harvard University Press, 1981), 66.

20. Homer, *The Iliad* 16.703-7, 407-13, trans. Robert Fagles (London: Penguin, 1990).

21. Homer, *Iliad* 16.415-19.

22. Lord Byron, "The Destruction of Sennacherib," in *The Poetical Works of Lord Byron, the Only Complete and Copyright Text in One Volume*, ed. E. H. Coleridge (London: John Murray, 1905), 467.

23. Enrique Banchs, "El tigre," in Banchs, *La urna* (1911) (Buenos Aires: Proa, 2000), 77.

24. Ogden Nash, "Very Like a Whale," in *I Wouldn't Have Missed It: Selected Poems of Ogden Nash* (Boston: Little, Brown, 1975), 45.

25. Paolo Vivante, *Homer* (New Haven: Yale University Press, 1985), 172-73.

26. Madame de Staël, *De la littérature considerée dans ses rapports avec les institutions sociales* (1800), ed. P. van Tiegham, 2 vols. (Geneva: Librairie Garnier, 1959), 54.

THIRTEEN. HOMER AS IDEA

1. Donald Phillip Verene, *Vico's Science of Imagination* (Ithaca: Cornell University Press, 1981), 32-35.

2. Giambattista Vico, *La scienza nuova*, sect. 819, ed. Paolo Rossi (Milan: Rizzoli, 1977), 495.

3. Richard Ellmann, *James Joyce*, rev. ed. (Oxford: Oxford University Press, 1983), 661.

4. Homer, *The Iliad* 2.573-82, trans. Robert Fagles (London: Penguin, 1990).

5. Verene, *Vico's Science of Imagination*, 180; Vico, *La scienza nuova*, sect. 873, p. 577.

6. See Ulrich Joost, "Friedrich August Wolf," in Walther Killy, *Literatur Lexicon*, vol. 12 (Munich: Bertelsmann, 1992), 396.

7. Johann Joachim Winckelmann, *Gedanken über die Nachahmung der griechischen Werke in der Malerei und Bildhauerkunst* (1755) (Stuttgart: Philipp Reclam, 1995), 149.

8. Denis Diderot, "Salon de 1767," in Diderot, *Oeuvres complètes* (Paris: Garnier frères, 1875–79), 278; Denis Diderot, "Grecs (philosophie des)," in *L'Encyclopédie de Diderot et d'Alembert* (Milan: Franco Maria Ricci, 1977–78), 908.

9. Cicero, *On the Orator. Books 1–2*, no. 62, trans. E. W. Sutton and H. Rackham (Cambridge: Harvard University Press, 1942), 243–45.

10. *Conversations of Goethe with Eckermann and Soret*, trans. John Oxenford, 2 vols. (London: Smith, Elder & Co., 1850), 1:362.

11. J. W. von Goethe, "Brief an Schiller, 17 Mai 1795," in *Goethes Werke: Briefe*, vol. 10 (Weimar: Verlag Hermann Böhlaus Nachfolger, 1887–1919), 260.

12. J. W. von Goethe, "Brief an Schiller, 27 December 1797," in *Goethes Werke: Briefe*, vol. 12, 385–86.

13. Goethe, "Brief an Schiller, 17 Mai 1795," 259–60.

14. See, among many others, Herder's *Auch eine Philosophie der Geschichte zur Bildung der Menschheit* (1774), *Älteste Urkunde des Menschengeschlechts* (1774), and *Ideen zur Philosophie der Geschichte der Menschheit* (1784–91); Wieland's *Geschichte des Agaton* (1766–67), *Die Abderiten* (1774), and *Neue Götter-Gespräche* (1791); Heinse's *Ardinghello* (1789); Schlegel's *Über die Diotima* (1795), *Über das Studium der griechischen Poesie* (1797), and *Die Griechen und Römer* (1798); Moritz's *Die Götterlehre* (1791); and Hölderlin's *Hyperion* (1797–99) and *Empedocles* (1797–1800).

15. Edmund Burke, *Hints for an Essay on Drama* (ca. 1761), in *The Writings and Speeches of Edmund Burke*, vol. 1: *The Early Writings*, ed. T. O. McLoughlin and James T. Boulton (Oxford: Clarendon, 1997), 553.

16. Goethe quoted in E. R. Curtius, *Europäische Literatur und Lateinisches Mittelalter* (Bern: A. Francke AG, 1948), 397; J. W. von Goethe, "Der ewige Jude," in *Goethes Werke*, vol. 2 (Stuttgart: J. G. Cotta'sche Buchhandlung Nachfolger, 1882), 121.

17. Curtius, *Europäische Literatur und Lateinisches Mittelalter*, 16.

FOURTEEN. THE ETERNAL FEMININE

1. See Nicholas Boyle, *Goethe, the Poet and the Age*, vol. 1: *The Poetry of Desire* (Oxford: Oxford University Press, 1992), 78.

2. J. W. von Goethe, *Die Leiden des Jungen Werther*, in *Goethes Werke*, vol. 6 (Munich: Beck, 1981), 10.

3. Friedrich Schiller, "Über naive und sentimentalische Dichtung," in Schiller, *Sämtliche Werke*, vol. 5 (Munich: Carl Hanser Verlag, 1962), 710.

4. Carl Gustav Jung, "Schiller's Ideas on the Type Problem," in *Collected*

Works of C. G. Jung, vol. 6: *Psychological Types*, ed. Gerhard Adler and R. F. C. Hull (Princeton: Princeton University Press, 1971), 87.

5. Schiller, "Über naive und sentimentalische Dichtung," 750; Jung, "Schiller's Ideas on the Type Problem," 132.

6. Goethe quoted in David Luke, "Introduction"; Goethe, "Unpublished Synopsis (1826) of an Early Conception of Act II (from Paralipomenon BA 73*)," both in J. W. von Goethe, *Faust, Part Two*, trans. David Luke (Oxford: Oxford University Press, 1994), xii, 244.

7. Homer, *The Iliad* 2.189–90; 3.219, trans. Robert Fagles (London: Penguin, 1990).

8. Anne Carson, *Norma Jeane Baker of Troy: A Version of Euripides's "Helen"* (New York: New Directions, 2019).

9. Homer, *Iliad* 3.187–90.

10. Osip Mandelstam, "Sleeplessness. Homer," in Mandelstam, *Black Earth: Selected Poems and Prose*, trans. Peter France (New York: New Directions, 2021), 18.

11. Homer, *Iliad* 6.424–26.

12. Homer, *Iliad* 3.151–54; Bettany Hughes, *Helen of Troy: Goddess, Princess, Whore* (London: Jonathan Cape, 2005), 341.

13. Christopher Marlowe, *Doctor Faustus* (1588?, first published 1604), ll. 62–63, 1354–56, in *The Plays of Christopher Marlow* (Oxford: Oxford University Press, 1939), 153, 192; Homer, *Iliad* 3.191.

14. See Zacharias Hogel, *Chronica von Thüringen und der Stadt Erffürth*, in Philip Mason Palmer and Robert Pattison More, *The Sources of the Faust Tradition: From Simon Magus to Lessing* (New York: Haskell House, 1965), 108–10; Eugenio Battisti and Giuseppa Saccaro Battisti, *Le macchine cifrate di Giovanni Fontana* (Milan: Arcadia, 1984), 99–100.

15. Edgar Allan Poe, "To Helen" (1848), in *The Complete Works of Edgar Allan Poe*, vol. 10: *Poems*, ed. Edmund Clarence Stedman and George Edward Woodberry (New York: Scribner's, 1914), 77.

16. Homer, *Iliad* 3.200; Goethe, *Faust, Part Two*, ll. 8838–40, p. 134.

17. Goethe, *Faust, Part Two*, l. 6197, p. 50; Goethe, *Die Leiden des Jungen Werther*, 10.

18. Saint Jerome, "Against Jovinianus," in *A Select Library of Nicene and Post-Nicene Fathers of the Christian Church*, ed. Philip Schaff and Henry Wace, trans. W. H. Fremantle, Second Series, vol. 6: *The Principal Works of St. Jerome* (New York: Parker and Company, 1893), 382.

19. Giulia Sissa, *Sex and Sensuality in the Ancient World*, trans. George Staunton (New Haven: Yale University Press, 2008), 30.

20. J. W. von Goethe, *Dichtung und Wahrheit*, in *Goethes Werke*, vol. 9 (Munich: Beck, 1981), 538.

FIFTEEN. HOMER AS SYMBOL

1. Friedrich Nietzsche, "What I Owe to the Ancients," in *Twilight of the Idols*, in *The Portable Nietzsche*, ed. and trans. Walter Kaufmann (London: Penguin, 1954), 561; Nietzsche, "Homer und die klassische Philologie," in Nietzsche, *Werke in drei Bänden* (Munich: Carl Hanser Verlag, 1973), 163.

2. Friedrich Nietzsche, "Homer Contest," in *The Portable Nietzsche*, 33; Nietzsche, *The Birth of Tragedy out of the Spirit of Music*, trans. Shaun Whiteside, ed. Michael Tanner, rev. ed. (London: Penguin, 2003), 22–24.

3. See Lesley Chamberlain, *Nietzsche in Turin* (London: Quartet Books, 1996), 216.

4. Sigmund Freud, "Our Attitude Towards Death," in *Civilization, Society and Religion: Group Psychology, Civilization and Its Discontents and Other Works*, translated from the German under the general editorship of James Strachey (London: Penguin, 1985), 85; Peter Gay, *Freud: A Life for Our Time* (New York: Norton, 1988), 45.

5. Homer, *The Odyssey* 11.550–52, trans. Robert Fagles (London: Penguin, 1996).

6. Homer, *The Iliad* 2.269–72; 21.123–26, trans. Robert Fagles (London: Penguin, 1990).

7. Freud, "Our Attitude Towards Death," 85.

8. Gay, *Freud*, 170.

9. Quoted in Gay, *Freud*, 171.

10. Gay, *Freud*, 427.

11. Freud, "Our Attitude Towards Death," 89.

12. Sigmund Freud, "Moses and Monotheism" (1939), in *The Origins of Religion*, translated from the German under the general editorship of James Strachey (London: Penguin, 1985), 314.

13. Bruno Bettelheim, *Freud and Man's Soul* (New York: Knopf, 1983), 16.

14. Carl Gustav Jung, "On the Relation of Analytical Psychology to Poetry," in Jung, *The Spirit in Man, Art and Literature*, trans. H. G. Baynes (Princeton: Princeton University Press, 1966), 70.

15. Rupert Brooke, "The Soldier," in Brooke, *The Collected Poems* (New York: Dodd, Mead, 1923), 111; Brooke, *The Letters of Rupert Brooke*, ed. Geoffrey Keynes (London: Faber and Faber, 1968), 662; Brooke, "Menelaus and Helen," in Brooke, *The Collected Poems*, 77.

16. Yannis Ritsos, "Penelope's Despair," in *Repetitions, Testimonies, Parentheses*, trans. Edmund Keeley (Princeton: Princeton University Press, 1991), 91.

SIXTEEN. HOMER AS HISTORY

1. Philip Smith, "Introduction," in Heinrich Schliemann, *Troy and Its Remains: A Narrative of Researches and Discoveries Made on the Site of Ilium and in the Trojan Plain*, ed. Philip Smith and trans. L. Dora Schmitz (New York: Arno Press, 1976), xx.

2. Schliemann, *Troy and Its Remains*, 3–4.

3. Michael Wood, *In Search of the Trojan War* (London: BBC Books, 1985), 49.

4. Wood, *In Search of the Trojan War*, 4, 9, 12, 59.

5. Noah Carney, "Lost Art: Homer's Troy and Priam's Treasure," *Art Newspaper*, May 6, 2018.

6. See Konstantin Akinsha and Grigorii Kozlov, *Beautiful Loot* (New York: Random House, 1995), 6–11; Susan Heuck Allen, "Calvert's Heirs Claim Schliemann's Treasure," *Archeology* 49, no. 1 (January–February 1996).

7. Arnold, Gobineau, and Curtius quoted in Wood, *In Search of the Trojan War*, 49–50; Michael Schmidt, *The First Poets: Lives of the Ancient Greek Poets* (New York: Knopf, 2005), 47.

8. Schliemann quoted in Smith, "Introduction," xxiv.

SEVENTEEN. MADAME HOMER

1. Samuel Butler, *The Authoress of the Odyssey: Who and What She Was, When and Where She Wrote* (1897), 2nd ed. (London: Jonathan Cape, 1922), 4.

2. Butler, *The Authoress of the Odyssey*, 6.

3. Butler, *The Authoress of the Odyssey*, 9. A. T. Murray explained the apparent muddle about the boat by suggesting that the two rudders were in fact one, and the ship had been turned around in the described action. See *Odyssey*, vol. 1, trans. A. T. Murray, rev. George E. Dimock (Cambridge: Harvard University Press, 1919), 13.

4. Butler, *The Authoress of the Odyssey*, 157.

5. Homer, *The Odyssey* 9.23–29, trans. Robert Fagles (London: Penguin, 1996).

6. See Robert Bittlestone, *Odysseus Unbound: The Search for Homer's Ithaca* (Cambridge: Cambridge University Press, 2006), 40; Butler, *The Authoress of the Odyssey*, 177.

7. Moses Finley, "Et tu Teddy White," *New York Review of Books*, November 21, 1968.

8. Samuel Butler, *The Notebooks*, ed. Henry Festing Jones (London: Jonathan Cape, 1912), 225.

9. T. E. Lawrence, "Translator's Note," in *The Odyssey of Homer*, trans. T. E. Shaw (Colonel T. E. Lawrence) (Oxford: Oxford University Press, 1956), iii.

10. Emily Wilson, "Introduction," in Homer, *The Odyssey*, trans. Emily Wilson (New York: Norton, 2018), 53.

11. Margaret Atwood, *The Penelopiad: The Myth of Penelope and Odysseus* (Edinburgh: Canongate, 2005), xv.

12. Butler, *The Authoress of the Odyssey*, 155.

13. Atwood, *The Penelopiad*, 161.

14. Homer, *Odyssey* 22.494–95.

15. Pat Barker, *The Silence of the Girls* (London: Hamish Hamilton, 2018).

16. Atwood, *The Penelopiad*, xv.

17. Butler quoted in Mary Josefa MacCarthy, *A Nineteenth-Century Childhood* (London: William Heinemann, 1924), 98.

18. John Ruskin, *Sesame and Lilies*, in *The Complete Works of John Ruskin*, vol. 18, ed. E. T. Cook and Alexander Wedderburn (London: George Allen, 1905), 159.

19. Rudyard Kipling, "When 'Omer Smote 'Is Bloomin' Lyre," in Kipling, *The Seven Seas* (London: Methuen, 1896), 162.

20. [Thomas Bridges], *A Burlesque Translation of Homer in Two Volumes*, vol. 1 (1762) (London: G. G. and J. Robinson, 1797), 3.

21. Sir Walter Scott, *Ivanhoe: A Romance*, chap. 29 (Edinburgh: Constable, 1820), 311; Matthew Arnold, *Culture & Anarchy: An Essay in Political and Social Criticism* (London: Macmillan, 1894), 38.

22. See Rachel Bryant Davies, *Victorian Epic Burlesques: A Critical Anthology of Nineteenth-Century Theatrical Entertainments After Homer* (London: Bloomsbury, 2019), 1.

EIGHTEEN. ULYSSES' TRAVELS

1. Durs Grünbein, *Galilei vermißt Dantes Hölle und bleibt an den Maßen hängen* (Frankfurt-am-Main: Suhrkamp Verlag, 1996), 38; Joyce quoted in Richard Ellmann, *James Joyce*, new and rev. ed. (Oxford: Oxford University Press, 1982), 436.

2. Joyce quoted in Ellmann, *James Joyce*, 103, 408.

3. W. B. Yeats, "The Autumn of the Body," in *Ideas of Good and Evil*, quoted in Richard Ellmann, *The Consciousness of Joyce* (Oxford: Oxford University Press, 1977), 10.

4. Vladimir Nabokov, "Ulysses," in *Lectures on Literature*, ed. Fredson Bowers (New York: Harcourt Brace Jovanovich, 1980), 336.

5. James Joyce, *Ulysses* (London: Bodley Head, 1960), 382; A. E. Housman, "Fragment of a Greek Tragedy" (1883), *Greece & Rome* 6, no. 1 (1959): 14.

6. Joyce quoted in Ellmann, *James Joyce*, 435. Neither anecdote is in Homer: Ulysses' story is told by Hyginus, *Fabulae* 95, Achilles' in Apollodorus (attrib.), *The Library* 3.13.8. For the Ulysses story see Robert Graves, *The Greek Myths*, rev. ed., vol. 2 (London: Penguin, 1960), 279.

7. Elizabeth Cook, *Achilles* (London: Methuen, 2001), 83.

8. Homer, *The Odyssey* 1.1, trans. Emily Wilson (New York: Norton, 2018), Robert Fagles (London: Penguin, 1996), Robert Fitzgerald (New York: Farrar, Straus and Giroux, 1961), Richmond Lattimore (New York: Harper Perennial, 1991).

9. Sarah Caudwell, *The Shortest Way to Hades* (New York: Dell, 1995), 193.

10. Homer, *The Iliad* 265–68, trans. Robert Fagles (London: Penguin, 1990); Alfonso Reyes, "Odiseo," in *Algunos ensayos*, ed. Emmanuel Carballo (Mexico City: Universidad Nacional Autónoma de México, 2002), 84.

11. See Bruce Louden, *Homer's "Odyssey" and the Near East* (Cambridge: Cambridge University Press, 2011), 31–32.

12. See Michael Grant, *History of Rome* (London: Weidenfeld Nicolson, 1978), 82, 102; Virgil, *Aeneid* 2.164, trans. C. Day Lewis (Oxford: Oxford University Press, 1952), 33.

13. Homer, *Odyssey* 11.138; Dante Alighieri, *Inferno*, 26:90–142; Alfred, Lord Tennyson, "Ulysses," in Tennyson, *Selected Poems*, ed. Michael Millgate (Oxford: Oxford University Press, 1963), 88–90.

14. Tennyson, "Ulysses"; Mario Vargas Llosa, "Odiseo en Mérida," *El País*, July 30, 2006.

15. Kemel quoted in Barry Tharaud, "Yasar Kemal, Son of Homer," *Texas Studies in Literature and Language* 54, no. 4 (Winter 2012): 563–90.

16. Nikos Kazantzakis, *The Odyssey: A Modern Sequel*, trans. Kimon Friar (New York: Simon & Schuster, 1985), 775.

17. Homer, *Iliad* 6.277; José Hernández, *Martín Fierro* (Buenos Aires: Centro Editor de América Latina, 1979), 150.

18. Victor Bérard, *Les Phéniciens et l'Odysée*, 2 vols. (Paris: Armand Colin, 1902–3), 18–61.

19. Joyce, *Ulysses*, 279; see George K. Anderson, *The Legend of the Wandering Jew* (Hanover, N.H.: Brown University Press, 1991). Anderson argues that to associate Joyce's Bloom with the Wandering Jew is an oversimplification (11, 117). Homer, *Odyssey* 1.2.

20. Samuel Johnson, *A Preface to Shakespeare* (1765), in Johnson, *The Major Works*, ed. Donald Greene (Oxford: Oxford University Press, 2000), 420.

NINETEEN. HOMER THROUGH
THE LOOKING-GLASS

1. See Jean Paulhan and Dominique Aury, eds., *La patrie se fait tous les jours* (Paris: Éditions de Minuit, 1947), 67, 95; Jean Giraudoux, "Note sur le texte," in Giraudoux, *Théâtre complet*, ed. Jacques Body (Paris: Gallimard, 1982), 1490–1502.

2. Jean Giraudoux, *La guerre de Troie n'aura pas lieu*, in Giraudoux, *Théâtre complet*, 551.

3. Giraudoux quoted in Colette Weil, "Préface," in Jean Giraudoux, *La guerre de Troie n'aura pas lieu* (Paris: Grasset, 1991), 12.

4. Jean Giraudoux, "Bellac et la tragédie," quoted in Weil, "Préface," 13; Marguerite Yourcenar, *Les yeux ouverts: entretiens avec Mathieu Galey* (Paris: Éditions du Centurion, 1980), 93; Doris Lessing, *African Laughter: Four Visits to Zimbabwe* (London: Harper Collins, 1992), 35.

5. Derek Walcott, *The Antilles: Fragments of Epic Memory: The Nobel Lecture* (London: Faber and Faber, 1993); Homer, *The Odyssey* 11.1, trans. Robert Fagles (London: Penguin, 1996); Derek Walcott, *Omeros*, 1:1:1 (London: Faber and Faber, 1990), 3; Ezra Pound, "Canto 1," in *The Cantos*, rev. ed. (London: Faber and Faber, 1975), 3.

6. Walcott, *Omeros*, 3:27:3, pp. 146–47.

7. Walcott, *Omeros*, 1:3:2, pp. 17–18.

8. See F. Létoublon and L. Fraisse, "Proust et la Descente aux Enfers: les souvenirs symboliques de la *Nekuia* d'Homère dans la *Recherche du temps perdu*," *Revue de l'histoire littéraire* 97 (1997): 119–33.

9. Italo Calvino, *Perché leggere i classici* (Milan: Arnoldo Mondadori, 1991), 14.

10. C. P. Cavafy, "Trojans," in Cavafy, *Collected Poems*, bilingual edition, trans. Edmund Keeley and Philip Sherrard, ed. George Savidis, rev ed. (Princeton: Princeton University Press, 1992), 22.

11. C. P. Cavafy, "Ithaka," in Cavafy, *Collected Poems*, 36–37.

12. C. P. Cavafy, "The City," in Cavafy, *Collected Poems*, 28.

13. Jonathan Shay, *Odysseus in America: Combat Trauma and the Trials of Homecoming* (New York: Scribner's, 2002), 87.

14. Timothy Findley, *Famous Last Words* (Toronto: Clarke, Irwin, 1981); Ezra Pound, *Hugh Selwyn Mauberley* (London: Faber and Faber, 1920), 425; Findley, "Famous Last Words," in *Inside Memory: Pages from a Writer's Workbook* (Toronto: Harper Collins, 2002), 181.

15. Findley quoted in David Ingham, "Bashing the Fascists: The Moral Dimensions of Findley's Fiction," *Studies in Canadian Literature* 15, no. 2 (1990): 33–54.

16. *Grand Hotel*, directed by Edmund Goulding, MGM, 1932; Findley, *Famous Last Words*, 386.

17. T. S. Eliot, "The Hollow Men," in Eliot, *Collected and Uncollected Poems*, vol. 1: *1909–1962* (London, Faber and Faber, 2015), 84; Ezra Pound, "Canto 74," *The Cantos*, 425.

18. Findley, *Famous Last Words*, 386.

TWENTY. THE SHIELD OF ACHILLES

1. François Albera, "The Heritage We Renounce: Eisenstein in Historiography," in *Sergei M. Eisenstein: Notes for a General History of Cinema*, ed. Naum Kleiman and Antonio Somaini (Amsterdam: Amsterdam University Press, 2016), 280; Joanna Paul, *Film and the Classic Epic Tradition* (Oxford: Oxford University Press, 2013), 38.

2. Alberto Moravia, *Il Disprezzo* (Milan: Bompiani, 1954), 133, 135, 133.

3. "Reviews of Independent Films," *New York Dramatic Mirror* 65, no. 1687 (1911): 34.

4. See Michael G. Cornelius, ed., *Of Muscles and Men: Essays on the Sword and Sandal Film* (Jefferson, N.C.: McFarland, 2011), 4; Peter Bondanella, *The Eternal City: Roman Images in the Modern World* (Chapel Hill: University of North Carolina Press, 1987), 201.

5. Richard Davenport-Hines, *Auden* (New York: Pantheon, 1995), 200; W. H. Auden, "Nature, History and Poetry," lecture delivered four times in the early months of 1950 at several American colleges, in *The Complete Works of W. H. Auden, Prose*, vol. 3: *1949–1955*, ed. Edward Mendelson (Princeton: Princeton University Press, 2008), 642.

6. *The Shield of Achilles*, in W. H. Auden, *Collected Poems*, ed. Edward Mendelson, 2nd ed. (London: Faber and Faber, 2007), 596.

7. Christopher Logue, "The Art of Poetry," interview with Shusha Guppy, *Paris Review* (Summer 1993). Further quotations by Logue are from this interview. George Steiner, review of Christopher Logue's *War Music*, *Sunday Times*, December 2, 2005. Miller quoted in James Campbell, *NB by J.C.: A Walk Through the "Times Literary Supplement"* (Manchester: Carcanet, 2023), 205.

8. See Amy C. Smith, "Athenian Political Art from the Fifth and Fourth Centuries BCE: Images of Political Personifications," in *Dēmos: Classical Athenian Democracy*, ed. C. W. Blackwell (ed. A. Mahoney and R. Scaife in *The Stoa: A Consortium for Electronic Publication in the Humanities*, January 18, 2003), https://www.stoa.org/demos/article_personifications@page=1&greekEncoding=UnicodeC.html.

9. Christopher Logue, *War Music* (London: Faber & Faber, 2015), 9, 14.

10. Christopher Logue, *War Music*, 67, 271, 175.

11. Christopher Logue, *All Day Permanent Red: The First Battle Scenes of Homer's "Iliad" Rewritten*, part 1 (London: Faber and Faber, 2003), 37; Alexander Pope, "An Essay on Criticism," ll. 299–300, in *The Poems of Alexander Pope*, ed. John Butt (London: Methuen, 1963).

TWENTY-ONE. THE NEVER-ENDING WAR

1. Alessandro Baricco, *Omero, Iliade* (Milan: Feltrinelli, 2004), 157.

2. Baricco, *Omero, Iliade*, 157.

3. Homer, *The Iliad* 2.250–55, 262–82, 313–14, trans. Robert Fagles (London: Penguin, 1990) (suspension points in original).

4. Zbigniew Herbert, "El repugnante Teristes," in *El rey de las hormigas: mitología personal*, trans. into Spanish by Anna Rubió and Jerzy Sławomirski (Barcelona: Acantilado, 2018), 57.

5. Camões, *Os Lusíadas* (Porto Alegre: Editorial Concreta, 2019), 4:90–104.

6. Adam Nicolson, *The Mighty Dead: Why Homer Matters* (New York: Henry Holt, 2014), 188. Nicolson is quoting from Bruce A. Jacobs and Richard Wright, *Street Justice: Retaliation in the Criminal Underworld* (Cambridge: Cambridge University Press, 2006).

7. Carlos Fuentes, *Aquiles o El guerrillero y el asesino* (Barcelona: Alfaguara, 2016), 191.

8. Stendhal, *La Chartreuse de Parme* (Paris: Divan, 1929), 78, 82.

9. Stendhal, *Oeuvres intimes*, vol. 1, ed. Victor Del Litto (Paris: Gallimard, Bibliothèque de la Pléiade, 1981), 31.

10. Leo Tolstoy, *War and Peace*, book 10, chap. 19, trans. Louise and Aylmer Maude (London: Macmillan, 1943), 459.

11. Tolstoy quoted in George Steiner, *Tolstoy or Dostoevsky: An Essay in the Old Criticism* (New York: Vintage, 1959), 71.

12. See Judith E. Kalb, "Homer in Russia," in *A Handbook to Classical Reception in Eastern and Central Europe*, ed. Zara Martirosova Torlone, Dana LaCourse Munteanu, and Dorota Dutsch (Hoboken, N.J.: Wiley, 2017), 470.

13. Dostoyevsky quoted in Kalb, "Homer in Russia," 473.

14. See Judith Kalb, "Homer in Russia," 474.

15. Tim O'Brien, *The Things They Carried* (New York: Houghton Mifflin, 1990), 76.

16. Heraclitus quoted in Diogenes Laertius, *Lives of Eminent Philosophers*, vol. 2: *Books 6–10*, trans. R. D. Hicks (Cambridge: Harvard University Press, 1925), 409; Heraclitus quoted in Celso, *Discurso verdadero contra los cristianos* (Madrid: Alianza, 1988), 125.

17. Dante Alighieri, *De monarchia*, in *Le opere di Dante*, vol. 2, 5:22, ed. M. Barbi et al. (Milan: Mondadori, 1921–22).

18. Homer, *The Odyssey* 22.474–77, 319–20, trans. Robert Fagles (London: Penguin, 1996).

19. Simone Weil, *The Iliad; or, The Poem of Force*, trans. Mary McCarthy, Pendle Hill Pamphlet no. 91 (Wallingford, Penn.: Pendle Hill, 1956), 66.

20. Herbert Read, ed., *The Knapsack* (London: George Routledge and Sons, 1939), vi; Charles Simic, "My Weariness of Epic Proportions," in Simic, *Selected Early Poems* (New York: George Braziller, 1982).

21. Homer, *Iliad* 15.557; 6.612; 20.180; 5.960; 8.523. Or perhaps the slaughter can be defended: in the *Spectator* of July 30, 2005 ("Giving Thanks for Hiroshima"), Andrew Kenny published an obscene defense of the bombing of Hiroshima, saying that in the long run it saved lives.

22. Émile Zola, "Nos auteurs dramatiques," in *Mélanges et discours* (Paris: François Bernouard, 1929), 283.

23. Homer, *Iliad* 6.52, 64–70, 74–75, 76–77.

24. Homer, *Iliad* 22.183–88, suspension points in original.

25. Homer, *Iliad* 2.535–38.

26. Homer, *Iliad* 23.100–102, suspension points in original.

27. Homer, *Iliad* 23.195–201, suspension points in original. This sacrifice makes a curious counterpoint to the twelve handmaids sacrificed by Odysseus on his return to Ithaca.

28. Homer, *Iliad* 24.695–99.

29. Homer, *Odyssey* 11.79–85.

30. Wallace Stevens, "Phases," *Poetry*, November 1914.

TWENTY-TWO. EVERYMAN

1. Jorge Luis Borges, "El inmortal," in Borges, *Obras completas*, vol. 1 (Buenos Aires: Emecé, 1996), 533–44. Quotations in the text are from this edition.

2. Homer, *The Iliad* 2.935–36, trans. Robert Fagles (London: Penguin, 1990).

3. Lewis Carroll, *Sylvie and Bruno Concluded* (New York: Macmillan, 1893), 131.

4. Claudio Magris, "Dos apuntes en torno a Borges," *Casa del Tiempo* (September 2005).

5. Robert Fitzgerald, "On Translating Homer," in *Critical Essays on Homer*, ed. Kenneth John Atchity, Ron Charles Hogart, and Doug Price (Boston: G. K. Hall, 1987), 50.

6. Homer, *Iliad* 6.530–33; 9.385–88.

7. Homer, *The Odyssey* 3.263–64, trans. Robert Fagles (London: Penguin, 1996); Homer, *Iliad* 18.126–27; Homer, *Odyssey* 9.346; 17.359–60; 23.343–53; Homer, *Iliad* 6.591–92; 24.740–44.

8. Bruce Louden traces these plots back to the *Epic of Gilgamesh* and several Ugaritic myths, and forward to the books of the Bible. See Bruce Louden, *Homer's "Odyssey" and the Near East* (Cambridge: Cambridge University Press, 2011), 1.

9. Heraclitus, *Homeric Problems*, ed. and trans. Donald A. Russell and David Konstan (Atlanta: Society of Biblical Literature, 2005), 3.

ACKNOWLEDGMENTS

Several readers have helped me in my research: Antonio Basanta Reyes, Carmen Criado, Silvia Di Segni Obiols, Lucie Pabel, Gottwalt Pankow, Arturo Ramoneda, Professor Marta Royo, Jean-Christophe Saladin, Guillermo Schavelzon, Takis Théodoropoulos, Mario Claudio Vicario: to them my deepest thanks. To Toby Mundy of Grove Atlantic for suggesting the book in the first place, and to Bruce Westwood and the staff of WCA, who were the first enthusiastic emissaries. Further thanks to the Schavelzon Agency, *semper fidelis,* and to John Donatich and Heather Gold at Yale University Press, who believe in the doctrine of resurrection. Also to Ben Cassell, who helped me update the bibliography, and to Suzie Tibor for her keen detective work. Many thanks to the relentless proofreader, Roberta Klarreich, and to Meridith Murray for her splendid index. And thanks once again to the indispensable Susan *Oxuderkēs* Laity for her scrupulous reading.

CREDITS

The Credits constitute a continuation of the copyright page.

W. H. Auden: Excerpt from "The Shield of Achilles," from Auden, *Collected Poems*, ed. Edward Mendelson, 2nd ed. (London: Faber & Faber, 2007), quoted with the permission of The Estate of W. H. Auden.

C. P. Cavafy: Excerpts from "The City," "Ithaka," and "Trojans," used with permission of Princeton University Press, from *Collected Poems*, by C. P. Cavafy, bilingual edition, translated by Edmund Keeley and Philip Sherrard, edited by George Savidis, revised edition, copyright 1975, 1992 by Edmund Keeley and Philip Sherrard; permission conveyed through Copyright Clearance Center, Inc.

Homer, *Iliad:* Excerpts from *The Iliad* by Homer, translated by Robert Fagles, translation copyright © 1990 by Robert Fagles. Used by permission of Viking Books, an imprint of Penguin Publishing Group, a division of Penguin Random House LLC. All rights reserved.

Homer, *Odyssey:* Excerpts from *The Odyssey* by Homer, translated by Robert Fagles, translation copyright © 1996 by Robert Fagles. Used by permission of Viking Books, an imprint of Penguin Publishing Group, a division of Penguin Random House LLC. All rights reserved.

Philip Larkin: Excerpts from *The Complete Poems of Philip Larkin* by Philip Larkin, edited by Archie Burnett. Copyright © 2012 by The Estate of Philip Larkin. Introduction copyright © 2012 by Archie Burnett. Reprinted by permission of Farrar, Straus and Giroux. All Rights Reserved. Published by Faber and Faber Ltd.

Christopher Logue: excerpts from *War Music: An Account of Homer's Iliad* by Christopher Logue. Copyright © 1981, 1991, 1995, 2003, 2005 by Christopher Logue. Copyright © 2015 by Rosemary Hill. Reprinted by permission of Farrar, Straus and Giroux. All Rights Reserved. Published by Faber and Faber Ltd.

Ogden Nash: Excerpt from "Very Like a Whale," first published in *The Primrose Path* (New York: Simon and Schuster, 1935), copyright © 1935 by Ogden Nash, renewed. Reprinted by permission of Curtis Brown, Ltd.

Yannos Ritsos: "Penelope's Despair," used with permission of Princeton University Press, from *Repetitions, Testimonies, Parentheses,* by Yannis Ritsos, translated by Edmund Keeley, first edition, copyright 1991 by Princeton University Press; permission conveyed through Copyright Clearance Center, Inc.

Charles Simic: "My Weariness of Epic Proportions," from *Selected Early Poems.* Copyright © 1982 by Charles Simic. Reprinted with the permission of George Braziller, Inc. (New York), www.georgebraziller.com. All rights reserved.

Virgil: Extracts from *The Aeneid: A New Verse Translation* by C. Day Lewis reprinted by permission of Peters Fraser & Dunlop (www.petersfraserdunlop.com) on behalf of The Estate of C. Day Lewis.

Derek Walcott: Excerpts from OMEROS by Derek Walcott. OMEROS by Derek Walcott. Copyright © 1990 by Derek Walcott. Reprinted by permission of Farrar, Straus and Giroux. All Rights Reserved. Published by Faber and Faber Ltd.

INDEX

Index

Index

Index

Index

Index

Index

Index

Index

Index